Crying

THE NATURAL AND CULTURAL HISTORY OF TEARS

Crying

THE NATURAL AND CULTURAL HISTORY OF TEARS

Tom Lutz

W. W. NORTON & COMPANY

NEW YORK   LONDON

For information about permission to reproduce selections from this book,
write to Permissions, W. W. Norton & Company, Inc.,
500 Fifth Avenue, New York, NY 10110

The text of this book is composed in Berling
with the display set in Elspeth
Desktop composition by Platinum Manuscript Services
Manufacturing by Quebecor Printing, Fairfield Inc.
Book design by Chris Welch

Library of Congress Cataloging-in-Publication Data

Lutz, Tom.
Crying : the natural and cultural history of tears / by Tom Lutz.
p.   cm.
Includes bibliographical references and index.
ISBN 0-393-04756-3
1. Crying. 2. Crying—History. I. Title.
BF575.C88L87   1999   99-21295
152.4—dc21   CIP

W. W. Norton & Company, Inc., 500 Fifth Avenue, New York, NY 10110
www.wwnorton.com

W. W. Norton & Company Ltd., 10 Coptic Street, London WC1A 1PU

1 2 3 4 5 6 7 8 9 0

To Laurie, with love

I have full cause of weeping, but this heart
Shall break into a hundred thousand flaws
Or ere I'll weep.
—William Shakespeare, *King Lear* (1606)

Excess of sorrow laughs. Excess of joy weeps.
—William Blake, *The Marriage of Heaven and Hell*
(1790)

As for the other things in life, the more we weep for
them, the less they merit our tears, and the fewer tears
we shed for them, the more we ought to weep for
them.
—St. Augustine, *Confessions* (397)

Acknowledgments

I want to thank especially Paul Mandelbaum and Rick Maddox for their friendship, advice, and reading. Linda Bolton, Ed Folsom, and Judy and Roger Aiken quite literally helped me keep body and soul together during the writing of this book, as have the very understanding and supportive University of Iowa Department of English and College of Liberal Arts. I want to thank my parents and siblings, each of whom continues, in inimitable, individual style, to be truly inspirational, no matter the distance. My agent Melanie Jackson and editor Jill Bialosky both helped me see what kind of book this could be. To Jessie, Yarri, and Cody, once again, thank you for raising me so well. And Laurie Winer, thank you for everything, including the suggestion that I write about crying: not just this book is dedicated to you.

I owe much to the following for their help along the way: Betsy Amster, Hans Breder, Ken Cmeil, Antonio Damasio, Pam Galvin, Julian Hanna, Jerry Harp, David Hay, Sam Lopez, Abby Metcalf, Vance Mews, Jon Miller, Steven Molton, E. N. Nieves, Martha Patterson, Donna Pall, Jonathan Penner, Thomas Scheff, Carol Spaulding, Ned Stuckey-French, Cathy Weingeist, Barbara Welch-Breder, and Holly Welker.

And for research assistance, stories, ideas, inspiration, and comfort, thanks to: Ritch Adams, Abby Adorney, John Adorney, Cari-esta Albert, Doug Anderson, Bridgette Andrew, Susanna Ashton, Kathy Balmer, The Blues Patrol, Leo Braudy, Tim Bryant, Kathleen Diffley, Barry Glassner, Beth Gwynn, Mark Henderson, Ellen Jagg, Joni Kinsey, Josh Kotzin, Ginger Makela, Kim Marra, Mary Moran, Jerry Neeley and the staff at Jerry's Video, Sky Palkowitz, Judith Pascoe, Joann Quinnones-Perdomo, Laura Rigal, Helen Ryan, Nina Sadowsky, Paul Sadowsky, John Stefaniak, Andy T., Stacy Title, Jennifer Travis, The staff of Video Journeys, Tom Weingeist, and Jon Wilcox.

Contents

List of Illustrations

Crying

THE NATURAL AND CULTURAL HISTORY OF TEARS

Introduction

Why Tears?

Weeping is a human universal. Throughout history, and in every culture, emotional tears are shed—everyone, everywhere, cries at some time. People weep during funeral rituals, for instance, in every culture except in Bali, and even there people weep in mourning—tearless funerals are made possible only by postponing the rites until two full years after the death. Around the globe, infants cry in hunger and pain and children in frustration and disappointment. However much the rules governing emotional display may vary from time to time and place to place, adults weep for myriad reasons and sometimes, a few claim, for no reason at all. In American culture, even those rare people (usually male) who claim they never cry can remember doing so as children.

And weeping is exclusively human. As far as we know, no other animal produces emotional tears. Some people have claimed that elephants cry, weeping at being reunited with their handlers, for instance, or after being scolded. But no independent confirmation of these rare and anomalous tears has ever been made. In his autobiography, the elephant trainer George Lewis, for instance, tells the story of Sadie, a young elephant who wept when she was punished. Sadie has since been offered as evidence that emotional tears occur in other species, but she is a poor offering. Lewis mentions only this one case in a lifetime of elephant handling, and since Sadie never cried a second time, Lewis is not entirely sure that what he saw was actual emotional weeping. Poodles have been reported to weep, but only by their owners. Arguments have been made for seals, beavers, and dolphins, all of them unsubstantiated. Even Jeffrey Moussaieff Masson and Susan McCarthy, who set out to establish the nature of animal emotion in their teasingly titled book, *When Elephants Weep*, are forced to admit, after telling the story of Sadie the sobbing elephant in some detail and with great pathos, that it is very probable that elephants never do actually weep. The cover photo shows two elephants not weeping but apparently snuggling, with their trunks wrapped around each other. Only elephants have those trunks, and only humans sob. Weeping is, as Darwin said, one of the "special expressions of man," crying a human peculiarity.

And yet we know surprisingly little about it. We know some of the basic physiological processes involved, a bit about the glands and ducts used and the hormonal activity that accompanies it. We know some of the major nerves that fire, and some of the brain systems that are activated. Physiologists have studied the chemical content of emotional tears and shown that they differ from the tears, called basal or continuous tears, that lubricate our eyes when we are not crying. We know that women in this culture cry more than men, and that infants cry more than either.

But beyond this we know very little. The psychological and sociological studies and theories are intriguing but often contradict each other. The philosophical speculations, however suggestive, are by their very nature inconclusive. History, anthropology, physiology, neurology—each discipline asks its own questions and arrives at its own answers. In 1760 the poet Edgar Young suggested that his readers should study the "Philosophy of Tears" because it was "a Science, yet unlectur'd in our Schools!" And until recently tears have been remarkably neglected as a subject of investigation. No lamentology or lacrimology has developed, no academic fields devoted to their study, no science of tears. The closest is the medical subfield of dacryology, or the study of the lacrimal system, which Juan Murube-del-Castillo declared was emerging in 1983, but which has yet to spawn a journal or a Library of Congress subject heading. Recent studies in Sweden, Texas, and Australia, finding that tears occur with great regularity in doctor-patient and nurse-patient relationships, have regretted the lack of courses in medical and nursing schools which deal with crying. Therapists, even those for whom crying is a central therapeutic activity, admit that they never studied crying in their undergraduate or graduate degree programs.

Our best understandings of tears come not from the medical and psychological sciences but from innumerable poetic, fictional, dramatic, and cinematic representations of the human proclivity to weep. Although this cultural record is extensive, many questions remain. Why do we cry? Tears of happiness, tears of joy, the proud tears of a parent, tears of mourning, frustration, defeat—what have they in common? What does it mean that at times of victory, success, love, reunion, and celebration, the outward signs of our emotional interiority are identical to those of our most profound experiences of loss? Why do certain ways of feeling make us cry and why does crying feel the way it does? How do we understand other people's weeping? Why have tears been considered sacred and redemptive? Why and how do we stop crying? When is crying neurotic or pathological? When is the inability to cry pathological? What, exactly, do tears express?

Tears often resist interpretation, and an explanation that is obvious to the crier may be lost on the person whose shoulder is getting wet. Conversely, what an observer might find patently obvious often passes unrecognized by the blurred eyes of the crier. We all at times misread or are stumped by emotional cues—is she angry? is he hurt? is she ashamed? is he hysterical?—and sometimes we just ignore emotional displays, or allow them to go uninterpreted. But tears are so obviously *there*, and often so obviously significant, so clearly meant to communicate intense emotion, that we at least try to understand them. When an infant cries, or when a friend cries in the course of an intense conversation, we know among other things that a serious demand is being placed upon our attention: tears demand a reaction. And we almost

*Van Eyck, renowned
as the most realistic
painter of his day,
shows the weeping
mourners removed
from the fray.*
Jan van Eyck, *The Cruci-
fixion* (c. 1430). The
Metropolitan Museum
of Art, Fletcher Fund,
1933. (33.92a) Photo-
graph © 1998 The
Metropolitan Museum
of Art.

always give one, even if that sometimes means studied inattention rather than gestures of comfort or sympathy.

Some tears are indisputably readable. A child's tears at a scraped knee, a parent weeping at the death of a child—these do not require any ingenious or tortured acts of interpretation. We see such tears, we comprehend them, we understand what they mean. But even then, our reactions to other people's tears are to some extent improvised. Even in cases when crying is expected—at a funeral, say—many people feel at a loss when asked to respond directly to a weeping mourner. Weeping often occurs at precisely those times when we are least able to fully verbalize complex, "overwhelming" emotions, least able to fully articulate our manifold, mingled feelings. We recognize in crying a surplus of feeling over thinking, and an overwhelming of our powers of articulation by the gestural language of tears.

If tears supplant articulation, it is small surprise that it is difficult to articulate their meaning, and this unreadability is exacerbated by crying's great variety of kinds and causes. Tears are sometimes considered pleasurable or profound, and sometimes dangerous, mysterious, or deceptive. In all cultures, some tears, like those we call crocodile tears, are a breach not just of etiquette but of ethics. Some weeping, like that of the medieval Christian fathers in prayer, was considered sacred: "tears of grace" were considered both a gift from God and a tribute to Him. The cultured European elite of the eighteenth century thought crying a sign of the moral worth and exceptional sensitivity of the crier. At other times, as when Stan Laurel, Art Carney, or any number of other clowns cry, tears are a source of mirth, sometimes poignant, sometimes not.

This vast array of tears share some common threads. Just as the infant's first tears signal its desire for nourishment or comfort, tears usually signal a desire, a wish, or a plea. People suffering from certain kinds of clinical depression do not cry precisely because they have, by their own report, given up all hope of their desires being answered. Fully detached and hopeless, they have lost the impetus to cry, because without desire there are no tears. A severely neglected infant, like the depressed person, will stop crying altogether. It is the infant who believes it will be picked up that wails, energized by its fear that it will be left alone.

It is often just such mixed emotions or competing desires—fear mixed with desire, hope mixed with despair—that can trigger the release of tears. The tears that lovers shed can express the desire for intimacy and, at the same time, a corresponding fear of that intimacy. Tears of mourning signal our desire to turn back time and magically redeem our loss, as well as the bitter knowledge of the impossibility of that desire. Our tears of pleasure and joy can express our desire to remain in the state of bliss we know full well will vanish all too quickly, leaving us to our more mundane lives, the lives we are, in effect, crying to escape.

The dry-eyed mourners attend the body, while the weeper stands removed.
Gerard David, *The Deposition* (c.1520). Copyright The Frick Collection, New York.

In van Eyck's painting *The Crucifixion* (c. 1420), we see what was for centuries a familiar artistic trope. There is a group of women in the foreground, with Christ on the cross behind them. One of the women looks up at the cross, and the others look away. The woman gazing at the dying Christ has a look of extreme anguish, while the others are turned away in tears. These figures are repeated in innumerable paintings of this scene. In Gerard David's version of the deposition (the lowering of the dead Christ from the cross) a hundred years later, for instance, Mary Magdalene kisses Christ's hand in dry-eyed anguish, while the Virgin Mary looks at the ground and cries, contemplating her own sorrow and loss. A more primitive Pietà from the fourteenth century by a follower of Konrad Witz shows two women attending to Christ's body and a third looking away, weeping. In these and scores of similar paintings, it is the dry-eyed women who seem most anguished and are focused on the dead body, while the crying women are in fact looking away or down. Crying allows us to turn away from the cause of our anguish and turn inward, away from the world and toward our own bodily sensations, our own feelings. Our feelings overwhelm the world, or at least our ability to process any new information from our world.

Tears express complex, contradictory desires, then, and we cry at least in part because it makes us feel better. A theory of cathartic tears has been with us since before Aristotle, suggesting that we feel better because of the "release" that tears afford. It may be more correct to say that rather than releasing them, tears redirect our emotions. By encouraging us to shift our attention from our thoughts to our bodies, crying can wash away the psychic pain we feel simply by diverting our attention from it. Like the teardrops that a shrinking Alice in Wonderland cries and then floats away on, our tears can be our deliverance even as they express our distress. And weeping can also make us feel better because it is satisfying in and of itself, a physical pleasure. Many cultures, from ancient Babylonia to fourteenth-century Japan to eighteenth-century Europe, have known this well. And now, as teenagers flock again and again to watch and weep once more at *Titanic*, it may be that we are in the process of returning to an understanding of the pleasures of tears.

If this is true, it is still only part of the story. "My words are my tears," Samuel Beckett said, and for many of us the opposite is equally true. Tears are a kind of language, a primary, and often primal, form of communication. The language of crying can accomplish many different ends, expressing not just our distress but our demands, not just our desire to be understood but our desire to evade detection. Our crocodile tears can be used to ensnare, to confuse, to extort, to deceive. Even those tears we cry when we are alone often have an imagined audience. Even in our deepest moments of grief, we can be well aware of the effect our tears are having on those around us.

Given the communicative function of tears, they rarely remain

Tears were primarily a religious subject in early modern and Renaissance painting. This is one of hundreds of paintings of this scene in which a weeping woman averts her eyes from the tragedy. Follower of Konrad Witz, *Pietà* (fifteenth century). Copyright The Frick Colection, New York.

where they begin, at the level of wordless gestures and sounds. They often demand an explanation, and in order to offer one, we necessarily revert to verbal language. The language is rich with synonyms and sayings, and crying has become the stuff of a million metaphors. "There is no use crying over spilled milk," "cry me a river," "I'm crying my eyes out," "crying for mercy," "read it and weep," "big girls don't cry"—all such catchphrases, proverbs, and song lyrics express a facet of our culture of tears, and in turn affect our understanding and experience of crying. Part of crying's elusiveness has to do with the ornate, complex culture that has grown up around weeping, as it does around all our most profound human activities—birth, love, sex, death—and as in the case of all such cultural elaboration, our ways of talking can both explain and obscure.

The forced migration of the Cherokee tribes from Georgia to Oklahoma in 1838, for instance, has always been known as the "Trail of Tears." When we refer to similar forced migrations during the Holocaust, we call them death marches (although Germans now call the train station on Friedrichstrasse in Berlin, where East meets West, the "Palace of Tears"). The "Trail of Tears" sentimentalizes the horror of the Cherokee death march, putting an emphasis on sorrow, as if the trail were marked not by starvation and brutality but by a comparatively delicate emotional state. A hundred years later, the image of a crying Indian chief in a television antilittering campaign exploited not just the idea that Native Americans have a special relation to the land stolen from them but also a special, emotional relation to nature itself. (The weeping Indian was about to reappear in commercials this year but was withdrawn under protest.) In each case, tears are used as a synecdoche—a metaphor in which a part stands for a whole—and are meant to offer an irrefutable argument.

As such metaphors, images, and arguments proliferate in our culture, our understanding of tears themselves continues to evolve. In any time and any place, the meaning of tears is rarely pure and never simple, and thus no simple translation of the language of tears is ever possible. The best we can do is to translate tears into a variety of languages—historical, physiological, psychological, sociological, anthropological, literary, and philosophical, for instance, as the chapters that follow do. None of these disciplinary lenses puts the full depth of crying in focus, but each achieves its own kind of clarity.

Tears have been central to myth, religion, poetry, and fiction through the ages, but until recently, remarkably little has been written in an attempt to explain and understand tears themselves. Perhaps no other fundamental human activity has received so little direct and sustained attention. There are a dozen books on laughter, for instance, for every one on tears. Only one book, *Crying: The Mystery of Tears* (1985) by physiologist William Frey, has attempted a general overview. Arthur Koestler contributed one important chapter in his *The Act of Creation* (1964). Psychotherapists have contributed a couple of books, and a half dozen literary critics have focused on particular centuries.

Almost all of these have been published in the last decade, which has also seen a new wave of articles on crying by social psychologists, physiologists, and others in professional journals. We are, in fact, in the midst of a renaissance in emotional research, both humanistic and scientific, one that promises clarified perspectives and exciting if undoubtedly far from permanent insights. The scientists and the humanists tend to disagree with each other, as is their wont, and within each group there is widespread disagreement on fundamental issues. Some scientists have argued that crying is a form of elimination, no different than urination, since tears contain chemicals and proteins that, in concentration, can cause problems like depression or ulcers, and which therefore need to be evacuated. Others have suggested that Darwin was right to see tears as a simple cooling system for eyes overheated or overgorged with blood by excessive emotion. Some psychologists, anthropologists, and philosophers have found crying to be a sign of health and progress, while others have argued that we should strive to eliminate crying from our lives. Still others have gone so far as to imagine utopias in which emotion has been completely abolished, so that we might live rationally ever after.

Several things are clear from this new wave of research, much of it done with a sophistication of method and measurement never before possible. One is that however universal crying might be, and however much similarity there may be with respect to occasion—funerals, weddings, partings—weeping has nonetheless been understood in remarkably different ways in different times and places and among different groups and individuals sharing the same time and place. Weeping's dense psychological, social, political, and cultural meanings are always in flux, and often in competition.

Those who study tears tend to concentrate on one aspect of this fluid mix at a time, in accord with the rigors of scientific or academic specialization. As in the case of many other areas of academic study, this specialization comes at a cost. With a few exceptions, the psychologists do not read the anthropologists or the sociologists, the sociologists do not read the historians, and the anthropologists, historians, and literary critics tend to read only each other, and then only a select group of anointed representatives. Cognitive psychologists who construct categories of fundamental emotions seem oblivious to the insistence of linguists that such categories are necessarily culture- and language-specific. Anthropologists contrast the emotional cultures of the societies they study with "Western" understandings of emotion, as if a solid line of thought connected Plato to Danielle Steel. Several have argued, for instance, that in the West the "emotions" are associated with the "female," unaware of the history of male "sensibility" and its attendant weeping, unaware of the literary record of massive weeping by medieval warriors and monks, and unaware of the emotional expressivity of ancient warrior heroes like Odysseus and Aeneas. The lack of interchange among the different forms of knowledge is most striking when theoretical partisans feel justified in dismissing whole schools of endeavor. The most striking example of this is the large contingent of "social constructionists," who assume that all culture is socially constructed, and therefore ban any talk of physiology and other such attempts at understanding the empirical bases for human behavior—a widespread error of judgment that affects many different disciplines. The result is that while physiologists have now described in great detail the relation between crying and the reduction of tension, psychotherapists have not integrated these findings into their practices or theories, and continue to employ an understanding that the physiologists abandoned decades ago.

In describing the various arts' and sciences' understandings of tears, in this book I have tried to demonstrate the value of each perspective, its history, and its shortcomings. Coming from the humanities, I have a certain prejudice in favor of the richness and complexity of literary and philosophical texts, but I find the scientific literature equally compelling and the combination necessary. The first chapter traces three different strands in the history of tears: the history of tears as a form of pleasure, as a form of religious expression, and as a central activity of warrior heroes. The second chapter surveys the physiology of tears and its history, the third the psychology of tears over the last century, the fourth the sociology of tears. The fifth chapter concentrates on anthropological reports of weeping in the rituals of other cultures and on our own ideas about mourning. The sixth chapter looks at the uses of tears: the ways in which tears can be deployed in politics or in romance, for instance, and the way weeping can be used to reorder our own sense of the universe. The seventh chapter looks at the history of literary and artistic tears and is followed by a conclusion about how and why we stop crying, or sometimes don't.

Today, when asked about attitudes toward crying, the vast majority of Americans fall into one of two camps, the criers and the dry. The dry group—much, much smaller than the criers and almost entirely male—tends to feel shy about forwarding theories and understandings of tears. The criers tend to be prolific theorists. Most criers insist on the one hand that crying is a profoundly mysterious activity, and yet they are very sure about a number of things: they are sure that crying is "good for you," that it "releases pent-up emotions," and that a good cry has positive health benefits. These benefits, they say, are not mysterious but commonsensical.

Often the dry group, and those criers who happen not to be crying, feel a certain contempt for tears, seeing criers as oversentimental, hysterical, manipulative, or "emotionally disturbed." We can often feel this negatively about our own tears. As our emotions pass, they leave us with memories of the experience that are at best shaky, and as we enter a new state of mind we often reevaluate our tears, usually finding them less compelling than we did while we were crying. Introspection about the nature of our own crying while we are crying can often, in fact, stem the flow, providing a kind of distraction from our distraction.

And this leads us to another great puzzle. Even if we think we do know why we cry, why do we stop crying? The mystery of tears lies not just in the fact of their perennial, and perennially unexpected, arrival. It lies as well in their thieflike tendency to suddenly disappear. The conspicuous physicality of tears and the impossibility of ignoring them when we see them are complicated by their ability to quickly evaporate, leaving only the slightest of crystalline traces. Tears are the most substantial and yet the most fleeting, the most obvious and yet the most enigmatic proof of our emotional lives.

1

Tears of Pleasure,
Tears of Grace,
and the Weeping Hero

An anonymous British pamphlet from 1755, *Man: A Paper for Ennobling the Species*, proposed a number of ideas for human improvement, and among them was the idea that something called "moral weeping" would help:

> We may properly distinguish weeping into two general kinds, genuine and counterfeit; or into physical crying and moral weeping. Physical crying, while there are no real corresponding ideas in the mind, nor any genuine sentimental feeling of the heart to produce it, depends upon the mechanism of the body: but moral weeping proceeds from, and is always attended with, such real sentiments of the mind, and feeling of the heart, as do honour to human nature; which false crying always debases.

In this text and throughout human history, some tears have been considered good, and some, like those that are not "genuine," have been held in contempt. Some tears do honor to human nature, some debase it. This distinction is one of the perennial strands of the cultural history of crying, found in ancient fables, medieval monastic treatises, court culture, and our own films and sitcoms. But while it is fair to say that the "good cry" and the debased cry have always been with us and always will be, what constitutes a good cry changes over time. If a young woman were to fall on the ground weeping in a restaurant, say, and wash her father's feet with her tears while begging for his forgiveness, few people would find it as appropriate or heartwarming a sight as a group at an eighteenth-century British inn might have, or as eighteenth-century novel readers clearly did. And the same is true for the other judgments we make about tears, as when we deem them to be normal or excessive, sincere or manipulative, expressive or histrionic.

As historians of everyday life know well, the mundane does not lend itself to historical recovery the way politics or diplomacy or technological change does. The minutiae of daily living, documented only in passing, leave less of a paper trail. Food historians, for instance, need to pull descriptions of meals from journalistic accounts, fictions, diaries, and other sources that are primarily interested in what was said at the table between bites. The historian of emotion is further hampered by the fact that so much emotional interaction relies on implicit knowledge, on rules of appropriateness and meaning that most people never consider, much less articulate, however well adjusted and eloquent they may be emotionally. As Johan Huizinga, the great historian of everyday life in the Middle Ages, points out, representations of emotion are also prone to exaggeration (or, we might add, understatement), so that direct statements about people falling on the ground sobbing may or may not mean that people actually did so. Add to this the fact that in all places, and all times, any given emotional reaction or expression can be interpreted in vastly different ways, even by people who share the same culture and values, and we have a historian's nightmare. Roast beef is roast beef, but the line between weeping and sobbing is unclear, crying is not always sincere, and when it is sincere it is not always a sign of sadness.

What follows, then, is less a history than a series of related anecdotes, designed not so much to recapture the specific meanings of tears in different historical epochs as to defamiliarize them, to disrupt this century's belief in the naturalness of tears, and to allow them to appear strange, odd, anomalous. I have relied in part on the few historians who have done extensive work: Fleming Friis Hvidberg's study of Old Testament tears, Sandra McEntire's history of "holy tears" in the third through tenth centuries, Marjory Lange's study of seventeenth-century England, and Sheila Page Bayne's and Anne Vincent-Buffault's studies of crying in seventeenth- and eighteenth-century France. And I have concentrated on just three aspects of crying, three kinds of "good" tears: heroic tears, tears of exceptional sincerity, and tears of pleasure.

"Drinking of Them Like Wine"

The earliest written record of tears is found on Canaanite clay tablets dating from the fourteenth century B.C. Named after the village in northwestern Syria where they were found by archaeologists, the Ras Shamra Texts are a series of clay tablets and fragments of tablets from the ancient city of Ugarit, which was destroyed by an earthquake in the early thirteenth century B.C. Although ancient Greek and other texts spoke of Ugarit as a fabled city of advanced civilization and learning, no one was sure of its exact location until an Ugarit tomb was uncovered in Ras Shamra in 1931. The tablets found in the ensuing excavations contain a narrative poem about the death of Ba'al, an earth god worshiped by several ancient Middle Eastern cultures. One of the fragments tells the story of the virgin goddess Anat, the sister of Ba'al, as she hears the news of his death. Quite naturally, she weeps at the news. The accepted scholarly translation is that Anat "continued sating herself with weeping, to drink tears like wine." This, the earliest mention of tears in history, suggests that they are induced by grief, and that they offer satiety, even a kind of intoxication.

Hvidberg, the scholar who produced this translation, argues that this version of the story of Ba'al and Anat is related to a ritual of laughing and weeping in ancient pre-Hebrew Canaan, traces of which show up in the Hebrew Bible and a number of other sources. In this springtime ritual, a whole tribe would remove themselves to the desert and together begin to slowly moan and cry, moving from whimpering to weeping to wailing and then, over the course of several days, to frenzied hysterics and finally to laughing exhilaration before dissolving into giggles and resuming everyday life. In these rituals, frantic crying and raucous laughter are not opposed emotional displays but part of a continuum, a continuum based on a belief in emotional expression as a source of fundamental pleasure and social cohesion.

Crying also has a powerful effect in the story, for Anat's tears bring Ba'al back to life. In the Egyptian story of the death of the god Osiris, something comparable happens: the goddess Isis finds her brother Osiris dead and weeps over him. Her tears, too, bring the dead god back to life. Similar stories are told of the Mesopotamian gods Marduk and Tammuz and of Ishtar and Gilgamesh. Each of these myths, scholars have long assumed, is related to specific seasonal rituals, in which the death of the god represents the autumn and its harvests, and the tears represent, among other things, the renewal that comes with spring rains.

But the association of tears with renewal and new life went well beyond equinox celebrations. We can see in the Hebrew Bible traces of these crying rituals which the Hebrew immigrants to Canaan adopted from the worshipers of Ba'al. "May those who sow in tears reap with shouts of joy!" as the writer of the Psalms put it, "He that goes forth weeping bearing the seed for sowing, shall come home with shouts of joy, bringing his sheaves with him." The Old Testament belief that "they that sow in tears shall reap in joy" is repeated with new emphases in the New Testament. In the Gospel of Luke— "Blessed are you who weep now, for you shall laugh"—and John— "your sorrow will be turned into joy"—the ideas have been lifted out of their mythic context and reintroduced as axioms for everyday life. The sowing and reaping in these passages suggest sustenance, as in Psalm 42, which claims that "my tears have been my food day and night." The psalmist here is not just constructing a complex spiritual metaphor but suggesting a general attitude toward emotional tears, one that assumes them to be nourishing, sustaining.

Transformative rituals and axioms about the sustaining pleasure of crying are found in many Greek sources as well. In *The Iliad*, Homer talks of the "desire for lamentation" and "taking satisfaction in lament."

According to classicist W. B. Stanford, the function of poetry in Homer is to give pleasure to the listener even if the audience finds the story painful. Odysseus cries in pleasure, for instance, when the bard Demodokos tells the story of the Trojan horse, despite the pain he experiences in remembering lost comrades and lost time. And the pleasure of tears goes beyond such aesthetic response. Meneláos tells Odysseus that when he thinks of the men who died in the war, "nothing but grief is left me for those companions. While I sit at home sometimes hot tears come, and I revel in them, or stop before the surfeit makes me shiver." The tears here are somehow compensation for grief, and are the opposite of purgation—Meneláos was empty of everything but grief until his tears came, and then he reveled in them until he was surfeited, satiated. Euripides is even more explicit in *The Trojan Women:*

> *How good are the tears, how sweet the dirges,*
> *I would rather sing dirges than eat or drink.*

Here the "desire for lamentation" is a desire for pleasure and sweet satisfaction, more satisfying than food or drink. Weeping is so pleasurable that it can make one "shiver" with delight.

In the Latin love elegies of the first century A.D., the pleasures of tears were linked to the pleasures of romance. Virgil was perhaps the first, in *The Aeneid*, to make tears a mark of beauty, suggesting that *lacrimaeque decorae*, or decorative tears, make the crier more beautiful to a lover. Ovid was the first to suggest tears as a form of seduction for young men: "Tears are a good thing too; you will move the most adamant with tears. Let her, if possible, see your cheeks wet with tears. . . . Let her dry mouth drink your tears." Ovid also suggests that women who cannot easily cry should learn to fake tears. Such tears have utility in providing pleasure because they are forms of persuasion, but they work as persuasion because of their link to pleasure. As Propertius, another first-century elegist writes: "Happy the man who can weep before his mistress's eyes; Love greatly delights in flooding tears."

Such images of amorous pleasure, and of nourishment, satiety, and

autointoxication through tears, can be found throughout Western history. The pleasure of tears was often religious in origin, and often only
tangentially related to pain, sadness, or suffering. St. Thomas Aquinas,
in his grand and gothic *Summa Theologica* (1267–73), asked whether
tears assuage suffering and came to the conclusion that they do
because they provide pleasure. First, tears assuage sorrow "because a
hurtful thing hurts yet more if we keep it shut up . . . whereas if it be
allowed to escape, the soul's intention is dispersed as it were on outward things, so that the inward sorrow is lessened." We feel better, in
other words, because our negative feelings are "dispersed." And second, Aquinas writes, any action "that befits a man according to his
actual disposition, is always pleasant to him. Now tears and groans are
actions befitting a man who is in sorrow or pain; and consequently
they become pleasant to him." Laughter gives pleasure when it is fit-
ting, and so does weeping.

Aquinas was being slightly disingenuous here, since he was well
aware of another tradition of lamentation in the Catholic Church.
The early Christian churchmen developed elaborate theories of the
different kinds of tears. One system divided them into four types:
tears of contrition, tears of sorrow, tears of gladness, and tears of
grace. Others developed slightly different taxonomies, but all
included a category of tears full of sweetness and pleasure. In Book 4
of the *Confessions*, St. Augustine asks how it "can be that there is
sweetness in the fruit we pluck from the bitter crop of life, in the
mourning and the tears, the wailing and the sighs." He wonders if
tears derive their sweetness from the possibility that God will notice
them. "Or is weeping, too, a bitter thing, becoming a pleasure only
when the things we once enjoyed turn loathsome and only as long as
our dislike for them remains?" He asks God to tell him "why tears are
so sweet to the sorrowful." Jerome's letter to Eustochium in the
fourth century describes religious tears of joy: "When I had shed copi-
ous tears and had strained my eyes towards heaven, I sometimes felt
myself among angelic hosts," he told his readers, and so "sang in joy
and gladness." Gregory I (or Gregory the Great, of Gregorian chant
fame), the sixth-century church leader, called crying *gratia lachry-
marum*, which can mean either tears of grace or the gift of tears. John

Man Ray's photo is the prototypical modernist representation of tears.
Man Ray, *Larmes (Tears)* (1932–33). The J. Paul Getty Museum, Los Angeles. © Man
Ray Trust / Artists Rights Society (ARS), New York.

of Fecamp prayed to God: "Give me the pleasantness of tears . . . give
me the gift of tears." Isidore of Seville, in interpreting the Psalms in
the seventh century, seconded the idea that tears produce satiety.
"Lamenting," he wrote, "is the food of souls." Whenever St. Louis
received the "gift of tears," according to the French historian Jules
Michelet, his tears "seemed to him delectable and comforting, not
only to the heart but to the tongue."

E. M. Cioran called this "voluptuous suffering." Cioran, a Romanian
writer living in Paris, made the sensual pleasure of crying central to his
examination of religious emotions in *Tears and Saints*, first published
in 1937. He decided that it was not the saints' piety or accomplish-
ments or worthiness that makes them attractive to us hundreds of
years later, but the voluptuousness of their suffering, a voluptuousness
demonstrated by their tears. "Were it not for their tears," he writes,
"saintliness would not interest us any more than a medieval political
intrigue in some little provincial town." The "blissful ignorance" that
tears afford is the source of their pleasure, according to Cioran, since
crying's "flame of ecstasy annihilates any kind of intellectual activity."
Cioran suggests that this sublime overcoming of cognition is an aesthetic experience, and it is thus that tears provide aesthetic pleasure.

Following Nietzsche, who said that "I cannot differentiate between tears and music," Cioran suggests that tears, like music, are an art form in themselves, a kind of aesthetic production as well as an aesthetic experience. "Tears," he writes, "are music in material form." Man Ray's famous photographs of stylized tears, sitting on his model's cheek like plastic pearls, spring from the same Parisian culture as Cioran's book and suggest something similar, highlighting and obscuring the relation between tears as art and tears as experience.

This modernist aestheticizing of tears hearkens back to Virgil's "decorative tears," but for the medieval saints, monks, and mystics, tears were real and substantial. They were not art but experience, and they provided a certain kind, or kinds, of experience, whether voluptuous, akin to laying one's head in "God's soft pillow," as Augustine said, or horrible, as in the bitter-tasting, hot, painful tears cried in penance and contrition. In some cases, the bitter was transformed into the sweet, as in the fourteenth-century English mystic Walter Hilton's oddly titled *The Prickynge of Love* (c. 1375): "As water in the vine through the heat of the sun is turned to wine, just so shall bitter tears truly through fervor of charity be turned into the wine of spiritual comfort." And sometimes the sweet tears of the mystics were indistinguishable from aesthetic weeping. Margery Kempe, who wrote (or actually dictated) the first woman's autobiography in English in the 1430s, described her response to celestial music she had heard in a mystical trance: "It surpassed any melody that ever might be heard in this world, without any comparison, and caused this creature to have plenteous and abundant tears of high devotion, with great sobbings and sighings after the bliss of heaven."

In the seventeenth century, religious writers continued to use and add to such imagery. Henry Hawkins, in *Partheneia Sacra* (1633), wrote that tears are an oasis in the "Libian Desert" of the world; they are the "Milk of Nature, wherewith she is disposed to suckle creatures at her own breast." And secular poetry, fiction, and drama are full of references to the pleasures of tears. One critic has called the tears of Racine's heroines *pleurs aphrodisiaques*, and it is clear that in the seventeenth and eighteenth centuries, inducing abundant and pleasurable tears was a primary goal of actors, directors, dramatists, novelists, and poets, and theatergoers and novel readers praised those productions that drew the most tears. And these tears had an aphrodisiac effect. A medieval woman in a convent, her body wet with tears, squirming in ecstasy on her cot, penetrated to the core by a visitation from her "betrothed," Jesus himself, as she weeps with joy, appears to us to be an obviously sexualized image. But the mystic herself saw it differently, and in the eleventh century, when John of Fecamp prayed, "Sweet Christ . . . Give me the pleasantness of tears . . . give me the higher wetness and the lower wetness," we can also safely assume he was oblivious to any sexual overtones. The secular writers of the eighteenth century were considerably more attuned to the connections. The wetness, the "liquid expansion," the convulsing of muscles, the transport, and what we might even call the ejaculatory nature of crying were all used to suggest its sexual nature, especially in tales of romance.

One of the messiest sentimentalists of all time was the titular hero of Goethe's *The Sorrows of Young Werther* (1774). Werther writes of his love for Lotte to his friend Wilhelm, saying, "Oh, if only I could fall on your neck and describe with a thousand joyous tears all the emotions that are storming in my heart." Lotte grants him "the comfort of crying [his] eyes out over her hand," and as Werther describes such scenes to Wilhelm, he again begins "weeping like a child" remembering the joy and the despair he felt. When Lotte and Werther read the Romantic poet Friedrich Gottlieb Klopstock's odes to each other, they touch and weep. Roland Barthes has discussed Werther's "propensity to dissolve in tears" at the slightest emotion as a patently sexual act. In Barthes's words, "By releasing his tears without constraint, [Werther] follows the orders of the amorous body, which is in liquid expansion, a bathed body: to weep together, to flow together: delicious tears finish off the reading of Klopstock which Charlotte and Werther perform together."

With the coming of Romanticism in the late eighteenth and early nineteenth centuries, tears of pleasure only increase. William Wordsworth's first published poem, "On Seeing Miss Helen Maria Williams Weep at a Tale of Distress" (1786), contains the following quatrain:

> *She wept.—Life's purple tide began to flow*
> *In languid streams through every thrilling vein;*

Dim were my swimming eyes—my pulse beat slow,
And my full heart was swell'd to dear delicious pain.

Helen Maria Williams was herself a poet, and was also fond of "thrilling veins" of tears and their "dear delicious pain." In this era's literature, crying is widely seen as pleasure, even in such unlikely places as James Fenimore Cooper's novels. In *The Spy* (1821), when Henry asks his sister's pardon for doubting her loyalty, he cries, "pressing her to his bosom, and kissing off the tears which had burst, in spite of her resolution, from her eyes," thus causing both sister and brother to experience a profound pleasure. And this was not just literary hyperbole: Thomas Jefferson, coming of age during the height of Romanticism, knew well the pleasures of tears. In a letter to a prospective mistress in Paris, for instance, he wrote that there was no more "sublime delight than to mingle tears with one whom the hand of heaven has smitten!" He fully expects this sentiment to meet with complete acceptance, and in fact offers it as a form of seduction, as a kind of proof that he is a connoisseur of love.

Abbé Prévost, a French monk who left the monastery to become a novelist in the mid-eighteenth century, and whose novels probably influenced Jefferson's understanding of tears, said that tears had "an infinite sweetness." Prévost and his audience knew that this sweetness, like Jefferson's "sublime delight," was erotic; and in the novels of Sterne, Mackenzie, and Chateaubriand, and the plays of Fénelon and Racine, lovers fall happily weeping on each other's necks in recognition of their mutual bond. The reader and theatergoer are then privy to this most intimate of acts, which, like sex, involves the exchange of fluids.

After the eighteenth century, although indulgence in the pleasures of weeping did not end, talk about it became less common. The distinction in the 1755 pamphlet between purely physical crying and "moral weeping" again came to the fore, and the pleasure of tears in literature, drama, and discussion became gradually less central and less blatantly sexual over the course of the nineteenth century. Alfred Austin wrote in 1881 that "Tears are Summer showers to the soul," and Ella Wheeler Wilcox included in her *Poems of Pleasure* (1892) one called "The Lady of Tears," about the "mystical Lady of Tears" who saves people from broken hearts with her "bitter-sweet draught of relief." But the kind of sexual pleasure Thomas Jefferson or Goethe knew is lost.

The use of "soul" and "mystical" are significant, for the pleasure of tears was again, in the nineteenth century, figured in religious terms, as we'll see. People continued to appreciate the secular pleasures of tears, but those pleasures were not referred to with the sense of intensity and profundity that one finds in the records of the eighteenth and earlier centuries. In his "A Song of Joys," Walt Whitman, the great enumerator, lists the joy an orator feels in making people weep along with him. And George Copway in the 1850s recounted his tearful response upon hearing stories in his Ojibwa childhood in the 1820s: "Some of these stories are most exciting, and so intensely interesting, that I have seen children during their relation, whose tears would flow quite plentifully, and their breasts heave with thoughts too big for utterance. . . . To those days I look back with pleasurable emotions." This is tame stuff compared with the long history of tearful eroticism. Only a few writers managed to get the earlier sense of the sensual power of tears into the language of Victorian emotional culture, as when Henry James describes a character in *The Aspern Papers* (1888) who "clearly had been crying, crying a great deal—simply, satisfyingly, refreshingly, with a primitive retarded sense of solitude and violence."

Toward the end of the nineteenth century, psychologists began to study the psychophysiology of tears. According to Henry's brother William James, long bouts of crying tend to alternate between actual weeping and "dry sorrow," in which despair and desolation are felt but no actual tears are produced. It is during the weeping part of this cycle, James wrote in his *Principles of Psychology* (1890), that pleasure is possible. The dry sorrow is uniformly unpleasant, he writes, but "there is an excitement during a crying fit which is not without a certain pungent pleasure of its own." A few later physiological psychologists—especially Walter B. Cannon and Silvan Tomkins—would make suggestive arguments in the middle of the twentieth century about tears and pleasure, as we will see in the next chapter. But these remain more or less observations in passing, and no physiologist has seriously taken up James's suggestion. The pleasure of tears remains inexplicably unexplored.

In our own day, there are some signs that, at least among some communities, there has been a return to the pleasures of tears that early centuries knew. No one can have watched a figure-skating championship, for instance, and not noticed a craze for weeping. During some Pentecostal Christian prayer meetings, ceremonies are as steeped in tears as the ancient Canaanite festivals. During the middle of the twentieth century, as the chapter on psychology recounts, many schools of therapy sprang up that encouraged people to cry, and although pleasure was never discussed, they perhaps owed their success to the gratification that accompanied their patients' weeping. And at the same time, Hollywood was perfecting its recipes for "weepies."

That is where most of us continue to experience tears as pleasurable: in our response to art and entertainment. In the standard reviewing cliché, "I laughed, I cried," we recognize an axiomatic expression of aesthetic pleasure, a fundamental avowal of the kind of pleasure we get from books, plays, and films. The teenagers who are helping to make *Titanic* one of the few top-grossing films of all time clearly understand the relation between tears and pleasure. Journalist Deirdre Dolan interviewed teenagers in New York who had seen the film ten or more times, weeping voluminously each time. "The first time I saw it, I started crying when she jumped off the lifeboat," a sixteen-year-old boy said, "and the second time I started in the opening credits." A seventeen-year-old girl came home crying so uncontrollably that—in her words—"my parents came home and they were like 'what's wrong? This isn't right!'" These adolescents go to the film knowing that they are going to witness a horrible and melodramatic tragedy, and this, Dolan writes, is why they go, "*so that* they can weep." One girl who had seen the film "eleven and a half times" had stopped wearing eye makeup ("I usually wear a lot") and had begun bringing a box of tissues. Another young man claimed that his shirt got wet around the neck every time he saw it. Some of the teenagers understood their own crying in terms of release—the letting go of pent-up emotion. But others were clear that crying was important for the pleasure it afforded. As one girl explained, "It's so much better to cry because it makes the movie so much more enjoyable."

The History of Sincerity

Pleasure is, of course, hardly the first thing that comes to mind when most people think of weeping. We assume that tears are a sign of suffering, of loss, of pain, and in *Titanic* Leonardo DiCaprio's character cries much more often in grief, sadness, and despair than he does in joy or pleasure, although he does a little of that, too. DiCaprio plays the hero of the film, who rescues people (or tries to) and loses his life in the attempt, and who is otherwise an absolutely wonderful and sincere person. And we know this in part because he cries. As the Romantic poets knew, and as the anonymous author of the tract on "moral weeping" argued, some tears come from "genuine sentimental feeling" and others do not. When we are being cynically intellectual, "genuine" and "sentimental" can seem like antonyms, but we have all been on the receiving end of tears that are meant to establish the crier's genuine sincerity and do. In fact, more than with any other emotional display, we often assume that tears are the marrow of pure feeling, a sign of unsullied genuineness, the liquid gist of sincerity itself.

This idea, too, has a long history, and is also found in the Bible, where crying can be a form of petition. The writer of the Psalms, for instance, frequently uses his tears in prayer ("Hear my prayer, O Lord, and give ear to my cry; hold not they peace at my tears") and assumes that prayerful tears will be answered. These prayerful tears were often the opposite of pleasurable: some accompanied the most anguished entreaties made to God and they are regularly described as "bitter." Weeping was an attempt to influence Yahweh through a kind of self-abasement, an announcement of submission before God, like rending one's garments or donning sackcloth and ashes.

Crying prayers were regularly offered up before battles. "Then all the people of Israel, the whole army," we are told in Judges, "went up and came to Bethel and wept." In Maccabees 2:13, the Jews "besought the merciful Lord with weeping and fasting and lying prostrate for three days" before an attack. And the Lord answered such tearful prayers, not just in battle but at all times. When the sick Hezekiah "wept bitterly" in prayer, the Lord answered, "I have heard your prayer, I have seen your tears; behold, I will heal you." These prayerful tears in the Bible are innovations in Hebrew culture, gradually replacing such earlier offerings to God as animal sacrifices and the rending of garments. Joel, a prophet from approximately the fifth century B.C., recalled the Jews to worship after a plague of locusts. "Yet even now," Joel quotes the Lord, "return to me with all your heart, with fasting, with weeping, and with mourning; and rend your hearts and not your garments." Tears are not just an offering here but the purest form of offering, as Joel suggests—anyone can rend their garments, but only the sincere rend their hearts in prayer. Garments can be rent with minimal emotional investment, but tears take "all" of one's "heart."

By the time of the Gospels, tears are commonly used as marks of sincere faith, as in the story that appears in all four Gospels of "a woman of the city," commonly taken to be Mary Magdalene, "who was a sinner." The story is given its fullest rendition in the Gospel according to Luke: "Standing behind him at his feet, weeping, she began to wet his feet with her tears, and wiped them with the hair of her head, and kissed his feet, and anointed them with the ointment." A Pharisee objects, claiming that the woman is unfit to minister to a religious man, but Jesus rebukes him with a parable and says to the woman, "Your sins are forgiven. . . . Your faith has saved you; go in peace." The woman never speaks in these stories; her faith is demonstrated and proven by her submission and her tears.

These scriptural descriptions of sincere tears became even more important to the history of tears than the biblical representations of pleasure. Tears began to be granted a certain kind of power, both as a form of entreaty and as testimony to the crier's honesty and integrity. In his fourth-century *Confessions*, St. Augustine describes his mother crying for his salvation, crying in entreaty to him to mend his evil ways. Her priest told her not to worry, saying that "it cannot be that the son of these tears should be lost." His mother's sincere tears have the power to save her son's soul. In book 5, Augustine describes his inability to join "all who have left the hard path and come to weep upon your [God's] breast." Augustine is clear about why one would want to: "Gently you [God] wipe away their tears. They weep the more, but now their tears are tears of joy, because it is not some man of flesh and blood but you, O Lord and Maker, who remakes them and consoles them." To explain his inability to tearfully commune with God, Augustine invokes a notion of self-knowledge close to our own ideas of sincerity: "I could not find myself," he writes, "much less find you." The sincere man who knows himself knows God, and his crying is offered up to God as a prayer, which is answered in the form of consolation and renewal. Both the prayer and the consolation can take the form of tears.

Tears had gradually evolved from their Old Testament meanings, and Augustine's private relationship to God demonstrates one of the important changes. "If we could not sob our troubles in your ear, what hope would we have?" Augustine asks. Hezekiah cried aloud to the heavens and the lamentations of the Jewish armies resounded into the heavens, but Augustine's weepy prayers are offered directly, privately, to God. This separation of the public and private uses of crying is Augustine's most important contribution to the medieval culture of tears. When his mother dies, he wants to cry but forces himself not to, and at her funeral he sheds no tears. But later, alone and praying, he offers his tears to God, "for her sake and mine. The tears which I had been holding back streamed down, and I let them flow as freely as they would, making of them a pillow for my heart. On them it rested, for my weeping was for your ears alone, not in the ears of men who might have misconstrued it and despised it." Crying as a part of a public ceremony would have shown him "guilty of too much worldly affection," but his private crying is a sincere offering to God.

Following on Augustine's distinction and attempting to clarify it, the monastic leaders attempted to categorize the different kinds of weeping. According to Abbot Isaac, four different kinds of tears are produced by four different feelings or reflections. Some tears are "caused by the pricks of sin smiting our heart," while others arise "from contemplation of eternal good things and desire of that future glory." Sometimes, he says, we cry not out of actual guilt about a specific sin or sins but out of our fear of the day of judgment. And finally, "there is too another kind of tears, which are caused not by knowledge of one's self but by the hardness and sins of others." Guilt, awe, fear, pity: each feeling produces a different kind of tears. Alcuin, the eighth-century Anglo-Saxon prelate, describes four kinds of tears, based on their functions: "There are moist tears that wash away the filth of sin and restore lost baptism. There are salty and bitter tears that restrain the frailty of the flesh and moderate sweetness of pleasure. There are warm tears that prevail against the coldness of unfaithfulness. There are pure tears that build up those who are cleansed from previous sins."

But from the beginning of monasticism, one strand of thinking was central: that tears are both a gift from God and a tribute to him. St. Anthony, the father of monasticism in the early fourth century, writes to his disciples that they should weep in the sight of God. In the Rule

St. Francis is said to have gone blind from too much weeping. Imitator of Daniele Crespi, *St. Francis Weeping* (seventeenth century). Gift of Castiglione and Consonni families, in memory of Victoria Castiglione, Collection of the John and Mable Ringling Museum of Art, the State Museum of Florida.

of the Master, the monks are told that crying should always accompany penitence. In the sixth-century Rule of St. Benedict, the monks are told that crying should accompany heartfelt prayer. Not only were tears one means of prayer, according to Benedict, they were the only pure form: "We must know that God regards our purity of heart and tears of compunction, not our many words." Almost a millennium later, in the fourteenth century, the German monk Thomas à Kempis still counseled young monks to "seek the gift of tears" as a way to gain purity of heart. But the clearest example is St. Francis of Assisi: when he began to go blind in his old age, according to Cioran, "doctors found the cause to be an excess of tears." This apocryphal story shows the extent to which tears were associated with holiness. St. Francis was a man who had no pretense, a man so authentic that all nature responded to him, and thus he literally cried his eyes out.

The female mystics of the Middle Ages also took weeping to be a central aspect of religious experience. In Elizabeth of Toess's *Revelations* in the fourteenth century, Elizabeth "full bitterly wept her sins" on many occasions, and "wept so bitterly that she could not restrain herself from outward sobs and vocal cries." When Elizabeth experienced the "spiritual inebriation" of a visitation from Christ, she felt she needed to "weep and sorrow with much fear that she is so unfit for such a blessing." Margery Kempe, too, "wept extraordinarily bitterly, asking for mercy and forgiveness," and also cried for grace, sometimes for hours at a time, "very plenteously and very boisterously." Sometimes, she tells us, "the crying was so loud and so amazing that it astounded people."

Sincere tears have been important to many other religious practices, whether as private adjuncts to prayer or as ritual practice. The Wailing Wall, for instance, is a place of worship where tears are expected, as well as great solemnity. Weeping at the wall marks the profundity of one's religious feeling. A special class of weepers during the Islamic haj, the annual pilgrimage to Mecca, are known as the "Weeping Sufis," and their tears are considered signs of the authenticity of their mystical experience. And tears are still used to convey the authenticity of one's feelings in contemporary Christianity, which is why those most in need of such authentication, like television evangelists, are most likely to weep. Our Lady of Fátima and other miraculous visitations are represented as weeping, and tears are so powerful a guarantor of religious authenticity that even religious statues are said to weep.

William James, in *Varieties of Religious Experience* (1902), divides religious belief into two kinds: one that is "healthy-minded" and sunny and, he suggests, a bit frivolous; and one that is depressive and emotionally trying and much richer. The wailing at the temple wall in Jerusalem, weeping along with the crying statues of mystical Catholicism, and the tears of the medieval saints all fail to be "healthy-minded" in James's terms, and are instead the activities of "sick souls." This is not a criticism. In James's view, the neurotic weepers have more intense, more authentic, and more profound religious experiences than their healthy-minded counterparts. They have, in fact, a kind of authenticity that the dry-eyed, healthy-minded churchgoers lack.

St. Ignatius of Loyola, the sixteenth-century founder of the Jesuit order, is an example of someone James would consider a "sick soul." In one forty-page stretch of Ignatius's diary, he boasts of 175 episodes of crying. Of one he wrote: "I had an abundance of tears, without experiencing understandings or perceptions of any persons, but accompanied by a most intense love, warmth, and great relish for divine things and an exceedingly deep satisfaction of soul." This deep soul satisfaction and intense love of the divine obliterated any perceptions of the actual world, and even any conventional understanding. Deep, sincere, and disengaged from all others, Loyola's abundant tearfulness is at once both absorbed and detached, a communion and an intensely felt removal from the world. A kind of emotional monasticism, tears remove one from "understandings or perceptions of any persons" into a realm of pure religious abstraction. In Loyola's text, and in many other religious texts, engagement and evasion, absorption and detachment, self-knowledge and denial of the world meld in a powerful, tearful embrace.

Robert Southwell has been credited with introducing the idea of "holy tears" into English secular literature in the late sixteenth century. In *Saint Marie Magdalens Funeral Teares*, Southwell writes of tears as if

they were attorneys: "Thy tears will obtaine. They are too mighty ora-
tours, to let any suite fall, and though they pleaded at the most rigorous barre, yet haue they so persuading a silense, and so conquering a
complaint that they by yielding ouercome, and by intreating they
comaund." By figuring tears as attorneys, Southwell combines tears of
worship, tears of beauty and pleasure, and tears of petition in a slightly
new way. Tears will "overcome by yielding" and "command by entreat-
ing," even at the most rigorous bar. In an extremely mixed metaphor,
Southwell goes on to say, "The Angels must still bath themseules in *the
pure streames of thy eyes,* and thy face shall still be set with *this liquid
pearle,* that as out of thy teares may be the oyle, to nourish and feed
his flame." Rather than bathing away sin, tears are pools for angels to
bathe in, liquid pearls, as well as fuel, even while they continue to act
as the crier's advocates.

In the eighteenth century, this understanding of tears—as "mighty
orators," as pearls, and as the playground of angels—was further secularized but otherwise retained the same characteristics. Now the sincere man offered up his tears not to God but to other people, especially
his beloved, who answered them with consolation (or didn't) and
caused a new bout of tears of joy (or didn't), making possible the most
ideal form of communion (or the agony of unrequitement).

Goethe's Werther is again the perfect example. Moping around,
complaining of the slights and injustices of the world, Werther is
ridiculously self-involved and self-deluded, but his tears of entreaty
are perfectly sincere. Incapable of being insincere, unable to live without expressing his desire, and finally in despair when Lotte doesn't
answer his tearful prayers, Werther commits suicide.

As this suggests, Werther is a bit of a schlemiel as well as a Romantic hero, but his tears are true, and they are the direct descendants of
the holy tears of the Middle Ages. Werther looks "up to Heaven with
longing and tears." His "eyes filled with tears" as he tells Lotte, "We
shall meet again, here and beyond." And he tells Wilhelm, "God alone
knows how often, in my bed, I have prayed in tears that He might
make me her equal." Just as the saints' tears are protestations of love
to God and requests to God for consolation, so Werther's tears and
prayers protest his love, plead for Lotte's consolation, and vouch for

his sincerity and purity of feeling. His tears fail as orators in the end, but in the meantime they help persuade Lotte to spend time with him, and even to cry with him as they read Romantic poetry together. Lotte is already engaged to someone else and so cannot requite his love, but she never doubts the sincerity and truth of Werther's tearful protestations.

A novel published three years earlier in Britain, Henry Mackenzie's *The Man of Feeling*, is often considered the prototypical British novel of the cult of sensibility, the British equivalent of *Werther*. One of the weepiest books on record, it, too, assumes that tears are offerings. Remembering an old friend, the narrator says, "I gave thee a tear then: accept of one cordial drop that falls to thy memory now." When Harley, the character who is the man of feeling, hears a tale of woe, he gives it "the tribute of some tears." Harley is often moved by such stories, and gives away his money and his tears to the various wretches he meets in the course of his travels: "He put a couple of guineas into the man's hand. . . . —He burst into tears, and left." They in return, often give him the tribute of tears: "'I am sorry,' he said, 'that at present I should be able to make you an offer of no more than this paltry sum.' —She burst into tears." And these tributes enter into intimate relationships as well. When a father and wayward daughter are reunited, she falls to the ground and "bathe[s] his feet with tears," in an obvious reference to the story of Jesus at Bethel. The father, in return, "fell on her neck and mingled his tears with hers," forgiving her her sins.

Mackenzie makes explicit the monastic heritage of these tears. "The world, my dear Charles, was a scene in which I never much delighted," says Harley. Some feelings, he explains, are too tender for this world, and people tend to assume, wrongly, that weeping is a sign of melancholy or overromantic selfishness. In heaven, though, Harley says, tears will be considered not flaws but the essence of goodness. In the meantime, we can try to bring a little heaven to earth through sensitive tears. Tears are a way, in fact, of infusing the world with virtue. To a "fallen" woman crying in gratitude for a gift he has made to her, he says, "There is virtue in these tears." Her tears not only solicit his sympathy but prove her sincerity and her essential purity, even if she is not "pure" in the worldly sense.

Sometimes tears in the novel are the result of an unrestrained empathy, as when Harley accompanies a young girl he has just met to her parents' graves, where "the girl cried afresh; Harley kissed off her tears as they flowed, and wept between every kiss." Sometimes Harley's tears seem to be an aesthetic response: "At that instant a shepherd blew his horn: the romantic melancholy of the sound quite overcame him!—it was the very note that wanted to be touched—he sighed! he dropped a tear!—and returned." Sometimes it is a simple response to a sad story; when he hears of the death of the house dog, Trusty, his face is "bathed with tears." In all of these cases, though, Harley is shown to be a new kind of man, a man who is not a monk but who is removed from the world of lesser men and their petty concerns, who is in the aristocracy but wants to alleviate the suffering of the poor, who is not afraid that the world will find him oversensitive. He is the ideal man of the cult of sensibility in the eighteenth century: sincere, sensitive, and not quite of this world.

Other eighteenth-century writers reinforced this connection between tears and sincerity. Rousseau in his philosophical works and novels, for instance, made similar comments. Civilized emotions are pale imitations of the primitive emotions people feel in their natural state, according to Rousseau. When we cry deeply, we are closer to our natural and to our divine state than when we are in the grip of the guilt and pride that make up modern, civilized feelings. In just one of many examples from Samuel Richardson's *Pamela*, the heroine's old father cries at the compliments his daughter receives, and those watching are not surprised to see that his "honest heart springs thus to the eyes." In Jacques Henri Bernardin de Saint-Pierre's *Paul et Virginie* (1788), a very popular idyll, Paul tells Virginie, "Your touching tears put out the torch of superstition." For all of these writers, tears represent what Cioran calls, in describing those of medieval saints, "the criterion for truth."

In the Romantic revision of eighteenth-century sensibility, the body becomes even more obviously the seal of truth. Franz Schubert's song "Lob der Tränen," or "In Praise of Tears," with lyrics by the great German Romantic poet A. W. Schlegel, asks: "Words, what are they? One tear will say more than all of them." As they are for the other Romantic authors, tears in this song are true because they cannot be counterfeit, as words can. Roland Barthes, the last of the great Romantics, goes a step further: "By my tears, I tell a story, I produce a myth of grief, and henceforth I adjust myself to it: I can live with it because, by weeping, I give myself an emphatic interlocutor who receives the 'truest' of messages, that of my body, not that of my speech."

To say that tears have a meaning greater than any words is to suggest that truth somehow resides in the body. For Barthes and Schlegel, crying is superior to words as a form of communication because our bodies, uncorrupted by culture or society, are naturally truthful, and tears are the most essential form of speech for this idealized body. In the middle of the nineteenth century, Emily Brontë penned the following stanza in this Romantic vein:

> *Had there been falsehood in my breast*
> *No thorns had marred my road,*
> *This spirit had not lost its rest,*
> *These tears had never flowed.*

For Brontë, tears are impossible if any falsehood resides in the breast, and similar sentiments were expressed by all the major Romantic poets.

Later in the nineteenth century, explicitly religious tears and tearful expressions of faith continued to be part of religious practice and to be regularly represented in poetry and novels. Little Eva's deathbed scene in Harriet Beecher Stowe's *Uncle Tom's Cabin* (1850) and Little Nell's in Charles Dickens's *The Old Curiosity Shop* (1841) are just two of the many representations of the transformative, transcendent power of tears in mid-nineteenth-century sentimentalism. In fact, the best-selling American novels of the nineteenth century—Stowe's book, Dickens's novels, Lew Wallace's *Ben Hur,* and Elizabeth Stuart Phelps's *The Gates Ajar*—all make clear the connection between faith and tears: when the gates of heaven are ajar, one glimpses paradise, and one cries tears of fear and beatitude. The gates are ajar at the moment of death of a saintly or innocent person, and therefore tend to be seen by his or her attendants through already flowing tears of grief. In *Uncle Tom's Cabin*, Eva spends a few days on her deathbed dispensing spiritual advice and consolation, causing frequent tears of contrition and awe on the part of her family and retainers. Immediately upon watching Little Eva die, her hard-hearted spinster aunt Ophelia announces that she has finally learned to love because, she says, "I've learnt something of the love of Christ from her." And the narrator goes on to say that "Miss Ophelia's voice was more than her words, and more than that were the honest tears that fell down her face."

In these texts, tears of sincerity had never had so large an audience. And given the social criticism all of these authors were involved in— Stowe writing against slavery, Phelps and Dickens against the evils of industrialism—the quasi-religious tears they described were offered as a pure alternative to the compromises and corruptions of contemporary society, with the sincerity of tears functioning as a counterbalance to the falseness of society.

The testimony of readers confirms this. One member of Parliament, Daniel O'Connell, burst into tears when reading about Nell's death in *The Old Curiosity Shop*, crying out, "He should not have killed her!" He was riding on a train at the time and opened a window and threw the novel out. The actor William Macready said that Dickens had the ability to make us feel bad, but at the same time to "make our hearts less selfish." Francis Jeffrey, a critic at the *Edinburgh Review*, wrote, "I have so cried and sobbed over it last night, and again this morning; and felt my heart purified by those tears. . . . In reading of these delightful children, how deeply do we feel that 'of such is the kingdom of Heaven'; how ashamed of the contaminations which our manhood has received from the contact of earth." John Forster wrote to Dickens saying that "I felt this death of dear little Nell as a kind of discipline of feeling and emotion which would do me lasting good." The tears shed in fiction helped ease nineteenth-century heroines like Little Nell into their final escape from a degraded world, and helped purge her readers of their selfish contaminations.

When Little Nell and Little Eva die, the children weep not because they are afraid of death but because they are going to heaven, and the families and friends weep in recognition that they are watching a sanctified death. As their pure little souls leave their bodies, these holy children and those around them get a glimpse of heaven. And the readers (and the many who had these books read to them in the nineteenth century) wept as well, in a glory of revelation. These are tear-stained ceremonies of innocence, for the characters and for the readers, signal and proof of the crier's worth. Tears wash away the sins of the world and announce the arrival of reborn innocence.

For contemporary readers, these tears are a bit much. We know that emotional authenticity is not something we want too much of in our daily lives. We recognize an obsession with one's own feelings as narcissistic and childish, and in practice incredibly demanding. People who announce every desire or revulsion without regard to expressive conventions, who cry on the bus or in the supermarket, are often considered mentally ill or emotionally disturbed. And we know that expressing a particular emotion can have unforeseen consequences, both immediately and long after the emotion itself passes. We learn restraint in expression in the same way that we learn the conventions of emotional expression: we learn to express happy surprise at a gift we don't really like, to present a somber, perhaps even moist face at a funeral for someone we hardly knew, and to not cry in public except in very special circumstances.

Oscar Wilde, revolting against the sappiness of Victorian sentimental culture, wrote that "one would have to have a heart of stone to read the death of Little Nell without laughing." Aldous Huxley, too, was one of many who, from Dickens's heyday to the present, complained that his sentimentality was caused by a refusal to think, by "overflow, nothing else." Tears of truth, tears of tribute, tears of empathy, tears of devotion, tears as the ultimate mark of a sincere and truthful heart: these are not foreign to us; the basic ideas are still part of our culture of crying. But we also know that emotional life is more complex and less innocent than these eighteenth- and nineteenth-century texts would have us believe. And we also know about tears of humiliation, frustration, and manipulation—tears that have nothing to do with sincerity.

This flip side of tears was also present in the cultures that developed sensibility, Romanticism, and sentimentalism, which had their own share of critics and doubters. And similar critiques of what we would call the sentimental long predate these. Aristophanes' comedies, Aesop's fables, Apuleius's *The Golden Ass,* and Petronius's *Satyricon* make fun of the excessive validation of tears. Publius Syrus wrote in the first century that "behind the mask, the tears of an heir are laughter." The great early modern humorists—Chaucer, Boccaccio, and Rabelais—all wrote scenes of insincere crying. St. Peter Damien, prior of an Italian monastery in the eleventh century, voiced the general understanding of the medieval church when he wrote that "the sort of tears" produced by feigning "did not come from heavenly dew, but had gushed forth from the bilge-water of hell." According to Abbot Isaac, insincere tears are experientially and visibly, palpably different from sincere tears, and forced tears "never attain the rich copiousness of spontaneous tears."

The relation of tears to sincerity is far from simple, and this is in part because sincerity itself is far from simple. Pascal wrote that "nothing is simple which is presented to the soul, and the soul never presents itself simply to any object. Hence we weep and laugh at the same thing." A thoroughgoing sincerity, in other words, is impossible. One of the most famous epigrams on sincerity is from *Hamlet:*

> This above all: to thine own self be true
> And it doth follow, as the night the day,
> Thou canst not then be false to any man.

These words are spoken by Polonious, a fawning pedant who is unable to identify the most basic human emotions in front of him, and whose self-knowledge seems as abbreviated as his understanding of others. Like the used-car salesman who says "Trust me!" Polonious's paean to genuineness undermines itself.

Alongside the various representations of sincere tears, then, are a series of representations of insincerity and emotional machination. In British dramatist George Chapman's *The Widow's Tears* (1612), a character claims that everyone knows how "short lived Widow's tears are, that their weeping is in truth but laughing under a Mask, that they mourn in their Gownes, and laugh in their Sleeves." In Molière's *The Misanthrope* (1666), Alceste is a man who weeps readily, but although he claims that his "chief talent is to be frank and sincere," he is self-deluded, manipulative, and foolish. Choderlos de Laclos, in *Les Liaisons dangereuses* (1782), at the height of the culture of sensibility, dissected the cruelty and dissipation of the nobility in France by showing its use of tears as tactics in various petty power plays and deceptions. Joseph Roux, a French parish priest in the late nineteenth century, wrote that "there are people who laugh to show their teeth, and there are those who cry to show their good hearts." Lewis Carroll's Walrus in *Alice in Wonderland* (1865) is another version of sincere insincerity, since he feels sorry for the oysters while he eats them: "'I weep for you,' the Walrus said:/ 'I deeply sympathize.'/ With sobs and tears he sorted out/ Those of the largest size./ Holding his pocket handkerchief/ Before his streaming eyes." The critique of sincerity, and of tears as a mark of sincerity, has a history parallel to that of sincerity's enthronement as a prime virtue.

Fake tears can function, in the most obvious cases, as straightforwardly false protestations of sincerity, innocence, or love. Publius Syrus wrote in the first century A.D. that "women have learned to shed tears in order that they might lie the better," and Cato, in the second century, offered the maxim: "When a woman weeps she is constructing a snare with her tears." These general slanders against women were based on the idea that crying is an underhanded way to get what one wants. J. K. Morley was being both serious and facetious when he claimed that "the world's greatest water power is woman's tears." O. Henry said of one of his characters, "She would have made a splendid wife, for crying only made her eyes more bright and tender." Oscar Wilde wrote that "crying is the refuge of plain women, but the ruin of pretty ones." Wilde and O. Henry suggest that tears can add to a woman's allure for men, an idea, as I've suggested, with a long history: one proverb of unknown vintage claimed that "a woman wears her tears like jewelry," and like jewelry or makeup, tears have long been seen as part of the arsenal of women's wiles. In the proverb which ironically claimed that "every woman is wrong until she cries," tears are tools of self-justification as well.

These attitudes have persisted: the prominent psychologist Alfred Adler discussed what he called women's "tyranny of tears" at mid-century. One of men's jobs in the face of such tyranny and danger is to resist the allure. Humphrey Bogart does so when he sees through Mary Astor's teary display in *The Maltese Falcon:* "You're good, sister. Very good," he tells her with a smile of admiration for her skill, lighting a cigarette and shaking his head. Astor was using her moist expression of helplessness to get Bogart's help; when he sees through her ruse, she offers him money instead. But in many other films, books, musicals, and songs, men declare their helplessness when faced with female tears. In a thousand ways, men say, "Please, please, don't cry, I'll do anything you want, only please don't cry." Sometimes this is the stuff of comedy, sometimes it is played straight.

Women clearly do not have a monopoly on emotional blackmail, since men—think of the angry male tyrant, or, for that matter, the angry Othello—wield emotions as weapons as well. According to some feminists, crying is simply a stratagem women are forced to employ because of their lack of access to other forms of personal, cultural, and emotional power. From this perspective, tears are the weapons of the oppressed for several reasons. Tears can announce submission, as they do in the Bible or when children cry when reprimanded, and as such they suggest that the crier—like Mary Astor— is acting much more subservient to the wishes of her auditor than she plans to be. Tears here are not so much con as cover. Because they announce submission, tears have the power to deflect counterattack, again making them the weapon of choice for those who feel themselves to be vulnerable.

Given the source of the metaphor, the fact that crocodile tears mask other motives should not be surprising. When crocodiles fully extend their jaws to swallow a victim, the crocodile's lacrimal ducts are squeezed, and excess lubricating tears are produced. Real crocodiles' tears are in fact meaningless in emotional terms. Metaphorical crocodiles' tears are an emotional diversionary tactic, a kind of camouflage for metaphorical teeth. In *Othello* (1604), as Desdemona weeps, decrying her innocence, Othello rants, unconvinced: "O Devil, Devil! If that the earth could teem with woman's tears, / Each drop she falls would prove a crocodile." Othello is of course mistaken. Shakespeare was well aware that this figure, the perfidious weeping woman, was not, at its core, the truth of the matter. Desdemona is not crying crocodile tears, and she is not perfidious—Othello is being led to his perdition because he is so ready to believe in his wife's crocodile nature. Desdemona's tears are real and they are sincere. Othello believes the proverbs rather than his own eyes.

Tears can also announce our submission, the human equivalent of a dog putting its tail between its legs—please, we can say with tears, I am already abased, do me no further harm. This appeal can be sincere, it can be faked, and it can be both sincere and strategic at the same time. Tears can encourage people to empathize with us, whatever our ulterior motives. Othello's tragedy is that he withholds his empathy, refusing to respond to Desdemona's tears. But tears can also be used to keep people at bay, to keep them from getting too close, just as Othello, himself, pushes Desdemona away with tears in his eyes. Norman Mailer, in *The Gospel According to the Son* (1997), has Christ say, "Tears stood forth in my eyes like sentinels on guard," and tears can be a way to guard the self, to demand that people treat us with kid gloves, or to raise the cost of doing emotional business with us.

Even those novelists who were especially good at deploying sincere tears understood this flip side of tears. Little Eva's mother is a hypochondriac who is constantly bursting into tears as a way of manipulating the people around her, and Stowe makes clear that sometimes those who cry are less sincere than those who do not. Dickens gives us a classic example of tears as strategy in his picture of Mrs. and Mr. Bumble in *Oliver Twist*. Two months into their marriage, the couple has a fight that amounts to a full scramble for power: "Mrs. Bumble, seeing at a glance that the decisive moment had now arrived, and that a blow struck for mastership on one side or another, must necessarily be final and conclusive, dropped into a chair, and with a loud scream that Mr. Bumble was a hard-hearted brute, fell into a paroxysm of tears." But just as Mr. Bumble had failed in his earlier attempt to stare her down, so her attempt to shame or cajole him with tears falls short. "Tears were not the things to find their way to Mr. Bumble's soul; his heart was waterproof. Like washable beaver hats that improve with rain, his nerves were rendered stouter, and more vigorous, by showers of tears, which, being tokens of weakness, and so far tacit admissions of his own power, pleased and exalted him." He even encourages her: "'It opens the lungs, washes the countenance, exercises the eyes, and softens down the temper,' said Mr. Bumble. 'So cry away.'" Mrs. Bumble, in turn, had lost a battle but not the war. She "had tried the tears because they were less troublesome than a manual assault," but when they don't work, she grabs him by the throat with one hand and "inflicted a shower of blows (dealt with singular vigour and dexterity)" upon his head with the other.

Insincere tears take other forms as well. Weeping religious statues, for instance, have been regularly derided as manipulations, most recently in Carl Hiaasen's *Lucky You* (1997), in which a small town in Florida has a shrine that weeps as its owner pumps a foot switch. The owner regularly attempts to improve his business by adding perfume or red dye to the tears. Hiaasen doesn't exaggerate much. On March 10, 1992, Tony Fernwalt of Steubenville, Ohio, the janitor at the Shrine of St. Jude, which was housed in a converted barbershop, had a fifteen-minute conversation with the Blessed Virgin Mary. After the visitation, a statue at the shrine began to weep. Bishop Roman Bernard immediately contacted the local and national media. Thousands of people came to the tiny shrine, according to some news reports, and Bishop Bernard's tithe revenues so mushroomed that he told several friends that he was ready to "pack it in, sell the shrine, and move to Florida." Fernwalt, we assume, and the believers who stuffed the bishop's coffers marveled at the sight or the idea of a crying icon, and found it inspirational or awesome; Bernard was obviously just a tad cynical, and the often ironic news reports found it all ludicrous.

In 1995 a total of thirteen different statues were reported to be weeping in Italy, and when one in Civitavecchia was reported to be weeping blood, the Catholic Church ordered DNA tests to see if the blood matched that of the owners, in an effort to replace what it saw as an outmoded and theologically questionable test of authenticity with a more modern one. Theologians and scholars of religion have long argued that the famous weeping apparitions of the Virgin—at Lourdes, for instance—are psychological phenomena which have no religious import in themselves, folk religion that is created around an aberration. The children who first saw this and other apparitions, for instance, did not identify them as Mary; this was an interpretation foisted on them by adults.

The other Madonna, in the video for her hit "Like a Prayer" (1989), shows a religious statue weeping. The statue then comes alive, and in a move that is even less theologically sound, it begins to respond to Madonna's sexual advances. Madonna uses the religious symbolism to heighten the sense of sexualized nonconformity that is a central part of her image—hers is a sociosexual heresy, not a religious one. And she uses the weeping statue to give a sense of tragic romance and significance to the odd encounter. But if weeping statues are regularly seen as scams or symbols by nonbelievers, they obviously speak quite persuasively and poignantly to those who do believe. For the audience that finds them profound and moving, they serve a perfectly authentic religious purpose. Sincerity, finally, is in the moist eye of the beholder.

Heroic Tears

In *Adam's Rib* (1949), the classic screwball comedy, Katharine Hepburn and Spencer Tracy play a wife and husband who are lawyers on opposite sides—she defending, he prosecuting a woman accused of attempting to murder her philandering husband. During the day they argue the case in court, and at home at night they go through a series of fights and reconciliations, both convinced that they have justice and reason on their side. During one fight, Hepburn begins to cry, and Tracy throws up his hands. "Here we go again!" he says. "The old juice! Guaranteed he-man melter: a few female tears, stronger than any acid. But this time it won't work. You can cry from now until the jury comes in but it won't make you right." Weeks later, when they are on the verge of divorce, he begins to cry, sees it has an effect, and cries some more. She joins him in tears and they decide to stay together. Later, he admits that he had faked the tears to get her not to leave. "But those tears were real," she insists, and he agrees. "Of course they were," he says. "But I can turn 'em on anytime I want. Us boys can do it too, only we never think to."

The fact is that neither Hepburn's nor Tracy's character turns them on artificially, and his claim to be able to control his tears is a bit of classic male bluster. He also, self-evidently, exaggerates when he claims that men never think to cry, since he obviously has. This dialogue was written at a time when the official line in American culture was that men didn't cry and women did, whether sincerely, strategically, or hysterically. But the simple fact is that men have always cried, and for many reasons.

In the Bible, men cried as we have seen, in prayer before battles, in lamentation for the fate of the Hebrews, and for many other reasons as well. David cried at the death of Absalom, Abraham wept when Sarah died, Joseph when meeting Benjamin, Jesus at the death of Lazarus. The shortest sentence in the Bible, famously, is "Jesus wept." In the Book of Lamentations, a collection of five psalms in which the author laments the destruction of Jerusalem in 587 B.C., the male narrator weeps unrestrainedly. "My eyes flow with rivers of tears," he sings, "my eyes will flow without ceasing, without respite, until the Lord from

Memling was the premier painter of tears in the fifteenth century. Hans Memling (after), *Christ Crowned in Thorns* (c. 1490). Philadelphia Museum of Art: John G. Johnson Collection.

heaven looks down and sees." (Weeping in these psalms is everywhere: Jerusalem itself is said to "weep bitterly in the night," the road to Zion is said to "mourn," and the ramparts and walls to "lament.") Men like the narrator of Lamentations were expected to cry, to cry hard and regularly.

In ancient Greek culture, both men and women could feel free to cry at the murder of a close relative or at reunions. But men were expected to cry if their family's honor was at stake while women were not, and women could cry out of loneliness or fear while men could not. Women could cry about a missing husband, as Penelope cries over Odysseus in *The Odyssey*, while the hero himself cries because he is separated from his homeland, from his vineyards, or from his kinsmen. In the Mycenaean civilization depicted in *The Odyssey*, it would have been an important part of Penelope's role to be a wife, but not a particularly important part of Odysseus's social responsibilities to be a husband. It was important that he be a good leader, a good warrior, a good friend, and have strong heirs, but to be a husband implied more rights than responsibilities; it was less a role to be fulfilled than a simple fact.

Odysseus cries quite a lot during his ten-year journey home. When he finally does return home, in disguise, he meets his childhood nurse, who tells him (thinking that he is a stranger) a story about the young Odysseus bravely hunting a wild boar. She notices that he has a scar on his leg that matches the one Odysseus received from the boar, but she only recognizes her former master for sure when he begins to cry in response to the story. His authentic, primary, tearful response to her story establishes his identity as both a man and a hero.

Penelope weeps when she thinks of the missing Odysseus. Unable to sleep "with all her cares" weighing upon her, Homer tells us, "she wept and cried aloud until she had her fill of tears." Odysseus never cries from the weight of his cares, and he is never sated by his tears. When Penelope finds that her son Telemakhos is gone:

> her eyes filled with tears, and she could find no utterance. . . . There were plenty of seats in the house, but she had no heart for sitting on any one of them; she could only fling herself on the floor of her own

room and cry; whereon all the maids in the house, both old and young, gathered round her and began to cry too.

Such worries did not make men cry, nor were men expected to faint from their tears, as women often did. Tears for women marked the end of action, as fainting would necessarily dictate; men's tears were instead more often a spur to action. And while women were not under any requirement to hide their tears, men sometimes were, as when Achilles "betook himself alone" in order to "cast forth upon the purple sea his wet eyes." Warriors were expected to cry, but they were also expected to know when to do so alone. And nothing made them cry quite so much as their own heroism.

Heroic epics from Greek times through the Middle Ages are soggy with weeping of all sorts. In the eighth-century Anglo-Saxon epic *Beowulf*, Hrothgar, king of the Danes, thanks Beowulf for helping to bring about peace by giving him twelve jewels, after which he "clasped the hero round the neck, and kissed him, tears pouring from his gray head." Roland, one of Charlemagne's warriors immortalized by the twelfth-century *Song of Roland*, cries freely, and is even allowed to faint. When Roland's friend Oliver dies in battle, "Lord Roland weeps, lamenting bitterly; / Many have grieved, but no man more than he," and he then faints in his saddle. When Roland himself dies, Charlemagne "pulls his beard in anguish and in pain;/The lords of France are weeping bitter tears,/And twenty thousand faint in their grief and fall. . . . There is not one among those noble lords/Who can refrain from shedding tears of grief." To mark the distance between our view of tears and that of eight hundred years ago, one need only imagine a film version of these twenty thousand weeping, fainting knights in armor falling off their horses—perhaps only Monty Python could accomplish it.

This kind of massive heroic weepiness is also found in medieval Japanese warrior epics. In the twelfth-century *Tales of the Heiki*, men cry copiously. The warrior Koremori declares, "I am forever undecided," and weeps. The monk Sonei weeps in abjection as he pleads to be told the way to escape the endless circle of death and rebirth, and weeps tears of joy when he is told. When the hero Hō-ō sees the exiled empress living poorly, "his voice became choked with sobs" and he "burst into tears." This is not just because she is an acquaintance who has been brought low but because her condition is the result of inadequate martial protection. Men also cry about high ideals. Upon hearing a woman sing a verse about the Buddha, "all the Princes and the Courtiers of the Heiki and the high officers and the samurai shed tears of admiration and sympathy." Women cry in the Japanese epics as well, but they tend to cry more about personal relationships than about eternal verities or social problems, more about love than ethics or aesthetics. As in the Western warrior tales, men cry most often about issues of war, peace, and ideals, women about domestic relationships.

The idea that tearlessness was the height of male stoicism and virtue, which we all recognize as a part, albeit a "traditional" or old-fashioned aspect, of our emotional culture, also has a long history, but as these three quick surveys of tears should make plain, tearlessness has not been the standard of manliness through most of history. The prohibition against male tears, in fact, only takes center stage in the middle of the twentieth century, and even then it was not fully observed, as we can see in the weeping of film stars and crooners. (Significantly, the same holds true for Japanese culture, where male reticence reaches its heights in the twentieth century, and where films, too, are full of male tears, usually excused by the character's drunkenness.) Male tears have continued unabated in our culture, and heroic tears have continued to be shed as well. One notable example is the scene of heroic weeping at the end of *First Blood*, in which Sylvester Stallone sheds tears of grief at his lost comrades-in-arms and in anguish at his own dubious place in history. Rambo was an ambiguous hero, of course, not the tough John Wayne type (who would get a little glassy-eyed on occasion, and sometimes wipe away a tear before it fell) or the neotough Clint Eastwood. Rambo straddled the cultural conflict between the peaceniks and law-and-order forces, a hippie Green Beret, a decorated macho killer with long hair and antiestablishment anger: when the film opened in 1982, *Variety* deemed the film itself "socially irresponsible." Rambo's position on the margin allows him to act in ways unavailable to the men around him, men in more obviously proscribed social roles. He knows no fear and feels no physical pain, but sobs and moans and cries out his emotional woe. Unlike the Greek hero who is expected to cry because he is heroic, Rambo earns the right to violate the macho prohibition against crying (as does Stallone's previous character, Rocky) through his heroism. Unlike the hippie he has been mistaken for, he can say to the man in authority, through his tears, "I did everything I was supposed to do, I have fulfilled my social role perfectly." This blissful sense of role fulfillment causes his tears, and is meant to cause tears in the audience as well. In one of the very few studies of men and women crying at films, done in 1950 in England, the majority of men who cried at films claimed that scenes of heroism, patriotism, and bravery were most likely to make them cry.

"Stormin' " Norman "the Bear" Schwarzkopf, plastered with macho nicknames and combat ribbons, was interviewed by Barbara Walters toward the end of the Persian Gulf War, and like most of Walters's interviewees, he welled up with tears as he answered personal questions. Walters said she was surprised. "Generals don't cry, generals don't get tears in their eyes," she suggested. Schwarzkopf answered, "Grant, after Shiloh, went back and cried. Sherman went back and cried. . . . And these are tough old guys. Lee cried at the loss of human life. . . . Lincoln cried."

Schwarzkopf added that generals cry not during battle but afterward. He didn't cry in front of his troops during the Gulf War, and not because he didn't feel things deeply but because his role demanded otherwise: "They don't want a general to cry and that's very important to me," he told Walters. But he could cry at a Christmas Eve service, he said, in front of his troops. He explained that at the service he was fulfilling a different role, acting not as a commanding officer but as a father figure, as a focus for communal emotions.

Pleasure, sincerity, heroism. The first is primarily subjective, the second interactive, and the third pretends to be objective. That is, if pleasure is a name we give to a particular way of feeling, and sincerity a display of one's inner state, tears of heroism are neither private nor explicitly meant to be seen. Heroic tears—Odysseus's, Rambo's, Schwarzkopf's—

are, the warriors and their chroniclers argue, reminiscent rather than strategic. Odysseus frequently tries to hide his tears, and when Beowulf, Rambo, and Schwarzkopf weep, their tears do not so much express an inner state as appear autonomously. Of course, Schwarzkopf's tears may indeed have been strategic, since on the heels of these interviews, Schwarzkopf began being mentioned as a political candidate, celebrated not just as tough guy but as a well-rounded man, one who could fulfill all aspects of his role as a leader. The tears he shed as a would-be politician testing the waters on a TV show known for making its guests cry are either sincere or the opposite. The tears he described himself crying during the war, however, are heroic. And all of these kinds of good tears—tears of pleasure, sincerity, and heroism—have their bad counterparts: tears of pain, crocodile tears, milksop tears.

As these three mini-histories of tears suggest, a very consistent mix of ideas about weeping has been with us for millennia, although the ratios have varied. Pleasure was sometimes seen as the prime virtue of tears, sometimes sincerity, and sometimes emotional heroism, and the flip side of each of these virtues—self-indulgence, insincerity, cowardice—was also always part of the cultural mix, again in varying measure. Even as the bases for judgment shift and reshift, the basic issues have tended to recur. The question most asked of tears is, in the words of the tract on moral weeping which began this chapter: Are they genuine or counterfeit, the route to heaven or the bilgewater of hell? It would be more correct, though, to say that tears are never simply a sign of pleasure, pain, sincerity, duplicity, fear, or heroism. There are no pure tears. Even at the most basic, physiological level, tears are mixed, impure. As the next chapter will show, not all tears are created equally, and none behave as our metaphors would suggest they should.

2

The Crying Body

The cornea of the eye has a far from perfect surface. It is pocked, wrinkled, uneven. Tears smooth out these irregularities in the surface of the eye and thus make possible vision as we know it. Without this everyday teary layer, we would see a world of weird diffractions and absences, be unable to move our eyes, and lose them to infection. Just as our emotional tears form a permeable barrier that can distance us from our social world even as they open us to its censures, rewards, pleasures, and pains, this continuous teary surface layer of the eye is a liquid membrane both protecting us from the world and allowing us access to it.

Tears are what Abraham Werb, an ophthalmic surgeon in London, has called a "fluid sandwich," with an inner layer of mucin against the eye surface, a middle aqueous layer, and an outer layer of oils that keeps the tears from evaporating too quickly. Physiologists and ophthalmologists recognize three different kinds of tears: basal, reflex, and psychic. Basal tears are the continuous tears that lubricate our eyeballs. Reflex or irritant tears are produced when we chop onions, for instance, or get poked in the eye. Psychic or emotional tears are those caused by, and communicating, specific emotional states. These different kinds of tears have not only different functions but different compositions—they contain differing concentrations of chemicals, hormones, and proteins.

The anatomy of the lacrimal system has only come to be understood in its present form in the last hundred years. It is made up of a secretory and an excretory system, the first producing tears and the second draining them away. The main lacrimal gland, located between a shallow depression in the frontal bone and the eyeball, is principally responsible for producing the great flow of tears caused by irritation or emotion. There are numerous smaller, accessory lacrimal glands that contribute primarily to basal tears: in each eye there are twenty or so glands of Krause in the conjunctiva and several glands of Wolfring near the upper border of the tarsal plate which produce the

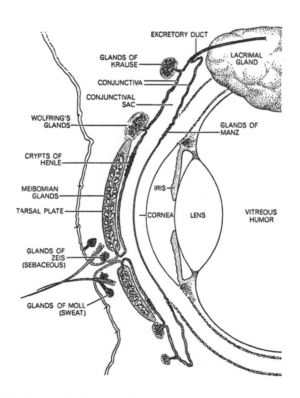

Diagram of the lacrimal glands. Tom Prentiss (1964). Courtesy Nelson H. Prentiss.

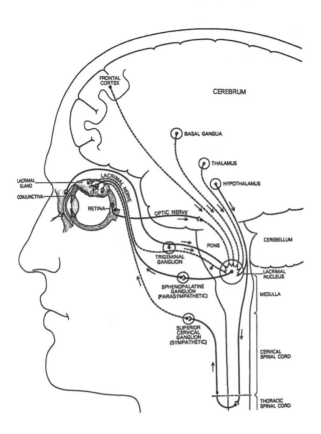

Diagram of the lacrimal and related nerves. Tom Prentiss (1964). Courtesy Nelson H. Prentiss.

aqueous layer. A combination of goblet cells and glands of Manz, also in the conjunctiva, secrete the mucin that forms the inner layer of tears. Finally, forty-six meibomian glands in the eyelids (along with glands of Zeis at the edges of the eyelids and glands of Moll at the eyelash roots) produce the lipids, or oils, that slow evaporation. All of these accessory glands put together are less than a tenth of the size of the lacrimal gland.

Basal tears are produced continuously, at the rate of one to two microliters a minute, or from five to ten ounces a day. As the tears are continually replenished, some of the fluid evaporates between blinks, and some is drained through the puncta—small, permanent openings at the nose end of each eyelid on a slight elevation of tissue known as

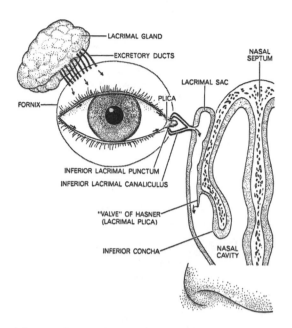

Diagram of the eye showing lacrimal ducts. Tom Prentiss (1964). Courtesy Nelson H. Prentiss.

the papilla lacrimalis. Tears drain through the puncta into the canaliculis, ducts that drain into the lacrimal sac. From the lacrimal sac the tears flow into the nasolacrimal duct, which empties into the nose. When tears are produced in exceptional quantities—due to emotions or irritants or disease—the puncta cannot handle the flow and tears drain outward over the eyelids. Because the puncta are about 0.2 to 0.3 millimeters in diameter, and therefore visible to the naked eye, they were very early on associated with tears, which were often assumed to be their source.

The physiology of emotion is, we might say, both a very old and a very new science. Physiological theories of emotion in the West begin with the Hippocratic writers of the fifth century B.C., and thus are as old as medical science itself. Contemporary physiology of the emotions, on the other hand, rightly begins only in the 1930s, on the heels of the development of endocrinology, the study of the hormone-releasing glands, a decade earlier. It is thus newer than the New Physics, and continues to be fraught with contention. As Jack George

Thompson notes in his textbook *The Psychobiology of the Emotions* (1988), "Scientific truths are probabilistic and not absolute," and there are not only numerous competing paradigms and fields—psychobiology, neuropsychology, and neurophysiology, just to name a few—but fundamental disagreements within those fields. Each of these subdisciplines has a slightly different approach to studying the body and the role of emotion, and no general theory of the emotions is accepted by them all. There are still some missing pieces of the basic anatomical puzzle as well: anatomists are unsure, for instance, of the exact pathway of some of the nerve fibers which control the lacrimal glands, and they are even further from coming up with a full map of the brain activity involved.

But we know that there are at least several interacting systems at work in any emotional experience. Peter J. Lang of the Center for Research in Psychophysiology at the University of Florida argues that any analysis of emotional life requires attention to verbal and cognitive activity, motor activity, and physiological activities such as changes in the tonic activity levels of the somatic muscles and viscera. Antonio Damasio, a professor of neurology at the University of Iowa College of Medicine and the Salk Institute for Biological Studies in La Jolla, California, suggests that researchers need to focus on these and several other neural and physiological systems and subsystems, including several different cerebral circuits. While these various systems might operate somewhat independently, emotions can produce activity in all of them concurrently.

Beyond such generalizations, there is much debate. Some researchers believe they have discovered basic human universals of feeling and facial expression; others believe no such universals exist. Some argue that there is an emotion-specific physiology, others that there is not. While all agree that emotions change as infants develop into children and then into adults, there is little agreement as to what exactly changes, how much is biological and how much cultural, and whether it is the emotions that actually change or just the ability to feel, express, and control them. Some researchers find this last distinction itself erroneous, arguing that an emotion is indistinguishable from its measurable feeling and expression. These debates have long histories, with some of the battle lines having been drawn two millennia ago. The history of physiological thinking about tears from the Hippocratic doctors through the early twentieth century is full of error and does little to inform the most advanced neurophysiological understandings of our own day. But the ideas of Hippocrates, Descartes, Darwin, and James have nonetheless had, and continue to have, profound effects on our general cultural understandings of tears.

The History of Lacrimation

The Hippocratic doctors thought that tears came directly from the brain. For the Hippocratic writers, and European medicine through the Renaissance, tears were related to the humors, the four fundamental bodily fluids—blood, phlegm, black bile, and yellow bile—that were thought to determine one's health and character. An imbalance among these four fluids, which were released by the glands, led to disease. The fundamental cure was the purging—through bleeding, enemas, emetics, or crying—of excess humors.

The emphasis placed on proper ingestion and purgation in Greek medicine is assumed by historians to be the effect of the influence of Egyptian physicians on the Greeks. In Egyptian medicine, feces were considered the prime pathogen. Fecal matter, or more precisely the *whdw*, which was thought to be the pathogen in feces, could, by entering and traveling through the veins or other bodily systems, infect any part of the body. Ensuring and increasing elimination were therefore considered the prime modes of medical prevention and intervention. Herodotus reports that Egyptians purged themselves with enemas and emetics for three consecutive days each month. Didorus Siculus claims that it was "sometimes every day and sometimes at intervals of three or four days."

The Hippocratic doctors elaborated on this basic idea, arguing that all excess humors needed purgation. The buildup of bile, which they believed could be brought on by a change in the winds or other environmental causes, might lead to an ulcer, and purging the bile would prevent the ulcer. Epileptic seizures were the result of the improper purgation of phlegm, which, blocking respiration, slows the flow of blood and air to the brain. The brain, becoming more and more "humid" and overheated as a result, further prevents the elimination of phlegm, which finally results in seizures. "Thus is this disease formed and prevails from those things which enter into and go out of the body, and it is no more difficult to understand or to cure than the others." Crying can help flush the excess phlegm from the body and is thus advised in this and other cases of "brain disease." But tears themselves need to be purged as well. "Tears," one Hippocratic text contended, "are humors from the brain," and thus any excess needs to be expressed, purged by weeping.

Hippocratic ideas held sway in Western medicine for another millennium and a half, and along with them notions of the curative power of tearful catharsis, a Greek word meaning "purgation" or "purification." Although Galen (c. 130–200 A.D.) mistakenly thought that tears were delivered through the puncta, he was also the first to suggest that tears were produced not by the brain but by glands. But most other physicians went with Hippocrates: Hunain in the ninth century, Al Rhazes in the tenth, and Casserius in the seventeenth century all still assumed that the brain secreted tears. Timothy Bright, a British physician, wrote in 1586 that tears were "the excrementitious humiditie of the brayne," and Laurent Joubert, a French physician, wrote in 1579 that "when the brain is compressed, it ejects great quantities of tears." Bright and Joubert assumed that emotions like fear and sorrow caused "contractions" that squeezed humors from the heart to the brain, and then helped expel, in Bright's words, "the brains thinnest & most liquide excrement."

In medical treatises from the seventeenth century on, the four humors gradually lost their central place in medical thinking as new models of physiology were introduced in medical writings. By the late seventeenth century, the term "catharsis" came to be used almost exclusively in relation to the evacuation of the bowels, and the adjective "cathartic" meant powerfully laxative. Robert Boyle, a seventeenth-century natural philosopher and chemist, therefore, wrote of the "purgative faculty of Rhubarb, Senna, and other Cathartic Vegetables" in 1667. It wasn't until Sigmund Freud and Josef Breuer reintroduced the term to psychology in the 1890s that it regained its earlier meanings.

Another seventeenth-century philosopher and scientist began the modern philosophical and physiological examination of emotion and he linked emotion, the soul, and the body in new ways. "My intention," René Descartes wrote in a prefatory letter to his *The Passions of the Soul* (1649), "is to treat the passions of the soul, not as a preacher, also not as a moral philosopher, but only as a physicist." He failed, of course, in terms of anything we might consider pure physics or physiology, in part because he, too, could not resist making unsupported claims for the benefits of emotional tears. He employed his age's new understanding of the circulation of the blood, and he knew that the nerves were connected to the brain and were necessary to all sensation and perception. But he believed that the brain and nerves contained "a certain very subtle air or wind which is called the animal spirits," which were "bodies of extreme minuteness" and which move through the body animating muscles and making action possible. For Descartes, this animating movement was more closely related to the spirit and spiritual entities than to the electrical and chemical understanding of the nervous system which would evolve in the centuries that followed, and he had a similar splay of information and misinformation about the limbic system and other aspects of neurophysiology.

His explanation of crying, not surprisingly, then, was partly right and largely wrong. He understood that tears had optical and lubricant functions. And he saw that extreme emotions cause an increased blood flow to the eyes, and understood that this blood flow can, as Charles Darwin rediscovered in the nineteenth century, stimulate tear production. But Descartes also believed that just as water vapor is condensed into rain, so the animal spirits, the vapors of the body, are converted into sweat and tears through condensation. Anything that causes an increased flow of blood also increases the flow of animal spirits, Descartes believed, and so as the hot blood meets the cool vapors in the eye, they condense into tears.

The Passions of the Soul attempts to determine the relations of the mind (and soul) to the body by isolating those things that bodies can do on their own, without any help from the soul or the mind. He uses the example of a friend thrusting a hand into our face: we shut our eyes and wince, even if we know our friend would never hurt us. We do so because the body, as a mechanism, reacts without intervention of the "soul" or the mind. Fear does not wait for any mental or moral middleman. An irritant in the eye, by causing pain and thereby calling for an increase in the flow of blood and tears to the injured part, acts in the same way.

This basic idea—that the body can react to stimuli without any cognitive activity whatsoever—is at the center of numerous theories of emotion that have followed, theories that are known as "peripheralist" or "somatic," as opposed to the "mentalist" theories that assume the mind to be the originary organ. (Mentalist theories would later split into cerebralist and cognitive orientations.) But Descartes was not just a somatic theorist. Though he suggests here that emotions are simple bodily reactions, that tears are physical events that occur without the aid of thought, reflection, or moral intent, he argues the mentalist position elsewhere in the same work. People who do not cry bear the mark of "an evil disposition," he wrote, and have "a tendency towards hatred or fear . . . for these are passions which diminish the material of tears." And by the same reasoning, since "we see that those who weep very easily are inclined to love and pity," crying is a sign of a more virtuous being. Pity is the passion that most inclines people to weep because it is a combination of love and sadness (for Descartes all emotions are combinations of the six basic passions: wonder, love, hatred, desire, joy, and sadness). "Love," writes Descartes, "sending much blood towards the heart, causes many vapors to issue from the eyes, and the coldness of sadness, retarding the agitation of these vapors, causes them to change into tears."

As this suggests, yes, tears are the result of purely physical processes. But those processes are set in motion by responses that are at their core ethical. We cry because of the condensation of vapors, and we have no control over that condensation—it simply happens at a certain temperature. But the excess vapors themselves were created because we became heated, and those who love easily and widely, and therefore become heated more often, will therefore be more inclined to tears. The more loving we are, the more prone to tears.

Each of the purely physical reactions to passion also has an ethical purpose, according to Descartes. "They dispose the soul to desire things which are of use," he writes, and to persist in those desires. And again, they do so by physical, rather than intellectual or moral, means. Passions work by causing the soul "to dispose the body to the movement which serves for the carrying into effect of these things." That is, fear can dispose us to run from danger, hate disposes us to avoid harmful relations, and so on.

Descartes's revision of classical theories of emotion was based on the new medical findings of Harvey and others, and was developed at a time when dissection became the prime tool of physiological research and the classical paradigm of humors was replaced by attempts to explain the physiology of glands, blood, and organs in new ways. Further scientific findings then paved the way for the next great physiologist of emotion, Charles Darwin: A generation after Descartes, Steno of Denmark (Niels Stensen), in his *Anatomical Observations of the Glands of the Eye & Their New Vessels thereby Revealing the True Source of Tears* (1662), based on dissections of sheep's heads, gave the first fully revised view of tears, and although he got important facts wrong (believing that tears were supplied by the puncta, rather than drained by them, for instance), he was the first to suggest the centrality of the lacrimal glands. The French anatomist and surgeon Jacques-François-Marie Duverney described important muscles attached to the eyelids and the lacrimal gland in the 1740s. It wasn't until 1792, however, that Janin conclusively demonstrated the source of tears in the lacrimal gland and their pathway. Johann Rosenmüller described the anatomy of the gland in 1797, and in 1844 Martini postulated (although he couldn't locate them) the accessory glands. Karl Ernst von Baer studied the embryology or development of the lacrimal excretory system in the 1820s. Jan Nepomuk Czermak, a Hungarian physician, identified some of the nerves that enervate the lacrimal glands in 1860.

But between Descartes and Darwin, many other less philosophical taxonomies of emotion were also developed, rewriting Descartes's scheme of six master passions with increasingly complex categorizations, each one a little goofier than the next. The most elaborate of these was presented in *The Passions of the Human Soul and Their Influence on Society and Civilization* (1851), by the French communitarian social philosopher Charles Fourier. Fourier argued that there were four classes of passions: five "sensitive" passions, each related to a basic sense organ, four "affectives" and three "distributives" that lead to twelve "radicals," or root passions, or, under another division, five "passions of the soul," related to the five senses, and seven "animic passions," which are divided into four groups—friendship, sectism, love, familialism. Within these twelve orders, there are 33 genera, 135 species, and 405 varieties of emotions, unevenly distributed within the orders. If this sounds like a very confused taxonomy, it is, and when Fourier went on to associate each of his twelve passions with specific notes on the musical scale (love is mi, or a major third) and specific alcoholic beverages (love is thick white wine), he lost all but his most faithful followers. Advances in anatomy and physiology soon rendered Fourier and his ilk historical curiosities.

Both the physiological discoveries and the philosophical speculations helped set the stage for Darwin's still influential contribution, *The Expression of Emotions in Man and Animals* (1872). Unlike Baer and Czermak and other experimental physiologists, Darwin was interested, like Descartes, in larger questions of the bodily origin and function of emotion in general, and crying in particular. We express emotion, he concluded, in order to alleviate distress. Infants, for instance, when they suffer even moderate pain, cry out violently for the sole purpose of communicating their discomfort. Such crying out has obvious evolutionary advantages: babies who can communicate when they are hungry get fed more regularly than those that can't. Hence crying out is standard mammalian behavior. And tears are simply the unintended side effects of these calls for help.

Darwin included six photographs of crying infants which he commissioned to illustrate his points, and notes that in all of them, the infants strenuously contract the muscles around the eyes:

> The corrugators of the brow (*corrugator supercilii*) seem to be the first muscles to contract; and these draw the eyebrows downwards and inwards toward the base of the nose, causing vertical furrows, that is a frown, to appear between the eyebrows; at the same time they cause the disappearance of the transverse wrinkles across the

PLATE II

Photographs demonstrating the facial muscles contracted during the expression of emotion. From Charles Darwin, *The Expression of Emotions in Man and Animals* (1872). Courtesy University of Iowa Libraries.

forehead. The orbicular muscles contract almost simultaneously with the corrugators, and produce wrinkles all around the eyes; they appear, however, to be enabled to contract with greater force, as soon as the contraction of the corrugators has given them some support. Lastly, the pyramidal muscles of the nose contract; and these draw the eyebrows and the skin of the forehead still lower down, producing short, transverse wrinkles across the base of the nose. . . . When these muscles are strongly contracted, those running to the upper lip likewise contract and raise the upper lip. . . . The raising of the upper lip draws upward the flesh of the upper parts of the cheeks, and produces a strongly marked fold on each cheek,—the naso-labial fold,—which runs from near the wings of the nostrils to the corners of the mouth and below them.

Darwin then goes on, in similar detail, to outline the muscular changes around the mouth, the changes in respiration and circulation, and other physical manifestations that accompany crying. Here he is following the lead of Herbert Spencer, who had made similar arguments in his *Principles of Psychology* (1855). But Darwin's physiology is both more detailed and more accurate than Spencer's, and Darwin's text remains a primary source for the study of facial expression.

His conclusions about what these muscular contractions mean are more debatable. Darwin's main conclusion is that "weeping is an incidental result, as purposeless as the secretion of tears from a blow outside the eye, or as a sneeze from the retina being affected by a bright light." Children cry out to their parents for help, and prolonged screaming leads to "the gorging of the blood-vessels of the eye" since during the increased respiration that accompanies cries and screams, the eyeball and surrounding tissue are flooded with increased blood. This engorgement leads, "at first consciously and at last habitually," to the contraction of muscles around the eyes in order to protect the veins and arteries from the increased pressure. These contractions squeeze the tear ducts, which, as they secrete, further help cool the overheated and engorged eyeballs. Weeping is the direct result of the contractions of these muscles in the face, which are themselves caused by "violent" respiration. Emotional tears are thus the same as reflex tears.

Darwin does not belittle the cultural differences in crying behavior. He cites a claim that women in New Zealand "can voluntarily shed tears in abundance; they meet for this purpose to mourn the dead, and they take pride in crying 'in the most affecting manner.'" He quotes the naturalist Sir John Lubbock's 1870 *The Origin of Civilization*, in which Lubbock wrote of a New Zealand chief who "cried like a child because the sailors spoilt his favorite cloak by powdering it with flour." He cites French foreign minister Charles de Freycinet's report that the Sandwich Islanders recognize tears as signs of happiness, not sadness. He quotes Sir James Crichton-Browne, the psychiatrist, to the effect that the insane weep more readily than the sane, and that cretins do not weep at all.

But despite these local variations in emotional culture, Darwin argues, the cause of tears is always the same and always purely physical: they result from the contraction of muscles, which squeeze the tear glands and force them to secrete. Different cultural beliefs or demands can set this process in motion, but it is a physiological process.

Darwin is aware that this scenario does not explain why we sometimes cry in quiet sadness, without the preparatory screaming and increased somatic activity that screaming induces. Here he posits habit: we cry because of the emotional and expressive habits we have developed. The habitual association of tears with certain actions (and the well-traveled neural highways that result from our habitual responses) combine to make tears appear even when the rest of the chain is only minimally in evidence, if at all. Darwin speculates that the Sandwich Islanders, for instance, must cry in laughter as infants (which also sends blood rushing to the eyes) more than they cry out in pain, and thus their tears become associated with joy rather than sorrow:

> If, during an early period of life, when habits of all kinds are readily established, our infants, when pleased, had been accustomed to utter loud peals of laughter (during which the vessels of their eyes are distended) as often and as continuously as they have yielded when distressed to screaming fits, then it is probable that in after life

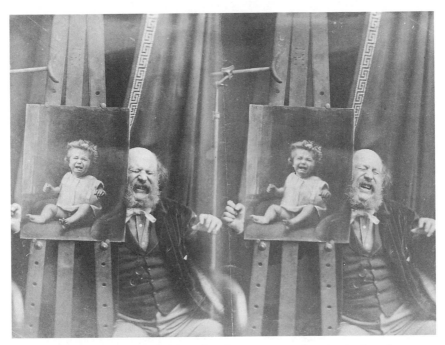

Darwin had an actor pose for these, laughing in one and crying in the other, to show the similarity of the facial muscle contractions. Courtesy Cambridge University Library.

tears would have been as copiously and regularly secreted under the one state of mind as under the other. Gentle laughter, or a smile, or even a pleasing thought, would have sufficed to cause a moderate secretion of tears.

And in the same way, we cry, moderately, without wailing, out of emotional habit. We acquire our emotional habits when young, when our eyeballs really were engorged each time we cried. But as adults, we can set the process off with any number of associated emotional states—as if our bodies trigger their own defense systems long before trouble actually starts, and begin to cool our eyes before they begin to overheat.

A similar combination of adaptive biology and habit informed the theories of William James, writing just a couple of decades later. James

at Harvard and Professor C. G. Lange at the University of Copenhagen
came to very similar conclusions in the 1890s, and although they
never worked together, their theories are often referred to as the
James-Lange theory of emotion, the most influential theory of emotion in the first part of this century. Like Darwin, James and Lange
argued that emotion was first and foremost bodily sensation. To feel
emotion was to feel one's own body, to feel its blushes, flushes, tin-
glings, and tears. Our emotions occur at first without the intercession
of rational thought; it is only after we feel the bodily sensations of
anger or fear that we cognitively register the emotion—we feel adrenaline rushing through our veins and only then do we conclude that we
are frightened or excited.

James's references to the body are not simply idle philosophical
speculation. He began his career at Harvard as a professor of comparative anatomy, and he was writing in the context of the latest physiological science and psychological experimentation. He argued that
emotions were similar to reflexes. Most people believe, writes James,
that we perceive something mentally, we have a mental reaction to it
which we call an emotion, and a set of bodily changes accompany that
reaction. But this, as the old pun goes, puts Descartes before the horse,
since without the bodily reactions, we don't yet have an emotion.
James sums up his own theory in a now famous passage in his *Principles of Psychology*:

> My thesis on the contrary is that *the bodily changes follow directly the
> PERCEPTION of the exciting fact, and that our feeling of the same
> changes as they occur IS the emotion*. Common sense says, we lose our
> fortune, are sorry and weep; we meet a bear, are frightened and run;
> we are insulted by a rival, are angry, and strike. The hypothesis here
> defended says that this order of sequence is incorrect, that the one
> mental state is not immediately induced by the other, that the bod-
> ily manifestations must first be interposed between, and that the
> more rational statement is that we feel sorry because we cry, angry
> because we strike, afraid because we tremble.

James's explanation seems to fly in the face of common sense, since it
is hard to support the notion that thought cannot give rise to feeling.

But the theory does account for some other aspects of emotion, such as the fact that it is impossible to imagine an emotion without an associated bodily state.

Imagine anger without a clenching of the jaw or the sense of blood rushing to one's head and chest. Whereas we might not agree with James that we are afraid simply because we tremble, it is true that if we are not trembling, if our heart is not pumping in our ears, if our hair is not standing on end, if we feel no rush of adrenaline, then we are not truly afraid. When we "feel" our bodies, when we get informa-

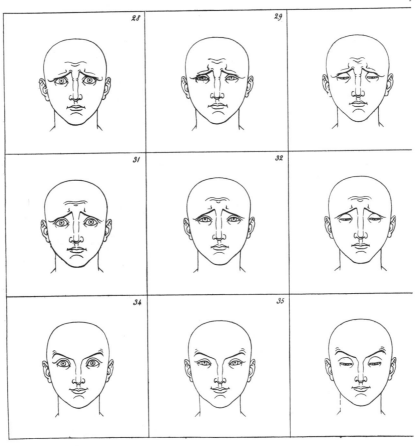

The nine possible facial expressions of emotion in the Delsarte system. From Alfred Giraudet, *Mimique, physionomie et gestes: methode pratique, d'apres le systeme de F. del Sarte pour servir a l'expression des sentiments* (1895). Courtesy Special Collections Department, University of Iowa Libraries.

tion from the inside of our bodies, we recognize our own emotional state, and without that information, there is no "feeling." The information is not always clear: are we crying from relief, from gratitude, from confusion? But if we are not feeling our bodies in a transformed state, then we are just thinking. As James puts it, if we remove all of the bodily signs that we are angry—the clenched fists and teeth, the increased heart rate, the adrenaline flow, the knotted brow—we may still have an idea or an attitude or a judgment, but we are no longer experiencing an emotion. Thus, to some extent, we are sad because we are crying, angry because we are fuming.

Historians have argued recently that James's theory was far from an unheralded stroke of genius but came into being in a culture infused with similar ideas about the relation between mind and body. Robyn Warhol has pointed out the similarities between James's theory of the emotions and the system of exercise, dance, and acting techniques based on the work of French philosopher François Delsarte. Delsarte's followers believed that a very discreet set of bodily changes expressed emotion, and that by performing those physical changes, the actor, and then the audience, would experience the corresponding emotion. These artificially induced emotions could be brought about with very simple movements. All expressions involving the eyes, for instance, depend on two muscle groups: one that raises or lowers the eyebrows and one that raises or lowers the eyelids. Since in each case there were only three pertinent positions (up, down, or normal), a total of nine different emotions could be had. As in James's theory, the body can have emotional reactions without the interpolation of specific thoughts. Joseph Roach has argued that the monistic views of a number of Victorian naturalists (such as George Henry Lewes) lead directly to James's view of emotions. And we can add that the widespread interest in eugenics at the turn of the century, and race-based understandings of human progress in general, signal a similar understanding of the body's primacy. But there is no denying that as an explicit theory of the emotions, the James-Lange theory did contain something new.

As commentators ever since (John Dewey as early as 1894) have noted however, we cannot be sad simply because we are crying. Very similar bodily states that in James's theory should determine our emotional experience can have very different emotional meanings. Dewey uses the example of two teams coming off the playing field at the end of a strenuous game, all of the players with their bodies in a state of extreme agitation and weariness from the prolonged contest, but the winning half of them jubilant and the losing half morose. What makes for the different emotions is different thoughts. And we can add a further wrinkle, since different emotions can have the same thought content. As the philosopher of music Malcolm Budd points out, "Pity and *Schadenfreude* both involve the thought of someone's misfortune or discomfiture," but they are radically different emotions. And we can cry with no particular thought content at all, as when we have just smashed our finger in a car door.

In the 1920s, scientists and social scientists of several persuasions attacked James's and Lange's conclusions. John B. Watson, the so-called father of behaviorism, said in 1924 that James's theory "gave the psychology of the emotions a setback from which it has only recently begun to recover." More importantly for physiological research, the Harvard physiologist James B. Cannon attacked James's theory and began in the 1920s and 1930s to develop a theory of the physiology of emotion based in part on Darwinian functionalism and in part on new findings concerning the workings of the endocrine system.

Cannon, using evidence collected by the British physiologist C. S. Sherrington, provided compelling arguments against the James-Lange theory. Sherrington surgically disconnected the internal organs of dogs from their central nervous systems so that their brains could receive no information from their hearts, lungs, or livers, and this had no effect on their emotional reactions: they exhibited the same kind of fear, happiness, and aggression that they had exhibited before the surgery. Cannon repeated Sherrington's experiments with cats and obtained the same results. He also cites a French study (it was actually a Spanish study, by Gregorio Marañon, published in a French journal) in which patients were given injections of adrenaline. They all reported feeling something *like* an emotion, but not the emotion itself: "I feel as if afraid," "as if I were going to weep without knowing why." None reported feeling an actual emotion. Thus, says Cannon, the bodily state alone does not constitute the emotion.

Central to Cannon's work was the idea of homeostasis, the process by which the body regulates itself to maintain a steady state of functioning. Earlier physiologists had offered similar theories. George W. Crile, for instance, argued in 1915 that crying, and all emotional expression, results when we develop tension anticipating some physical action which we then do not carry out. Crying then releases that nervous energy and allows us to return to our normal state. But Crile's explanations were based on simple measurements of muscle enervation. Cannon (and a bit later Philip Bard) helped establish the fact that these muscular effects are secondary to the regulation of the body by the autonomic nervous system and the endocrine system. Cannon believed that the thalamus, in the diencephalon—the part of the brain that connects the primitive structures of the brain stem to the evolutionarily more advanced cerebrum—was the center of emotional activity. That the thalamus was a phylogenetically ancient part of the brain, Cannon thought, helped explain our sense of being overwhelmed by emotion. "These powerful impulses originating in a region of the brain not associated with cognitive consciousness and arousing therefore in an obscure and unrelated manner the strong feelings of emotional excitement, explain the sense of being seized, possessed, or controlled by an outside force."

According to Cannon, emotion, far from being simply a disruptive and antirational force, is part of what he called "the wisdom of the body" in responding directly to emergencies of various kinds (the fight-or-flight response being the most obvious) and in recovering its balance after the emergency is met. Cannon successfully shifted the debate from the logical or inferential terms that James and Dewey had primarily relied on to an emphasis on localization of brain structures and patterns of nerve firing and hormonal action. In other words, Cannon modernized the body-centered study of emotion, and since he also studied the activity of the brain, he had enormous impact on the cognitive study of the emotions. Later cognitive theories, like the appraisal theory of Magda Arnold of Loyola University and the cognitive arousal theory of Stanley Schachter and Jerome Singer, psychologists at Columbia University, dominated much of the research into emotions in the 1960s and 1970s, as cognitive psychology dominated academic study in general. Schachter, Singer, Arnold, and other cognitive theorists all built on Cannon's findings but moved the discussion away from physiology and toward the implications of this work for cognitive psychology. Silvan Tomkins followed Cannon's lead as well in psychology, and developed a theory of crying to be discussed in the chapter on psychology. In the meantime, the physiological aspects of Cannon's studies have been greatly expanded upon, thanks in large part to new methods of observing brain activity and other technological advances. The emotional body and the emotional brain are much more complex entities than they were believed to be even a half century ago.

The Emotional Brain

The anatomy of the brain is difficult to summarize, and not just because it houses somewhere between ten billion and one trillion neurons, and over one hundred trillion synapses, where the sending end of one nerve is in communicating proximity to the receiving end of another. In the peripheral nervous system—that is, the part of the nervous system outside the brain and spinal cord—physiological function and anatomical structure are easy to identify, fairly simple in operation, and usually correlated. The afferent (sensory) nerves that register feeling in the tips of our fingers, for instance, clearly begin in the tips of our fingers and send information to the central nervous system along a nerve route that is relatively easy to follow; the efferent (motor) nerves that send commands to the finger muscles travel a parallel route in the opposite direction. The brain itself, on the other hand, is composed of a much more complex web of neural relationships, few of which can be reduced to one of simple identity of structure with function.

Ever since the nineteenth century, physiologists have been attempting to construct a map of the brain's functions, and for a while it seemed that we would be able to draw a full map of specific anatomical locations for specific neurological functions. Famous cases of brain

Crying

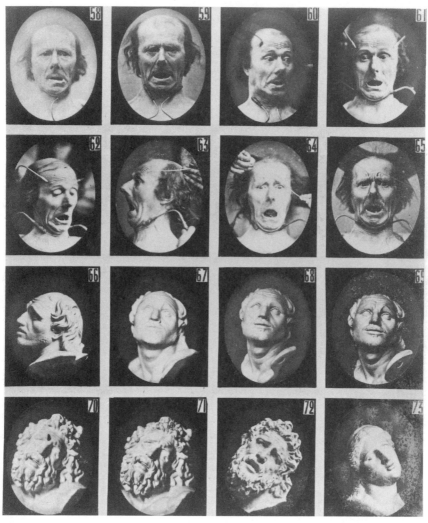

*Duchenne, whose physiological researches led to electrotherapy and biopsy, simu-
lated emotional expressions in subjects by applying electric shocks to facial muscles. He provided the classical sculpture as evidence of the universality of
emotional physiology.* G.-B.Duchenne, *Mécanisme de la physiognomie humaine; ou,
Analyse électro-physiologique de l'expression des passions, par le docteur G.-B. Duchenne
(de Boulogne) Avec un atlas composé de 74 figures électro-physiologiques photographiées*
(Paris, 1862). Getty Research Institute, Research Library.

damage, autopsies of brains with recorded dysfunctions, and animal experiments all pointed to specific locales in the brain where different sorts of activity took place. Damage to the Wernicke area, for instance, disrupts language processing: people with such damage will still produce words, but in nonsense sequences. Damage to Broca's area interferes with speech but not with language comprehension. Paul Broca and Carl Wernicke, for whom these areas are named, were pioneering neurologists who identified the relation between specific, localized brain damage and specific disabilities in the middle of the nineteenth century. Since then, however, a complex web of other brain structures have been identified as being involved in the comprehension and production of speech, including, for instance, the six different centers involved in hearing and the many brain structures involved in sight.

Several decades ago, researchers realized that damage to a particular neural center might disrupt a system enough to keep it from functioning and yet not necessarily be the "control" center of that system. The rear coupling on a boxcar may break and leave the string of cars behind it stranded, as one neurophysiologist explained, but the boxcar is not the engine. As more complex systems and subsystems have been identified by neurophysiologists and psychiatrists, the notion of a simple one-to-one relationship between location and function has been replaced by more complicated models that stress the interrelationships among neural centers. Even the three main anatomical divisions of the brain (traditionally identified as the hindbrain, midbrain, and forebrain) do not have completely separate physiological functions.

In general, the hindbrain, the oldest part of the brain in evolutionary terms, has been associated with basic, low-level processes, and the forebrain with more complex rational activities. The hindbrain helps coordinate motor activity, digestion, heart rate, blood pressure, and respiration, all suggesting its importance to emotional response. But raising a hand, for instance, or emotional tears, for that matter, involves activity in all three of the main divisions. Instead of taking a purely anatomical approach, therefore, neurologists have been attempting to catalogue a variety of local circuits, systems, and systems of systems involved in emotional experience.

The midbrain is the main conduit between the forebrain and the hindbrain. Three of the midbrain's tracts are central to emotions: the pain tract (or periventricular system), the pleasure tract (or medial forebrain bundle), and the reticular activating system (RAS). The RAS receives information from the sense organs which it uses to help regulate the state of arousal of the central nervous system.

Anatomists, following the work of James W. Papez in the 1930s, called the collection of brain systems that are activated during emotional experiences (the hindbrain, these three tracts, and a few small structures deep in the forebrain) the limbic system, and some neurologists continue to use the term; it is handy in that it includes many of the most important brain structures associated with emotion, no matter where they are located. The medulla oblongata, an evolutionarily ancient part of the hindbrain implicated in many nonconscious processes, like control of the heart rate, is an important part of the limbic system, as is the amygdala, for instance, an almond-shaped node of gray matter deep within the temporal lobes of the cerebrum, and fairly recent in evolutionary terms. Papez was instrumental in changing the focus of emotional physiology from neural centers to neural circuits, especially the limbic system, the circuit he also called the "emotional brain."

Paul D. MacLean, who was heavily influenced by Papez, has studied the limbic system in different species and notes that the mammalian brain is an elaborated version of the earlier, reptilian brain, with the fundamental evolutionary change being the addition of those parts of the brain that make vocalization possible. The evolutionarily oldest vocalization, he suggests, was the "separation cry," and since the earliest mammals were nocturnal forest dwellers, this crying helped parents find their infants and made possible communication within the group. MacLean also suggests, although this is more obviously speculative, that crying as a response to separation is linked to other basic facts of human evolution. Since there is some evidence that the remarkable development of the cerebrum in humans may be related to the discovery of fire, and since fire was so much a part of early hominid life, MacLean deduces that the smoke that got in these early human eyes helped ensure the evolution of a race that had great capacity for producing reflex tears, and that over time, especially when the dead were cremated, the association of reflex tears and sep-aration helped people develop tearful relations to loss.

Be that as it may, it is clear that the brain as it evolved developed a number of very specialized nodes, centers, and structures as part of the limbic system. Neurologists have recently isolated two different mem-ory systems, for instance, one declarative and one emotional, that use different parts of the system. Declarative memory has an important center in the hippocampus, a ridge of gray matter along the floor of each of the lateral ventricles of the cerebrum. Emotional memory has been linked to the amygdala. These two structures often work in tan-dem, but not always. Joseph LeDoux has shown that lesions in the hippocampus have no effect on implicit emotional memories, while J. P. Aggleton has shown that damage to the amygdala destroys those memories. A person with a damaged amygdala and a sound hippocam-pus may have clear memories of having been present at a traumatic event and of what happened, and even understand that he or she thought it was awful at the time, but still have no emotional memory of it. A person with a sound amygdala and a damaged hippocampus may react with great fear to a person who had hurt him or her with-out any explicit memory of the person or the injury.

But in normal emotional experience, many parts of the "emotional brain" are in use, and along with them other systems, including the endocrine system and its hormones. Especially when applied to moody teenagers, menopausal women, or aggressive men, the single word "hormones" serves for some people as a full explanation for com-plex, markedly emotional behavior. But hormones are not the control center either: the release of hormones can arouse or inhibit specific activity in the brain, but the hormones themselves can be triggered by the brain. The endocrine glands include the pituitary (which, since it regulates many of the other glands, is considered the "master gland"), the adrenals (unrelated to, but perched atop, the kidneys), the thyroid and parathyroids in the throat, the pancreas, the gonads, and the pineal. All are implicated in one way or another with emotional expe-rience. Increased thyroid secretion results in an increase in tears, for instance, whereas atrophy of the thyroid gland can stop the produc-tion of tears altogether. The pituitary gland releases (besides the tropic hormones that stimulate other glands to release their hormones) two main hormones, the first of which is human growth hormone, and the second of which is prolactin, the hormone that stimulates the production of breast milk and is also associated with the production of tears.

And so the nervous system, the endocrine system, the respiratory system, the thermoregulatory system, and the cardiovascular system all play important roles in emotional experience, and emotional experiences have effects on all of these systems. But while physiologists can identify the parts of the body involved in emotional experience, much is still unknown. Although they have identified a correlation between tears and pituitary activity, for instance, what this means is unsettled. Some studies have argued that the pituitary gland controls emotional response by releasing the hormones that activate the other major glands, many of which can induce emotional reactions (such as anxiety) if they are artificially stimulated. But other studies have shown that the pituitary gland is instead itself activated by emotions, so that the tears might in fact cause the corollary activity in the gland.

Another example: Emotionally deprived or traumatized children secrete less human growth hormone than other children. This led some researchers to conclude that growth-hormone deficiency caused emotional problems. In one case, however, a boy with low levels of growth hormone was removed from his depressed and therefore neglectful mother and placed in a foster home. He immediately experienced an increase in the hormone and a corresponding growth spurt. When his parents reconciled and he rejoined them, his growth again accelerated, so that in his case, at least, it appears that his emotional problems were causing the hormonal deficiency rather than the other way around. Hormones—and brain centers, heart and lung activity, and the other physical concomitants of emotion—all exist in a chicken-and-egg relation to emotional experience. They are obviously related, but we are unable to assign any ultimate priority or causality.

The same kinds of problems come into play in efforts to understand the brain systems employed during emotional experience. Phineas Gage is perhaps the most famous patient in the annals of neurology, in part because his peculiar case can be used as evidence for and against the localization of emotion in the brain. In 1848 Gage was working on the railroad in Vermont, detonating explosives to cut through some rock as his gang laid new track. One explosion went off prematurely, and Gage's tamping rod was blown through his left cheek, piercing the base of his skull, after which it tore through the front of his brain and smashed through the top of his head, landing a hundred feet away, trailing bits of brain, blood, and bone. Three and a half feet long, one and a half inches in diameter, and weighing over thirteen pounds, the metal rod, although it shot directly through his brain, somehow did not kill Phineas Gage. In fact, he managed to ride sitting upright in an oxcart almost a mile, walk with a little aid into the doctor's office, and sit up while he was examined. He talked coherently while his wound was being cleaned, describing the details of the accident that had occurred. Gage's remarkable survival has intrigued neurologists ever since, and his skull and the iron rod are in a museum case at Harvard University's Warren Medical Museum. Gage's accident took place at about the same time that Broca and Wernicke were independently discovering the functional specialization of the brain and beginning to map the different parts of the brain and their functions. Gage's physician, John Harlow, came to some tentative (and, as it turns out, erroneous) conclusions about brain function as well.

After the accident, Gage had a tough time of it. He recovered physically, and except for losing the vision of his left eye, he retained complete use of his perceptual, verbal, and motor abilities, according to the tests administered by doctors. But his personality underwent an enormous transformation. He had always been a responsible, amiable, cheerful man, well liked by the railroad crews he supervised and by the general community. After the iron rod passed through his skull, taking several cubic inches of brain matter with it, he not surprisingly became a different person. According to the physician who originally attended him and continued to examine him, he became "fitful, irreverent, indulging at times in the grossest profanity which was not previously his custom, manifesting but little deference for his fellows, impatient of restraint or advice when it conflicts with his desires, at times pertinaciously obstinate, yet capricious and vacillating, devising many plans of future operation, which are no sooner arranged than they are abandoned." None of the advice or admonitions given by his doctor or others had any effect. He no sooner found employment than he was fired for his temper or walked off the job in a fit. He spent some time as an attraction, along with his iron rod, at Barnum's Museum in New York. He died thirteen years later, at the age of thirty-eight, after wandering from Santiago to Valparaiso to San Francisco. His friends, claiming that "Gage was no longer Gage" after the accident, had long since ceased talking to him.

Dr. Hanna Damasio has conducted detailed clinical studies of patients with severe traumatic brain damage similar to Gage's. She has also studied Gage's skull and with the help of computer imaging has attempted to reconstruct the specific neural loss Gage suffered. She concluded that the most significant damage wreaked by the rod was a severing of important connections between the frontal cortex and the mid- and hindbrain. These lower structures fired at will, uninhibited by the decision-making and hierarchizing functions of the cortex, and thus "the balance between his emotions and his intellectual faculties [was] destroyed." His emotions, detached from his reasoning capacities, led him into fights and tantrums, while his reasoning, detached from his emotional faculties, could not properly factor in his own self-interest. Gage's story is the tragic enactment of Oscar Wilde's dictum that "the advantage of the emotions is that they lead us astray."

But the most significant conclusion that Damasio, her husband Antonio Damasio, and their colleagues have shown is that reason and emotion are not opposed to each other, that losing one's emotional abilities is itself detrimental to the ability to reason, that reason needs emotion to function properly. In an experiment designed by Antoine Bechara, Hanna Damasio, and Steven Anderson, patients who had suffered damage to the frontal lobe of the brain played a gambling card game devised by the team. The subjects were allowed to choose between a high-stakes and a low-stakes deck. A preference for the low-reward, low-penalty deck led to the greatest gain, and most of the patients in the control group made that choice and stuck to it, with the "high-risk" types in that group occasionally reverting to the first set of decks, after which they, too, came back to the low-risk cards. The patients with frontal lobe injuries routinely picked the high-risk deck and lost.

The neurologists argued that the problem was not one of information processing. In tests with a control group, patients whose mathematical and reasoning skills were impaired due to other kinds of injury managed to learn the game and come out ahead. The problem, Antonio Damasio explains, is that the frontal lobe patients did not have the normal amount of interplay between their limbic systems, the brain systems associated with feeling, and their cerebral cortex, the seat of rational cognition. All of the specific neural centers necessary to this level of decision making were intact. The patients, like Phineas Gage, had the ability to think, discuss their options, and process the necessary information. They all had the ability to feel, to experience emotion. But the connections between their feelings and their rationality had been severed.

Damasio suggests in his groundbreaking book on the current state of the neurology of the emotions, *Descartes' Error*, that Descartes's separation of mind and body, and his insistence on the purely cognitive aspects of emotion, have had a profound and deleterious effect on research into the emotions ever since. But Descartes, as we have seen, saw the fundamental emotions not just as reactions to stimuli but as constitutive forms of human thought and action. The real villain of this story of the mind-body split, if we were to name one, is not Descartes but Plato. In the *Phaedrus*, Plato gives his famous description of passion and reason as two mismatched horses pulling the chariot of the soul. The rational horse is white, "upright and clean-limbed, carrying its neck high . . . and needs no whip, being driven by word of command alone." Passion, on the other hand, is "a massive jumble of a creature, with thick short neck, snub nose, black skin, and gray eyes; hot-blooded, consorting with wantonness and vainglory; shaggy of ear, deaf, and hard to control with whip and goad." Plato's error is more stark than Descartes's, as he more clearly pits passion and reason against each other. What the physiology of the brain shows us is that any such mind-body dualism is always necessarily an error. The white horse of rationality is not enough to keep Phineas Gage in a job or Damasio's patients ahead in their bets.

Some emotional reactions can in fact bypass the rational centers of the brain, indeed bypass the brain entirely and cause bodily reactions through the spinal cord. The "startle" response is one clear example: infants will exhibit the startle response at any loud noise even while asleep. Cognition is not necessary. Or Descartes's example of the friend thrusting a hand in our face. We can experience fear *despite* whatever we may think of the situation. Sometimes, on the other hand, cognition is all. Damasio argues that, especially when it comes to more complex emotions, we develop "systematic connections between categories of objects or situations, on the one hand, and primary emotions, on the other." As certain images are stored in our memories, they are marked with "somatic information." As we file away certain images—of a fight or a moment of tenderness with another person, for instance—we also store information about the emotions and feelings we experienced at that moment. These feelings, which of course cannot be stored as such, can then be recalled along with the images and rekindled. A memory of a painful moment that had us in tears can thus be "marked" by tears, and remembering the moment can elicit tears in us again. If we associate weddings with a tearful joyfulness, for instance, when we attend a wedding we will begin to tear up, sometimes even if we are just passing by a church or flipping the channels on the television. People who get sappy around random babies do so for the same reason.

If Damasio is right, we can thus have an emotional response without any rational thought, even though it is based on a cognitive process of recall. We perceive a situation, which we recognize because it fits into a mental category, which is constructed by memories, which have "somatic markers" that trigger nuclei deep within the brain, which send messages to the autonomic nervous system, the motor system, the endocrine system, and so on, causing an emotional experience without an actual train of thought in the sense that cognitive psychologists would suggest is necessary.

In addition, Damasio shows that at times these brain structures can "mimic" bodily responses, relaying information that simulates the body's emotional reactions neurally without actually triggering them in the body. That is, our brain can send signals to itself suggesting that we are feeling a hormonal stimulus even though no hormones are present. And of course there are instances in which all of these systems are at work at once, in which primary emotional responses are triggered through the kind of Jamesian system in which the body reacts before the brain perceives, and at the same time secondary responses are triggered in which the brain causes an emotional reaction that has its origin and its end in the brain, and also triggers secondary responses that have their origin in the brain, but which then trigger bodily responses (or vice versa), which are then perceived by the autonomic system and relayed as more information, and so on, ad infinitum.

These multiple-feedback loops are central to what has become known as "method acting," as taught by Konstantin Stanislavsky, Lee Strasberg, and their followers. Method acting makes use of both the mentalist view and the peripheralist understandings of emotion. Actors are asked to find, in their "affective memories," an event approximating the one they are being asked to perform onstage. From this we get the much abused notion that an actor may try to remember his or her dog dying in order to cry onstage. But the actors are also instructed to concentrate on their "sense memories" of the event, including their memory of the feel of their clothes on their skin at the time, the temperature in the room, their sense of their own heartbeat, the feel of tears on their cheeks. Just thinking of the dead dog is not enough; one needs to remember and refeel the physical sensations of crying in order to stimulate, and thereby convincingly simulate, a person crying in grief.

The mix of cognition and feeling varies from actor to actor. One acting student told me she could cry whenever she wanted to simply by feeling it in her body, with no sad thoughts whatsoever. I asked her to demonstrate for me and she bent her head forward and began to breathe heavily. Within seconds, she was heaving with sobs and tears were running down her face, with no provocation save the increased respiration. Another actor who used a similar method told me he had begun his career remembering his dead dog in order to stimulate tears, but that now he, too, worked to remember the physical sensation of crying.

Most actors, in fact, are not fully, consciously aware of the emotional work they do, at where they find access along the complicated feedback loops of the various brain and bodily systems involved. Remembering sad thoughts can kick off a crying jag (one actor told me that she quite literally thinks of Old Yeller), as can re-creating the physical conditions. Even re-creating the facial contractions of crying or the heavy staccato breathing that accompanies it can cause a person to feel like crying, as Delsarte had suggested. Paul Ekman, who had developed a system of facial expressions that illustrate specific emotional states, performed experiments in which he asked subjects to contract certain facial muscles without telling them why. By assessing their mood before and after the experiment, Ekman showed that contracting the muscles of the face was enough, as Delsarte suspected, to increase the subjects' feelings of anguish.

The body and the brain, then, despite the history of philosophy, are inseparable—an idea that finds no argument from common sense. What we all know about extreme emotional experience should reinforce the ideas of physiologists from Papez through Damasio who insist on the complicated nature of interactions among the various parts of our bodies and brains. We might feel sometimes that love, or fear, or anxiety, as Plato suggested, represents the scruffy, wanton horses of our desires overwhelming the nice white horse of our rationality. But it is also easy to recognize that we could not love without our rational mind, nor can our rational mind intercept all of our fears. Our bodies may be overwhelming us, but they can do so only with the help of our minds, just as every time we make a rational, moral choice, we do so with the help of our emotions.

In Phineas Gage we have one powerful image of what it means to be overwhelmed by emotion, that is, to have one's anger or frustration take full control of one's actions, with no cognitive mediation. And one wonders what exactly it meant that he was so overwhelmed—was he inundated, confounded, defeated, overcome, routed, prostrated, submerged, bewildered? The metaphor we might choose has obvious implications for our understanding of tears, especially in a culture with a widely shared belief that to cry is to be overwhelmed, as seen in our common usages: to be overcome with tears, to break down into tears, to drown in our own tears, to overflow with tears.

Parasympathy, Pleasure, and the Content of Tears

Overflow, catharsis, pleasure: In order to understand these different functions of tears at the level of physiology, we need to look at their biochemical content and two more physiological systems: the parasympathetic nervous system and the pleasure tract.

Physiologists divide the nervous system into two parts: the central nervous system (the brain and the spinal cord) and the peripheral nervous system (made up of the rest of the nerve cells in the body). The peripheral nervous system is further divided into the autonomic nervous system and the somatic nervous system, each with its separate but related functions. The somatic nervous system is composed of the neurons that get information from and control the skin and skeletal muscles, and is susceptible to willful control. The autonomic nervous system controls the organs such as the heart, lungs, kidneys, and liver, which usually function with a great deal of autonomy, and under no direct influence of a person's conscious will. Both are obviously active in emotional experience.

The autonomic system is further divided into the sympathetic and parasympathetic nervous systems, and herein lies our quarry. These are physically and functionally separate systems: the sympathetic system sends messages to the eye, salivary gland, lungs, and heart, for instance, through a series of spinal nerves, while the parasympathetic system communicates with the same organs by means of a cranial nerve, the tenth cranial or vagus nerve. The sympathetic system, physiologists have shown, helps control physiological activity of the viscera during exceptional activity, the parasympathetic system when the body is returning to homeostasis or is at rest. The main job of the sympathetic nervous system, in other words, is to ready the body for specific action, while that of the parasympathetic nervous system is to restore the body to and help maintain equilibrium.

This distinction, which has been developed in detail in just the last half century, has obvious repercussions for our understanding of the physiology of emotion. One argument, as we have seen, is that the function of emotions is to ready the body for action, the paradigmatic case being the flight-or-fight readiness associated with fear. This would tie emotion to the sympathetic system, and several researchers have set out to prove as much, and thereby to prove that crying is regulated by the sympathetic nervous system. The opposing argument, as one might suspect, is that crying is regulated by the parasympathetic system, which would suggest that it kicks in after exceptional or strenuous activity and simply accompanies our recovery from such activity to a homeostatic steady state. At stake is the question of whether crying is part of the arousal process or part of the recovery process, and thus whether crying can effect some kind of significant change or is only a sign that some change has already taken place.

James Gross and his colleagues at the University of California at Berkeley showed a film to 150 women, 33 of whom cried in response. Those who cried registered "a complex mixture of sympathetic, parasympathetic, and somatic activation," which, Gross argued, because there was still sympathetic activity, supports "the physiological arousal model of crying rather than the physiological recovery hypothesis." But most of the other studies in recent years (and much of Gross's own data) point to the parasympathetic rather than the sympathetic system, and most researchers now assume that the parasympathetic nervous system controls tears. Paralysis of certain nerves important to the sympathetic nervous system have been shown to cause an increase in tears, for instance, whereas paralysis of the seventh cranial or facial nerve, which carries only parasympathetic fibers, causes a suppression of tears. In other words, a crier apparently needs, in order to cry, to have his or her parasympathetic system intact, but not his or her sympathetic system. The parasympathetic control of tears is supported by recent studies that have shown that crying occurs not at the peak of an emotional experience but at some point after the peak, during the return to a "normal" condition. If tears occur only after the body has already begun to return to homeostasis, then many psychological theories of cathartic tears (discussed in the next chapter) are in need of revision.

While studying the relation of emotion to homeostasis, Walter Cannon began looking at the physiology of pain and pleasure and their relation to emotional experience. For Cannon, fear induces emotions through the reflex secretion of adrenaline. Adrenaline was so central to his theory that he spoke of the "sympathico-adrenal system" instead of the sympathetic nervous system. Researchers studying pain since Cannon's time have focused instead on three parallel structures in the brain stem: the pain tract, the pleasure tract, and the reticular activating system. While all agree on the existence of these structures and their centrality to the experience of pleasure and pain, there is not a complete consensus about how they interact, or about their place in the larger scheme of things mental and emotional.

Both humans and animals with electrodes planted at specific points along the pleasure tract will self-stimulate at rates of up to one thousand times an hour. Stimulation at some points along the tract induces intense, orgasmic pleasure for some subjects, while others stimulated at the same points report much milder feelings of well-being. In some experiments, subjects continue to choose to stimulate a specific spot, even though they report no pleasure whatsoever, simply an undeniable desire to repeat the stimulus. Stimulation of the pain tract at different points leads to the same variety of responses: pain, mild depression, or no sensation save a desire to avoid repeating the stimulus. The pleasure tract and the pain tract are interconnected at several points, and while humans and other animals will most often strive to have their pleasure tract stimulated and to avoid having their pain tract stimulated, several experiments have suggested that the division between the two is not as stark as we might suppose. Another possibility is that pain and pleasure are so closely linked that sometimes only our interpretation separates them. This is the argument, of course, that masochists and sadists make, and physiologists give them some support. And it offers tantalizing possible explanations for the mystery of how tears might arise from both the most painful and the most pleasurable experiences. But the current state of physiological research into such matters leaves us with more questions than answers.

And we are still left with the most basic question: Why tears? Some physiologists have argued that the answer to that question lies in the specific content of tears. Along with water, mucin, and oils, tears contain a number of proteins, some of which are antibacterial, immuno-

Charles Le Brun (1619–1690), director of the Académie Royale, produced drawings of the passions for use in art instruction. They were first published in 1698. From *Heads representing the Passions of the Soul, selected from Mons. Le Brun, on twelve plates, in chalk* (London, 1794). Getty Research Institute, Research Library.

globins, glucose, urea, and a number of salts. In 1957 Robert Brunish, a researcher at UCLA, conducted a study which first established that emotional tears had a higher protein concentration than reflex tears and that the amount of various proteins—lysozyme, globulin, and albumin—varied in the two kinds of tears as well. Two subsequent studies failed to replicate his findings the next year. But twenty years later, William Frey conducted a study that confirmed Brunish's findings.

Frey exposed his subjects to onions and to classic tearjerker films in order to make them cry, and had them collect their tears in six-inch test tubes. He claims that his inspiration for the onions came from a scene in *The Taming of the Shrew* in which an actor is given the following advice:

> And if the boy not have a woman's gift,
> To rain a shower of commanded tears,
> An onion will do well for such a shift.

But instead of using a Shakespearean scene, Frey employed more contemporary stuff to induce emotional tears for his study: the movies
Brian's Song, The Champ, and *All Mine to Give,* this last the top tear-
getter of all the films Frey tried. The tears Frey's subjects collected
during the movies not only were more voluminous than those collected over the onions, but they had 20 to 25 percent more protein,
supporting Brunish's contention that emotional tears and reflex tears
have radically different compositions.

Following on Frey's study, N. J. Van Haeringen discovered in 1981
that emotional tears have four times as much potassium as plasma,
and Frey also measured the level of other substances. He found that
tears have thirty times the amount of manganese than is found in
blood. Concentrations of manganese have also been found in the
brains of chronic depressives after their deaths, which led Frey to theorize that since the lacrimal gland concentrates and removes manganese, crying may stave off depression. This would give a physiological
basis to the idea that we can cry our way to mental health, which is, in
fact, Frey's conclusion.

Frey also found several hormones in tears. One of them, adrenocor-
ticotropic hormone (ACTH), has been shown in blood levels to be
one of the most sensitive indicators of stress. Again, crying, by eliminating the excess ACTH, may relieve stress. According to Frey,
lacrimation, like urination or defecation, is simply one of the body's
ways of removing waste. Such arguments about tears as a means of
elimination ignore one important fact: unlike sweating or urination,
crying is not a very effective way to eliminate waste products, since
the majority of tears are reabsorbed by the body. As the tear ducts
pump out tears, much of the production flows into the lacrimal ducts
and from there through the nasolacrimal duct into the nasal cavity.
During intense emotional crying, the ducts cannot keep up with the
flow, and so some tears slosh out over the eyelids. But the nasolacrimal
ducts still drain a good deal of the emotional tears produced, making
crying a very inefficient form of elimination at best.

A few other medical studies have also concluded that crying has
healthful benefits. Margaret Crepeau, of the University of Pittsburgh
School of Nursing, for instance, has found that healthy people cry

more and have a more positive understanding of tears than people with colitis or ulcers. But each of these studies hinges on a simple correlation, which can in each case be explained in other ways. A person who cries regularly may be good at returning to equilibrium after emotionally trying experiences, and the crying they report may simply accompany their rapid return to equilibrium. In other words, both the lack of tears and the ulcer may be symptoms of the same condition—unalleviated stress or faulty nervous system functioning, for instance—and the failure to cry simply tells us that the person remains in a stressed state. A depressive disorder may cause manganese deposits to form in the brain and may limit a person's crying without one being the cause of the other, just as a severed spinal cord makes both walking and breathing difficult—obviously in such patients it is not the breathing problem that is causing the walking problem or vice versa.

And even if Frey and Crepeau have discovered a causal relation, their studies may still seem a bit reductive, treating the complexities of emotion simply as side effects of physiological processes over which we have little control and regarding health as an accident of emotional dispositions. We have assimilated the findings about Type A behavior and stress-related illnesses and know therefore that there is a relationship between emotion and health, and most of do believe at some level that the body is the seat of emotion. We understand, for instance, that the lie-detector test works by measuring visually unnoticeable bodily events—electrodermal changes based on nerve activity, pulse rate, and blood pressure—and thus believe that emotions which can be hidden at the level of observable behavior will nonetheless be detectable by closer measurements of the body. The growing array of drugs for emotional disorders—Prozac, Zoloft, and the rest—and their increasing acceptance are even clearer indications of our current understanding of the biochemical nature of emotion. And it is not just biochemistry but brain biochemistry. Before the discovery of these new psychotropic drugs, our imperfect understanding of the brain's role in emotional behavior was evident in the widespread use of frontal lobotomy, the radical surgical removal of the frontal cerebral cortex, to correct emotional problems. The discovery of Thorazine (chlorpromazine) in the 1950s put an end to the barbaric and ineffec-

tive practice, but Thorazine itself is understood as a drug that works
through changing brain chemistry; the study that the drug prompted,
in fact, resulted in the discovery of important neurotransmitters.
Whatever metaphors of the heart or the gut we might use, therefore,
we tend to assume that the brain is at the center of the body's emotional life.

And still, most people also believe, somewhat as Descartes did, that
the soul is the seat of the emotions, or, in a more modern idiom, that
emotions are deeply personal psychological phenomena. The latest
evidence in the social sciences suggests something else again, that one
cannot understand emotions without reference to the specific meanings emotional display has in a specific culture at a given time. Physiological knowledge of the body is obviously quite extensive and
detailed, and we have learned much in the last decades about the basic
physiological correlates of emotion: the firing of the different clusters
of neurons in various regions of the brain, spine, and body, the secretion of various glands, the production of neurotransmitters, chemical
reactions, and the like. But it is still a developing science, and once we
get beyond the simple act of registering activity within a cell, a gland,
or an organ to larger questions of physiology, much less psychology or
sociology, the professional consensus breaks down fairly quickly. Just
as Papez moved the inquiry forward by identifying a neural circuit
rather than a neural center as the mechanism controlling emotional
life, we now understand that the circuit goes beyond the nervous system into the entire body, and beyond the body into the social world.
The failure of lobotomies to effect cures was hard evidence of the
insufficiency of a brain-centered view of emotion. The most positive
estimate of "improvement" during the heyday of lobotomizing in the
1940s was only about 35 percent, and although the conscious experience of anxiety or depression was reduced for many, emotional behaviors like laughing and crying often increased dramatically. In light of
what neurophysiologists now know, this makes perfect sense: while
specific areas of the brain may have the ability to inhibit or induce
specific emotional experiences, they are only part of the full circuitry.
As even Descartes knew, the pineal gland and the thermoregulatory
system are involved, as are, as Darwin suggested, the respiratory sys-

tem and muscles throughout the body. As our common metaphors have always told us, the heart (and other organs) and nerves are very much involved. And as psychologists, sociologists, and anthropologists have shown, emotions are fundamentally social as well.

One of Frey's additional findings helps, inadvertently, to make this point. Frey found significantly more prolactin in emotional tears than in irritant tears. Prolactin controls the neurotransmitter receptors in the lacrimal glands, and while both men and women produce it, women generate significantly more, and women have twice as many of these receptors as men. Prolactin is also the hormone responsible for milk production (hence its root *lact-*, as in lactose and lactation), and the amount produced varies during the menstrual cycle, pregnancy, and nursing. Women with abnormally high levels of prolactin (hyper-prolactinemics) have been shown to have higher levels of anxiety, hostility, and/or depression than women with lower levels. This combination of facts leads Frey to conclude two things: one, that the difference in prolactin production accounts for the fact that women cry more often than men; and two, that another function of crying is to eliminate the excess prolactin, which we must do in order to stave off depression.

In another experiment (by O'Moore, O'Moore, Harrison, Murphy, and Carruthers), however, women who had been trained in relaxation techniques reported fewer negative emotions and less crying, and they had lower prolactin levels—in other words, the level of prolactin may be an effect, rather than a cause, of depression. Another experiment demonstrated that while men with higher levels of prolactin have higher levels of anxiety, the hormone has no discernible effect on their level of depression. The correlation between the levels of prolactin associated with depression and in tears is insufficient for us to theorize about the function of prolactin, depression, or tears; or at any rate, every theory like Frey's, which posits a direct causal relation between tears and physiological functions, is contradicted by other studies that posit a different control center.

Researchers in the Netherlands, for instance, tested Frey's hypothesis and found that women with high levels of prolactin were no more prone to weep than the control group, and their understanding of their own crying (in general, that it was a relief) was identical to the control group's. The same researchers, at the Helen Dowling Institute for Biopsychosocial Medicine in Rotterdam, did find a correlation in both men and women between weeping and "neuroticism," defined as self-esteem or coping problems, but not between weeping and physiological variables such as hormone levels. Psychology, not physiology, they suggested, held the answers.

Other researchers have found that physiological factors other than prolactin levels may explain the different rates of male and female weeping. Fumihiko Okada at Hokkaidō University in Sapporo, Japan, found that men normally have very different levels of blood flow to their right and left hemispheres when they are at rest than they do while performing a task, while women and depressed men tend to exhibit the same level of activity in both hemispheres. This may help explain, Okada says, why women weep more and why they are more prone to depression. But all of these findings are tentative at best.

Crying Too Much and Too Little

Oddly enough, women also have worse problems associated with *not* crying than men. Women suffer from dry eye, and from the most serious diseases associated with dry eye, such as Sjögren's syndrome, at a much higher rate than men. In both men and women, lacrimal glands shrink with age, so that by the age of sixty-five, the body is producing only 60 percent of the tears it did in the prime of life, and by eighty only 30 percent. As everyday basal tear production drops off, the eyes can get irritated and produce reflex tears. Watery eyes can thus ironically be a symptom of chronic dry eye. Dry eye syndrome results if the lacrimal glands don't produce enough tears (a condition known as keratoconjunctivitis sicca), or if they don't produce enough of the oils that keep tears from evaporating too quickly. Redness, burning, light sensitivity, and gritty sensations, as well as watery eyes, are all symptoms. Artificial tears and lubricating ointments are the primary treatments prescribed for mild dry eye, while more serious cases can require the temporary or permanent closure of the puncta, or drainage ducts, in order to slow the drainage of tears.

Sometimes, however, blocked drainage ducts are the source of the problem. The most common site of such obstruction is the naso-lacrimal duct, which can cause constant tearing, mucus buildup in the lacrimal sac, and eventually infection. If the supply ducts from the lacrimal glands themselves are obstructed by these infections, corneal surface erosion and corneal scarring can result. The most serious cases of dry eye are caused by Sjögren's syndrome, a degenerative disease of the lacrimal glands. Sjögren's syndrome leads to the chronic inflammation and the eventual complete destruction of the lacrimal glands, requiring constant manual lubrication of the eyes.

Sjögren's is obviously a horrible disease, with devastating effects. (Dr. J. Daniel Nelson, chief of ophthalmology and director of the Dry Eye and Tear Research Center at St. Paul-Ramsey Medical Center in St. Paul, Minnesota, among others, continues to study Sjögren's syndrome and offers assistance over the Internet and by mail.) And again, women contract the disease more often than men. As many as 10 million women suffer from at least intermittent dry eye, and the worst times for women are during increased hormonal activity: during pregnancy, lactation, menstruation, and oral contraceptive use. This has led researchers at the University of Southern California's Doheny Eye Institute to study the hormonal levels of dry eye sufferers.

Surprisingly, reports the study's lead author, Ana Maria Azzarolo, low levels of androgens are the most common physiological factor associated with dry eye in women. While the Doheny study agreed that the "female" hormone prolactin was necessary to tear production, it concluded that just as crucial were testosterone and other "male" sex hormones called androgens. Women produce these hormones in smaller amounts than men, and when their testosterone levels drop significantly, their lacrimal glands shrink and malfunction. Testosterone and prolactin interact in regulating the glands, and since men produce considerably more testosterone, and women considerably more prolactin, there are, according to one of the study's authors, Dwight W. Warren, "distinct structural and biochemical differences between lacrimal glands in men and women." But for both men and women, excessive *or* inadequate prolactin *or* testosterone can inhibit the proper functioning of the gland, which is why women often suffer from dry eye during lactation.

At the opposite end of the spectrum are cases of abnormally abundant tears. The average adult in America cries, according to the available studies, for about five minutes at a stretch around three or four times a month (with wide variations for men and women, as we'll see). Infants cry much more than that, of course, but it is not entirely clear how much more. Some studies have found the normal amount of crying to be around thirty minutes a day; others have found it to be slightly over two hours. Most physicians agree that anything over two hours a day is excessive, and call such excessive crying colic. Colic affects between 15 and 33 percent (depending on the source) of all infants in the U.S. and lasts from two to eleven months, during which time the infants cry from two to eighteen hours a day. Around the world the same patterns apply, including, for instance, the fact that the crying tends to peak in the late afternoon. Physicians and parents have assumed that colic, as the word implies, is related to pain emanating from the colon, and indeed the word comes from the Greek *kōlikos*, from *kōlon*, colon. Cynthia Stifter, of Pennsylvania State University, is now looking for the cause of colic by analyzing infant electrogastrograms to see if there is a locatable developmental problem in colicky babies. And some acoustic analyses of the cries themselves indicate she may be on the right track. The cries of colicky babies are higher in jitter, shimmer, proportion of noise, and tenseness than those of noncolicky babies, suggesting that the infants have a regulatory disorder rather than simply a temperamental one. Other physicians have proposed a variety of etiologies (psychosocial, intestinal, nervous, temperamental, hormonal), and some divide colic into two types: consolable and inconsolable, a distinction that finds no argument from common sense. In the first type, the rocking or baths or Snuglis make a difference; in the second type, they do not. But there is no established cause and no known cure.

In any case like this, when the symptom defines the disease, the chances of misdiagnosis increase. Some nurses claim that 90 percent of all colic is misdiagnosed, although it is unclear how this could be true, since colic is simply a name for excessive crying. Babies are often diagnosed by doctors as colicky when they in fact (also) have what is called gastroesophageal reflux, in which the lower esophageal sphincter fails and allows food and acid in the stomach to come back up the food pipe, causing heartburn, indigestion, and pain. But there have been cases of reflux in which the colic continued even after the reflux was treated, and therefore it is clear that colic can have other causes, even in babies with reflux.

Many explanations have been offered by laypeople and alternative practitioners, citing such possible causes as milk allergies, gas, gastric dysrhythmia, temperament, stress, overstimulation, calcium deficiency, hereditary predisposition, overfeeding, bad parenting, or, as one survey concluded, "the presence of excessive anger, anxiety, fear, or excitement in the household [and] probably a multitude of other factors as yet unknown." The length of this list suggests how little science and how much anecdotal evidence have gone into the discussion, and each of these causes has been discounted by other accounts. People don't agree on whether gas, for instance, is a cause or a symptom—the gas pains may cause the crying, but the crying itself may cause the infant to swallow enough air to cause gas pains. The anxious household could very well be the result rather than the cause of a baby screaming its lungs out for hours every day.

Colic is a "self-limiting disorder." That is, it disappears on its own with no intervention, often within three months, always by eighteen months. But neither date is soon enough for the harried parents, who try everything they can think of and follow every scrap of advice they hear in their attempt to get some peace: crib vibrators, car rides, swaddling, simethicone and other antigas medicines, low-allergy formula, a "positive attitude," pouch-style carriers, rocking, steady sounds (vacuums, clothes dryers, or even white noise), hot-water bottles or heating pads, herbal teas, pacifiers, thorough burping, mechanical swings, walking in the stroller, working the legs up and down to get the gas out or some other form of exercise, digestive enzymes, antacids, and warm baths. Breast-feeding mothers are told to avoid taking antibiotics and consuming milk products and caffeine, onions, cabbage, beans, broccoli, and other gas-producing, spicy, or irritating foods, and to take calcium supplements. Chiropractic adjustments and homeopathic remedies are touted, as well as rostrums like Nurse Harvey's Gripe Water, consisting of dill oil or dill water, sodium bicarbonate, and 3 to 5 percent alcohol. And of course each one of these remedies is strenuously criticized by someone else. In 1985 Terry Woodford, a former record producer and songwriter, began marketing tapes that feature the sound of a real human heart beating. According to his own promotional material, 94 percent of crying babies fell asleep without a bottle or pacifier as the tapes played, and he has sold over a million copies. But a study by Douglas K. Detterman of Case Western Reserve University found exposure to the sound of heartbeats to have no pacifying effect whatsoever in infants colicky or otherwise. The osteopaths condemn the chiropractors, and the medical establishment scoffs at the homeopathic remedies. "Gripe water" is in fact illegal in this country and is regularly seized by customs agents. On the Internet chat lines, parents recommend remedies that they say worked for them, and then offer a series of possible cures that, although they did not work for them, they feel might work for others.

Many people go through nearly the whole list of above-mentioned folk cures before hitting on something that "works." But since the syndrome eventually disappears anyway, parents can never be sure whether they hit on a cure or whether the baby stopped coincidentally. Since parents are forever trying something new, they are always in the midst of an experiment when their baby grows out of colic. As one doctor at the Nemours Foundation put it, "You can switch baby formulas around a lot. . . . Usually what's happened is that by the time you've switched them a number of times they're three months old, the normal period in which colic will go away, and people think it's because they switched formulas."

Some doctors prescribe for the parents rather than the baby, suggesting earplugs, for instance, or hiring a baby-sitter. Some parents try scores of remedies just to have the sense that they are doing something. One parent in an Internet support group suggested crying as a cure—she would call a friend and weep. Another, after recommending a long list of the standard remedies, said that "when all else failed, I'd go in the other room and punch the walls." In what sounds a bit like a parody of scientific precision, a study by pediatricians from the University of Utah Medical School published in the journal *Clinical Pediatrics* concluded that parents with colicky babies were 5.7 times more likely to score higher on stress tests. In a study at the Children's Hospital in Columbus, Ohio, Belinda J. Pinyerd found that mothers of colicky infants "reported more bodily dysfunction, fears, disordered thinking, depression, anxiety, fatigue, hostility, and impulsive thoughts and actions and had stronger feelings of personal inadequacy or inferiority." A study of infants and mothers by Cynthia Stifter and her graduate student Julia Braungart demonstrated that several months after the colic had subsided, the infants had no discernible aftereffects, but mothers often continue to feel inadequate as caretakers and nurturers. One mother, for instance, who reported that her baby had screamed for eighteen hours a day for four months, claimed that even at six months she had yet to feel fully connected to her daughter.

At the other end of the life span, constant crying can also occur due to a poststroke phenomenon known as pathological crying or pathological laughing and crying (PLC); it also is sometimes identified as emotional lability, pseudobulbar affect, and emotional incontinence. Under one or another of these names, pathological crying has been recognized as a manifestation of brain damage since the late nineteenth century. The lesions, or damage, can occur in many different parts of the brain—the pons, midbrain, diencephalon, the frontal lobe, the tracts descending to the bulbar nuclei—and the syndrome can take different forms, from continuous laughter and crying to paroxysmal or convulsive laughter and crying. Once the damage has been incurred, usually following a stroke, and therefore usually among older people, PLC happens spontaneously, with no apparent inciting cause, and often without any associated feeling. A patient can cry for hours and report to the physician that he or she feels perfectly indifferent, neither particularly happy nor sad.

And the crying is involuntary. Patients cannot will it into being, and cannot stop it voluntarily once it starts. Since the patient does not necessarily feel bad when crying, it is the children, grandchildren, and spouses who suffer the most. Some spells of crying can go on for twenty-four hours or longer, as those closest to the patient try to ignore what seem to be constant messages of anguish. Although we know that the tears are the result of brain damage, that is almost all we know. The specific reason for the tears and their relation to normal tears are still shrouded in mystery.

Colic and pathological crying are caused, we assume, by purely physical problems. They don't have the cultural or psychological determinants of, say, the dry eyes of men overtrained in stoicism or the "weatherless" state that in severe forms of depression is marked by a complete loss of the ability to weep. And yet colic has a social dimension as well, affecting basic relations between parents and children, husbands and wives. The physiological answer to these puzzles of abnormal crying will do little to alter them as social facts. Likewise with the new revelations about hormones. Women cry more often and for longer periods than men, and this is related to some of the physiological differences between men and women, but for now, that is essentially the sum of our knowledge on the subject. In other words, while we know that anatomy and physiology are a part of every crier's destiny, they are only a part. Much more important are the social distinctions, rules of behavior, etiquettes, and roles that organize the relations between men and women in different societies. Tear production is a physiological process, but we cannot understand weeping unless we also apprehend it in social and psychological terms.

3

The Psychology of Tears

Toward the beginning of Edward Albee's play *Three Tall Women* (1994), an old woman begins to cry. Her weeping, the stage directions inform us, "begins in self-pity, proceeds to crying for crying's sake, and concludes with rage and self-loathing at having to cry." When it is over, her nurse comes over, fluffs the pillows, and offers a very common, nursely platitude: "There. Feel better? A good cry lets it all out." The old woman shoots back: "What does a bad one do?" Too old and too crabby to be easily placated, she challenges the idea that a good cry allows pent-up, repressed emotions to find expression and bring relief. The nurse's brief homily covers a complex array of human invention and activity, and like most homiletic proverbs, it represents not just a core insight but a form of willful blindness: the very phrase "having a good cry" suggests that there are other kinds. Sometimes, as Albee suggests, crying is less a release than it is an indulgence in self-pity, rage, or self-loathing.

Still, the nurse is offering a piece of standard medical advice, as old as Hippocrates and as current as William Frey: crying is cathartic, and therefore, by definition, good for you. Catharsis has a long, complex history, one that weaves together physiological, moral, psychological, aesthetic, and spiritual thinking in a variety of promiscuous ways. "Having a good cry" in an ecstasy of aesthetic appreciation is obviously very different from Frey's sense of a good cry as a means of eliminating excess manganese. And although some psychologists might argue that the "holy tears" shed by medieval mystics are in fact very similar to the cathartic crying of a patient in therapy, St. Augustine might not agree.

Although cathartic ideas have been at the center of pop psychology and many therapeutic regimens in this century, the majority of experimental psychologists have concentrated on other aspects of tears. Ours is a psychological age, and there is little about crying that cannot be thought of in psychological terms, including the physiology we have just surveyed. But psychology itself is a far from unified science. In 1927 P. T. Young wrote that "the confusion and contradiction found to-day within affective psychology are notorious. Upon the most fundamental matters there is little agreement among psychologists." Seventy years later, multiplicity still reigns, as standard textbooks outline twenty or more competing psychological theories of emotion. What follows, then, is a necessarily selective review.

The cathartic, behaviorist, and cognitive theories discussed here have been, along with physiological theories, at the center of academic and clinical psychology in this century, and they encompass a multitude of possibilities. In some cognitive theories, crying is simply a physiological side effect of more significant mental processes, while in others it is an integral part of a person's social world and communication skills. In some behaviorist theories, weeping is never mentioned, while in others it is considered detrimental to mental health. Some psychologists, such as John B. Watson, have suggested that even infants should be ignored when they cry, since a child who is comforted will develop neuroses as an adult and end up spending its life weeping on a psychoanalyst's couch. In some forms of therapy, crying is a meaningless epiphenomenon, while in others it is considered the most important pathway to mental health.

Catharsis

A century or so after Hippocrates, Aristotle mentioned catharsis in his discussion of tragic theater in the *Poetics*. He used the term only once, and did so in what has been called the most often debated sentence in the history of aesthetics:

> A tragedy, then, is the imitation of an action that is serious, and also, as having magnitude, complete in itself; in language embellished with pleasurable accessories, each kind brought in separately in the parts of the work; in a dramatic, not in narrative form; with incidents arousing pity and fear wherewith to accomplish the catharsis of such emotions.

Aristotle might be using "catharsis" in this sentence to mean "purgation" or to refer to a more general sense of cleansing or purifying. Does watching tragedy "purge" these emotions, leaving us free of them? Or does it somehow "purify" them? We may want to be purged of fear, but why do we need to be purged of pity? What would it mean, on the other hand, to "purify" or cleanse such emotions?

This translation (by W. D. Ross) refuses to translate the key term, simply anglicizing the spelling. S. H. Butcher, in his influential 1895 translation, used "purgation," as have many translators before and since. Purgation, however, does not make complete sense. The capacity for fear and pity is not something Aristotle wants to eliminate, any more than Hippocrates wanted to purge people of all of their humors, which were necessary to life. The Hippocratic cathartic therapies were designed to eliminate excess humors, to purify the body of those waste humors that had been produced in surplus, keeping the proper amount of the four humors in the body in a purified and cleansed state. This, one can assume, is what Aristotle claimed for tragedy: that in the end it leaves us with neither too much nor too little pity and fear in our lives, and allows us to experience those emotions in some kind of pure and healthy way.

Aristotle's theory of tragedy has long been recognized as a response to Plato's condemnation of theater in *The Republic*. Tragedy and comedy both arouse the passions, according to Plato, and therefore they are among the destabilizing forces he felt should be banned from an ideal republic. He argued that just as in a perfect republic a philosopher would be head of state, so each person's head, each person's rationality, should rule his or her feelings and desires, which he saw as necessarily at war with the intellect.

It is drama's appeal to the passions that Plato—and a long series of censors since—wanted to abolish. Aristotle, in order to defend drama, theorizes that it does not stimulate such passions but instead purges or purifies them. Whatever passions it elicits, tragedy, according to Aristotle, has a cognitive conclusion; feelings of fear and pity are aroused, but since they are either purged or purified by the same process, they end up leaving the mind free from the vicissitudes of problematic passions. The tears we cry at a tragedy are a sign that we are cleaning up our psychic house in order to let rationality and our emotions resume their proper place. Thus Aristotle introduces the cognitive dimension of cathartic experience.

Some combination of the Aristotelian and Hippocratic views were invoked by many writers in the classical period. In the first century A.D., Ovid wrote that "by weeping we disperse our wrath. . . . It is a relief to weep; grief is satisfied and carried off by tears." A half century later, Seneca wrote that "tears ease the soul." The Greeks and Romans were not alone in understanding tears as beneficial, of course. An ancient Hindu proverb states that "tears are good for the complexion," and a Yiddish proverb of unknown provenance claims that "weeping makes the heart grow lighter." In these proverbs, too, weeping is good for the body, but also for the heart, the mind, the spirit, moods, dispositions—and all in different ratios. This inchoate combination of emotional, spiritual, mental, and bodily states, overlapping and blending into each other, has been at the center of our understanding and misunderstandings of tears for millennia, and at the center of psychotherapy throughout the last century.

Hippocrates' notions of purgation and purification of the four humors lasted into the Middle Ages, and so did the notion of catharsis in fields as diverse as aesthetics, nutrition, and religion. Alan of Lille wrote in the twelfth century that lamentation "is the first medicine in the cure of sin." The influence of cathartic thinking can clearly be seen in the Catholic ritual of confession, institutionalized in the thirteenth century. This original "talking cure" was conceived as purgative and purifying as well as penitential, and was often accompanied by tears. As we will see, weeping played other roles in prayer as well, but its cathartic virtues were always present. The theologian and philosopher Ralph Cudworth wrote in 1678 that "as this Earthy Body is washed by Water, so is that Spiritous Body Cleansed by Cathartick Vapors." The American divine Cotton Mather, in his combination guide to spiritual and physical health, *The Angel of Bethesda* (1724), urges purges of both body and spirit. By the nineteenth century, a slightly less religious and yet still recognizably cathartic view of tears was expressed by Sir Henry Maudsley: "Sorrows which find no vent in tears," he wrote, "may soon make other organs weep."

And so on down to our own day. In his recent book on crying in psychotherapy, the psychologist Jeffrey A. Kottler explains cathartic crying by saying that we have emotional reservoirs in which our tears gather until they are too full. Then the excess sloshes over the top and out of our eyes. This release of excess tears is necessary, Kottler explains, because without it we would build up pressure that can cause various forms of neurosis. Kottler is just using a metaphor, but it is one that permeates the psychological literature of the last century. Cathartic tears drain our bodies of the anxiety and negativity that gather there in our daily lives.

Mixed metaphors involving uncried tears building up pressure and then torrentially overflowing inform much physiological research as well, as in the case of Frey's arguments about the role of tears in removing the poisons that cause depression. Catharsis has been the single most persistent idea in this century's long march of new therapies. Every working therapist I interviewed agreed that crying was beneficial, and they used the familiar formulas to describe it. People need to be "in touch with their feelings." Repression, or "holding in" feelings, is harmful. We need to "let it all out." Most of the therapists admitted that crying was never addressed directly in their training, that it was never theorized or discussed in classes, and that the benefits of crying were simply assumed to be self-evident. And the therapists were not alone: medical doctors warning against stress, feminist critics of male reticence, and numerous other popular avatars of emotional expression have made crying not an end in itself but a means to health, success, relief, and redemption. One study of nurses in Texas found that across the entire profession—from beginning nursing students through staff nurses to nursing faculty—there was agreement that weeping was positive and healthy.

Despite its apparent simplicity, however, the idea that crying is beneficial implies a very complex set of assumptions, many of which will not hold up to extended scrutiny. After a century of therapeutic theorizing and research, there is still no hard evidence that tears are in fact cathartic, and there is some to suggest that they are not. We all know what it means to feel better after we cry. But most of us also know what it means to feel better after a couple of shots of booze, after eating a rich meal, or after smoking legal or illegal substances. We don't on that account construe these activities as necessary to ensure our mental stability and emotional health. Most of us, although we might not admit it, have felt better after a temper tantrum. But again, even if we feel it important not to repress our legitimate anger, we don't necessarily assume that expressing loud, abusive petulance is necessary to our emotional well-being. Being a brat is not recognized as cathartic. Only crying retains this special place in our emotional world. Just as we no longer consider bleeding with leeches to be a reasonable remedy, it is time to rethink the cathartic nature of tears as well. Sigmund Freud, who began his career believing in the value of catharsis, did just that.

As Freud began his medical training in the 1870s, he befriended Josef Breuer, a well-known and well-respected medical practitioner and researcher fifteen years his senior who specialized in the treatment of hysteria. Hysteria, a diagnosis given to a somewhat amorphous group of symptoms or dysfunctions, was still in the 1870s widely considered to be the result of either physical damage to the nervous system or hypochondriacal malingering. Breuer, along with Freud, argued that hysteria was instead a neurosis caused by psychological trauma. "Hysterics," Freud and Breuer concluded in their jointly authored *Studies in Hysteria* (1895), "suffer mainly from reminiscences." Thus the symptoms of hysterics were directly related to the inciting trauma: a woman whose arm had fallen asleep as she stood watch at a relative's deathbed was later afflicted with a hysterically paralyzed arm; a man who had observed his brother's hip operation was afflicted with a constant pain in his hip. Freud and Breuer's explanation relies on a Hippocratic notion of purgation. The memory of the trauma "acts like a foreign body," they wrote, "which long after its entry must continue to be regarded as an agent that is still at work." The goal of therapy is to purge the foreign agent, and to reach that goal they developed what they called the "cathartic method" of psychotherapy.

From 1880 to 1882, while Freud was finishing his medical examinations, Breuer treated a woman named Bertha Pappenheim. Renamed "Anna O." (following the practice of fictionalizing the names of patients in published case histories), Pappenheim became one of the most famous patients in psychoanalytic history. It was she, not Freud or Breuer, who first came up with the phrase "talking cure" to describe her doctor's method, and it is the talking cure rather than the cathartic method which eventually became central to Freud's work.

In cathartic therapy, the patient was encouraged to remember the traumatic event and reexperience the negative emotions "as vividly as possible." Anna O. had developed an aversion to drinking water and was severely dehydrated, eating nothing but watery fruits to lessen her thirst. Breuer put her under hypnosis. Unprompted, she began talking about a companion who had let her dog drink water from a glass. As she told the story, she felt and vocalized all the anger and disgust she had hidden from her companion and had never expressed. She straightaway asked for a glass of water and drank comfortably from then on. Breuer writes that he was "greatly surprised" by this sudden removal of a symptom, and marks this accident as the origin of the cathartic theory. Breuer then managed to remove each of her other hysterical symptoms—neuralgia, tremors, eye problems (diplopia, amblyopia, macropsia), coughing, an inability to read, "seeing a death's head instead of her father"—through this same method. Her horrible hallucinations disappeared, for instance, when she managed, "shaking with fear and horror," to reproduce under hypnosis the full experience of the hallucination and the full experience of the traumatic experience that had first induced the hallucination, leaving her mind completely "relieved."

The introduction to *Studies in Hysteria* sums up the method: "Each individual hysteric symptom immediately and permanently disappeared when we had succeeded in bringing clearly to light the memory of the event by which it was produced and in arousing its accompanying affect, and when the patient had described the event in the greatest possible detail and put the affect into words." In practice, this was far from simple. Remembering chronologically backward, Anna O. reexperienced almost three hundred instances of impaired hearing (all dutifully catalogued by Breuer) before getting back to the inciting traumatic event that had induced that symptom, which was only one among her many complaints.

It was almost a decade after Breuer saw Anna O. that Freud began to use cathartic therapy himself, modify it, and retheorize it. His first case involved a forty-year-old woman he calls "Frau Emmy von N." Freud describes her symptoms as he noted them during her treatment: violent tics and clacking sounds, and regular loud imprecations to "Keep still!—Don't say anything!—Don't touch me!" which he assumed were incantations to ward off hallucinations. He also describes his treatment regimen. She was given a bath every day, and Freud himself gave her full body massages twice a day while she was under hypnosis ("Don't touch me" indeed). During these hypnotized massages, Freud would prompt her to talk about what was bothering her and attempt to analyze the originating cause of her symptoms. She did "abreact" many memories—that is, she emotionally reexperienced painful events—and Freud felt he had found the cause of some of her symptoms, but he admits that despite successful catharses, he failed to effect a cure.

Thus, in writing up his very first case using cathartic therapy, Freud was already doubting its efficacy. Freud and Breuer had used the terms "catharsis" and "abreaction" somewhat interchangeably, as if any painful memory was necessarily therapeutic. In the years that followed, Freud came to use the latter term exclusively, with a decreased emphasis on emotional release. In later Freudian theory, emotional release alone can never effect a cure, since he saw that a cathartic experience can remove a particular symptom and still leave the fundamental problem untouched. Cathartic experiences can occur, in fact, even when a symptom is digging in for a longer stay. In a note added to the 1924 edition of the case, Freud wrote, perhaps prematurely: "I am aware that no analyst can read this case history today without a smile of pity."

Another case Freud discusses in passing in *Studies in Hysteria* comes much closer to a pure cathartic cure. "'Fräulein Mathilde H.'" was "a good-looking, nineteen-year-old girl" who was suffering from partial paralysis of the legs and, some months later, depression. Freud, as was common practice at the time, put her under hypnosis and gave her "commands and suggestions" for her improvement. "She listened to these in deep sleep, to the accompaniment of floods of tears," Freud writes, but his suggestions had no discernible effect on her condition. One day she did talk about the inciting cause of the problem—a broken engagement—and she cried voluminously. In subsequent sessions she could never be induced to speak of it again, despite Freud's prompting during and after hypnosis. Freud continued hypnotizing her and giving her pointed suggestions, after each of which she "burst into tears without ever answering." One day, about a year after breaking off the engagement, her depression vanished, and proponents of cathartic therapies have since argued that this is proof that emotional discharge is sufficient for a cure. Freud himself disagreed, writing, with some sarcasm, that the case "brought me the credit of a great therapeutic success."

This "success" is relegated to a footnote because Freud was already moving, in *Studies in Hysteria* (although the theoretical explication would wait some years), toward the realization that what was important in Breuer's cathartic therapy was not emotional release but the act of bringing the experience into words. The verbal descriptions are essential, Freud came to believe, because they prove that the experience, which had been repressed, was once again conscious. Emotions reexperienced during analysis insure the accuracy of the memory, but are otherwise beside the point, which is to revise the emotional associations with a particular memory, to dilute their power by reimagining them. That one cries during an analytic session means that one has accessed the full meaning and power of the memory. When one describes the traumatic memory in words, one rescues it from the irredeemable past and incorporates it into current consciousness. But the crying that might accompany such coming to consciousness has no therapeutic value of its own.

In the lectures Freud gave at Clark University in 1909 introducing psychoanalysis to the United States, he retold some of the stories from *Studies in Hysteria* and elaborated upon them slightly. In these lectures, he continued to argue that traumatic experiences arouse emotions which the patient represses and that these emotions are "imprisoned" and converted into symptoms. But Freud also introduced a new concept, not yet theorized in the earlier text, which is that of conflicting desires. A patient will tend to repress a desire that for ethical or aesthetic reasons is unacceptable in favor of the desire to remain within the bounds of propriety. It is the repressed wish, not the repressed feeling, that is converted into symptoms. Thus the psychic economy that analysis restructures is not emotional but libidinal—that is, we store frustrated desires, not frustrated emotions.

The difference is significant. If libidinal rather than emotional energy is redirected or repressed in neurosis, then the expression of emotion alone will change nothing. If a patient's crying expresses emotions repressed during the traumatic death of a parent, then crying will eventually allow the patient to "work through" the trauma and erase its effects. But if the patient cries because his or her very real desire for the presence of the parent is thwarted, then continued crying can never alter the now well-trod pathways to his or her grief. Patients need to come to terms with their desires rather than with their loss.

Hence Freud's dictum of the 1920s: where id was, there shall ego be. It is the unattainable dreams and desires of the id that must become conscious, he came to believe, in order for them to lose their power. The emotions we feel as we relive past experiences are simply a by-product of this coming to consciousness of one's desires. We cannot feel the same emotions because they are long gone. Emotions cannot be stored for years in our bodies, waiting to reappear like a virus or bottled-up carbonation. We might cry, of course, in a way very similar to the way we cried when our desires were first frustrated, but not because the tears have been waiting somewhere inside us during the intervening years. We cry because the events or the desires still evoke powerful feelings when they are remembered or recognized, in part because our understanding of the events has not evolved. As in the case of "Fräulein Mathilde H." or in the case of tears of grief years after a death, the crying has no therapeutic value in and of itself. And new crying can happen in analysis, too, a newly induced mourning for an object of desire that is "lost" in the process of analysis.

But even though Freud abandoned cathartic therapy, many others in the medical community did not. In 1939 Thomas M. French, M.D., claimed that in his patients asthma attacks ended when crying started, and thus suggested that crying was a cure for asthma. Saul and Bernstein observed in 1941 that in some patients, uriticaria (or hives) was absent when the patient was weeping, and present when not weeping. H. J. Shorvon and W. B. Sargent, writing in the *Journal of Mental Science* in 1947, spoke favorably of the Corybantes, a Greek sect that cured through orgiastic dancing. Gregory Zilboorg, although he was a historian and not a physician, in his *History of Medical Psychology* (1941) commended Greek and Roman physicians for stimulating frightening memories in their patients for purgative purposes. Moshé Feldenkrais, in *The Body and Mature Behavior* (1949), argued that the Freudian couch works by facilitating the cathartic ridding of bodily tension. In 1954, Percival Symonds reviewed the therapeutic literature in the *American Journal of Orthopsychiatry* and argued that catharsis was the most frequent cause of success in psychotherapy.

Feldenkrais, Symonds, and many others making these body-centered arguments about catharsis had come under the influence of Wilhelm Reich, who had been a close associate of Freud's and had vehemently returned to the concept Freud had left behind. Reich's wacky beliefs and behavior—rainmaking being just one of his more mundane activities—led to his expulsion from the psychoanalytic school and then from the ranks of professional psychotherapists altogether. He developed a theory that a mass-free energy called orgone permeated the universe. Orgone built up in human beings and caused neurosis, Reich argued, and only regular sexual intercourse could maintain one's orgone equilibrium. Reich encouraged crying, shouting, touching, kicking, pillow-punching, and stimulation of the gag reflex, among other physical therapies, to break down the body's "defenses," the armor people build up to avoid full participation in adult life. The act signaling and making possible a final cure for any patient, according to Reich, was pleasurable, fulfilling sexual intercourse. Freudian therapy is designed to break down psychic defenses, whereupon bodily symptoms, like the classic hysterically paralyzed arm, are removed. Reichian therapy instead attempts to attack the body's defenses, whereupon character change and psychological integration can take place. Although many of Reich's theories have been uniformly dismissed by mainstream psychologists, his emphasis on the body and aspects of his techniques found their way into various emotivist therapies that followed.

In the 1970s, cathartic therapies enjoyed a loud and splashy renaissance. A new slew of psychotherapeutic techniques and schools arose that owed much to the counterculture of the sixties, with its premium on self-expression and its intensification of what Philip Rahv called the "cult of experience" in American culture. A 1976 volume of conference essays with the unappetizing title *Emotional Flooding* explicitly gives credit for the resurgence of emotivist therapy to the demands of this "present young generation, a generation that has proclaimed in countless ways its distrust of verbiage and attempted intellectual solutions to emotional problems." Psychologist Paul Olsen, who edited the book, considers this a good thing. "Directly stimulating emotion in patients," he wrote, "is perhaps the most exciting and meaningful therapeutic trend that the mental health profession has witnessed in the past two decades." For Olsen and most of the therapies he discusses, "emotion" here is primarily a physical rather than a psychological entity, often stimulated by physical means and measured by the intensity of its physical manifestations.

As Olsen admits, the transfer of attention from the intellect to the body implied by such emotional stimulation owes much to Reich, but Reich's influence had taken many new turns. *Emotional Flooding* offers essays on Gestalt therapy, psychodrama, structural integration, bioenergetics, regrief therapy, and a number of other, shorter-lived schools. Their common ground is the expression of emotion as a necessary part of the therapeutic encounter, because, as one contributor put it, "neurosis is a disease of feelings."

Arthur Janov's primal therapy, for instance, requires "opening up the whole being to the fullest expression of the deepest and most primitive feelings." In the three-week crash course that begins primal therapy, the patient is cut off from the outside world and encouraged to regress to his or her infantile state, complete with crying and screaming. "Screaming and crying are civilized out of us," Sidney Rose, a primal therapist and psychiatrist writes. We are forced to cut off our emotional reactions by parents and caretakers, and primal therapy allows the patient to "finish off old scripts to attain closure . . . to feel the emotions that were denied consciousness at the time." In the year-long or longer therapy that ensues, the patient slowly "comes to terms with his deepest emotions, those that he has struggled over an entire lifetime not to feel."

Janov, in *The Primal Scream* (1970), makes clear that everyday crying is not enough. The tears we shed at a movie or a play, for instance, "are generally the result of the release of feeling rather than the expansion into total primal feelings. The release process is what helps make the complete feeling unfelt. It vitiates and aborts the feeling and thus mitigates the hurt." A much fuller and more extreme catharsis than any imagined by Aristotle is necessary, Janov said. The patient needs to scream and wail. Rose, who calls his offshoot "intense feeling therapy," believed that the effectiveness of the technique would eventually be established. Janov claimed that 90 percent of his patients were "cured" by this technique. No independent studies would ever confirm either claim.

Many other psychotherapeutic schools offered cures through crying. Daniel Casriel, in his New Identity therapy, also uses screaming as a basic therapeutic tool: "Screams can release emotions repressed since childhood, and the freedom of release can affect significant positive changes in personality." Vamik D. Volkan, a professor of psychiatry at the University of Virginia Medical Center, originated regrief therapy in the 1970s for patients who had not successfully mourned the death of an intimate. They are encouraged "to experience and to express the emotions generated by the loss," which is both the process of therapy and the cure. Henry Jackins was a former labor union organizer who had a friend he was trying to help through a tough time when he noticed that the friend always started crying when they tried to talk. He decided it was more important to just listen to his friend cry than to figure out the problem intellectually. Each time the man cried, he seemed to be better, more rational and more content, at least for a while. Jackins developed "reevaluation counseling" based on such insights. The more repressed the emotion, Jackins argued, the more irrational someone acts. Hence the discharge of emotion is in the service of more rational living. Reevaluation follows spontaneously upon catharsis.

Thomas J. Scheff, a professor emeritus of sociology at the University of Santa Barbara and a pioneer in the growing field of the sociology of the emotions, outlined his own theory of catharsis in *Catharsis in Healing, Ritual, and Drama* (1979). The research to date, he admits, is insufficient to form reliable conclusions about catharsis. But based on his own work as a lay counselor and then as a licensed marriage, family, and child counselor, Scheff came to believe that Freud and Breuer were right. "Emotional expressions such as crying are biological necessities," Scheff writes. "Crying itself is instinctual; the baby comes out of the womb with the ability to cry. This ability is unlearned. What is learned is the ability to suppress crying. I will argue that the suppression of crying and other cathartic processes, which is learned, has supremely important consequences, both for persons and societies." Although he has moved on to other projects, Scheff continues to believe that crying can have profound therapeutic benefits.

Two of the longest-lasting of the emotivist therapies that emerged in the 1970s are bioenergetics, originated by Alexander Lowen, M.D., and structural integration therapy, invented by Ida P. Rolf. Rolf, who developed what is popularly known as "Rolfing" at the Esalen Institute, used direct physical manipulation to induce intense emotion. "Psychological hang-ups," Rolf writes, dating herself immediately, "are recorded and perpetuated in the body, in flesh, and in bones." Her technique of "freeing" the joints through vigorous, extremely painful massage and manipulation was meant to help the body realign its four major "segments," which had been thrown out of whack by emotional upheavals. The pain and tears that accompany Rolfing are the necessary result of releasing both bodily and psychological tension.

The flood of emotion and tears that is experienced, according to people who have gone through Rolf's therapy, is much more profound than could be caused by the pain of the massage, although that is itself severe. Patients report having cried for half an hour or longer, and more intensely than they ever have in their lives. For the people I interviewed, the intensity of the experience was proof that "very deep stuff was getting accessed," as one told me, or that, in the words of another, "deeply buried emotions were brought back to life."

In the 1970s, Alexander Lowen, the founder of "bioenergetic analysis," had people all across the country beating and screaming into their pillows and practicing "deep" crying in therapists' offices, helping them to get in touch with themselves by getting in touch with repressed feelings. Lowen sees the body as the repository of psychological or characterological problems and reads the tensions in the facial muscles, the long skeletal muscles, and the joints as clues to the patient's troubles. Some practitioners of Lowen's method, like John Bellis of the Institute of Bioenergetic Analysis, encourage emotional flooding as part of a therapy that also includes cognitive work. But Lowen suggests that emotional experience is sufficient unto itself. In *The Language of the Body* (1958) and *The Betrayal of the Body* (1967), Lowen got rid of the distinction between psychic energy and physical energy in favor of one, "fundamental energy in the human body," that he calls "bioenergy." A feeling of loss calls for tears, Lowen wrote, and if the tears do not fall, that loss is transformed into bodily tension. Emotions get stuck in the body whenever they are not expressed, and so the raised shoulders of fear, the tucked shoulders of a load of guilt, the stiff, straight back of a person who is emotionally inflexible and unyielding are all the result of unshed tears. This bodily tension, in turn, inhibits emotional experience, starting a spiral that can lead to depression. Thus he encourages his patients to hit and kick the couch, releasing anger.

That release frees the body from its armorlike tension, allowing the patient to feel again, after which the patient cries.

Conscious understanding of one's own tension and repression does not help, Lowen claims, in contrast to Freud. The fits and tears are necessary: "It is one thing to be able to recognize that one is sad; it is another to be able to cry." Like many of the people who work in the field of pop psychology, Lowen throws such near tautologies around as if they prove his theory. "Crying, that is, sobbing, is the earliest and deepest way to release tension," Lowen writes, and "every stress that produces a state of tension in the body" thus needs to be released by crying. The analyst can, through massage and exercises, break through the tension-induced body armor and help the patient begin to cry, but it is the crying, not the massage, that does the work.

In one of his later books, *Narcissism: Denial of the True Self* (1983), Lowen again argues that "people in trouble need to cry." He recounts many cases in which people made extraordinary progress in their quest for mental health when he helped them release their tears. "Fortunately, I was able to help Mary get in touch with and release some of her sadness by crying," Lowen writes of one patient. "This enabled her to break through the denial, see the reality of her being, and make a connection to her bodily self which gave her a strength she had never previously possessed." Lowen offers no explanation as to why this might be so—the mere fact that it happened functions, instead, as an explanation.

In the self-empowerment vernacular of the 1970s and 1980s, then, crying had become a kind of technology of the psyche, a kind of ur-skill allowing one to tap into the fullness of human power. All of these therapies have patients or ex-patients who can vouch for their value. Indeed, they all have patients willing to proselytize for the therapies as earnestly as their therapists: The most forceful statements about the beneficial value of tears I have heard came from people who had had profound experiences while weeping during one of these therapeutic sessions. The experiences are, at one level, undeniably cathartic, since the people who experienced them feel them to have been so. They feel transformed, and so their weepy therapeutic sessions must have been cathartic at some level. But a recent doctoral dissertation by

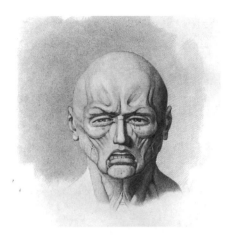

One of a series of engravings, produced for wealthy amateur artists, of the facial muscles used in emotional expressions, based on drawings by anatomist George Stubbs. From C. Knight, *Stipple engravings: Ecorche expressions of emotions* (1815), after H. Singleton and/or after George Stubbs. Wellcome Institute Library, London.

Wendy Ellen Davis suggests another possibility. Davis studied the crying habits and attitudes among close to two hundred college students and found that the women (who cried more often and used crying as a coping strategy more often than men) reported positive benefits from their crying, both psychologically and in terms of their "quality of life." But using standard stress inventories and health questionnaires, Davis found that crying was associated with *worse* rather than better health, and that tears did nothing to mitigate stress. The self-evaluation of their tearful episodes and the objective inventory of their health and stress levels simply did not match.

The idea of catharsis, of purification through purgation, does have obvious physical resonance—vomiting can remove poisons and pathogens; nobody likes constipation. The act of crying is obviously an act of excretion, most forms of which—urination, sweating, defecation, phlegm—are involved in removing unwanted waste from the body. And the religious connotations cannot be underestimated. Confession, baptism, exorcism, fasting, holy water, sweat lodges—such spiritual cleansings and purgings are very much alive as rituals and metaphors, however secularized some of them may be. None of the

explanations offered by therapists, however, square with contemporary neuroscience, and none have conducted replicatable studies of
their efficacy. Some psychologists have argued that this is because of a
basic confusion between the mental and physical forms of catharsis.
And others offer a simpler explanation: crying, these researchers
claim, accompanies, rather than causes, the release these patients feel.

Perhaps this is why the idea of catharsis persists, and why we continue to assume that a good cry will make us feel better. Despite the
fact that Freud and the majority of research psychologists and neuro-
scientists reject the catharsis hypothesis, it remains embedded in the
popular consciousness. It shows up in all sorts of imagery, from the cult film
Fantastic Voyage, in which a man must cry to expel the miniaturized
foreign craft motoring around in his veins, to the recent Joop! jeans
advertising campaign which announced, apropos of nothing, that
"tears are anti-freeze for the soul." But if the physiologists and experimental psychologists are correct in their conclusion that tears are
stimulated by the parasympathetic system, something else must
unfreeze the soul before tears can run.

Behaviorism

At the same time that Freud was developing ego psychology and Cannon was reimagining the physiology of the emotions, another new
school of psychology was emerging and it, too, had something to say
about weeping. Though it came out of Pavlov's studies of conditioned
response, behaviorism was named and first theorized as a general
method by James B. Watson. Using laboratory experiments with both
animal and human subjects, behaviorists completely rejected the
introspective and philosophical tendencies of Jamesian psychology
and the kind of ungrounded theorizing they found in Freud's work.
What psychology needed in order to become a true science, Watson
argued, was to stick to measurable, observable behavior and to purely
scientific methods of hypothesis and demonstration. In practice, this
meant, among other things, that Watson studied emotional response
by banging loudly on an enormous steel plate with a hammer directly
behind the heads of infants in order to measure their startle response,

taken to be an elemental emotional response. Although later critics like Noam Chomsky would argue that behaviorists using such methods could not tell a pigeon from a poet, from the 1920s through the heyday of B. F. Skinner in the 1960s, behaviorism was the dominant school of American academic psychology. Behaviorism transformed and has been fully integrated into the science of psychology, but like classic Freudianism or 1920s physiology, its excesses and blind spots become clearer with each passing decade. In the 1920s, though, behaviorism, with its insistence that psychology should be a science of behavior, not of consciousness, was considered to be at the forefront of social science, and Watson was the man who had pushed it there.

Watson, the "father" of behaviorism, was one of the most fascinating figures in the history of psychology. A professor at Johns Hopkins University, the editor of the *Journal of Experimental Psychology* and a controversial but respected researcher into animal and human behavior, Watson was also one of the best-known psychologists in the country, in part because he had written not just scholarly articles but several books and many magazine pieces for a general audience as well. In 1920 he was caught *in flagrante* with a graduate student (on his office desk, the unofficial legend has it) and was summarily dismissed from his Hopkins post. From there he took a job at the J. Walter Thompson advertising agency, where he became a vice president, applying psychology to the ad business. While in the advertising business, he continued writing books on psychology for mass audiences, and his child-rearing manual, *The Psychological Care of Infant and Child*, was a best-seller when it appeared in 1928. Although some reviewers found the book's prescriptions too modern for their taste, almost all deferred to Watson's authority.

In the nineteenth century, most writers on child rearing and childhood tears agreed that human beings were born basically good, and that while they might be led wrong, if properly taught they would develop into moral, well-adjusted adults. In the meantime, children lived in a kind of paradise, in which the tears of childhood were strewn like so many sentimental speed bumps in what was otherwise an idyll. Such thinking was a central strand in the culture of childhood from Rousseau and the Romantics on, and many psychologists in the twenties continued to hold similar views. The German psychologist William Stern, for instance, wrote in *Psychology of Early Childhood* (1924) that crying was a short interlude in an otherwise "chronic state of well-being and delight." Stern wrote consciously against the tide of psychoanalysis and what Freud himself called the "plague" of psycho-analytic ideas about childhood sexuality and aggression.

Freudian thought had already had an effect on popular child-rearing manuals by the 1920s, which meant a new emphasis on the natural depravity of children, and thus on parental control, strict discipline, and suspicion. In the manuals reflecting the influence of Freud, one sees a corresponding distrust of tears, an assumption that the crying of children was not simply expressive but manipulative. This more cynical understanding assumed that children were always on the verge of becoming petty tyrants in the home, an unholy situation that could only be averted by imposing some form of discipline. Using Freudian ideas but recasting them in behaviorist terms, Watson concluded that all crying should be completely ignored. Motherhood, Watson argued, should be considered not primarily as a relation of love but as a profession, just like engineering. Mothers, it seemed, had been bungling the job for millennia, doing all sorts of harm to their offspring and to mankind. Watson suggested that it was time to inject a little professionalism into the obviously important work mothers perform. Watson's beef is the opposite of the one most commonly heard today as mothers increasingly work outside the home and the family is once again in the process of being reinvented. If at present we believe that parents don't spend enough time with their children, Watson summed up his credo in one of his chapter titles: "Too Much Mother Love."

Too much mother love is responsible for, among other things, the excessive crying that babies do. "The fact that our children are always crying and always whining shows the unhappy, unwholesome state they are in. Their digestion is interfered with and probably their whole glandular system is deranged." And the mother is wholly to blame.

Mothers since Eve have watched their children come into the world and begin to grow up. They know that as time goes on more and more things around the house make it cry. When it cries a hundred times a day, as many millions of them do, we say it is "spoiled." And we put the blame on the child rather than upon our own shoulders where the blame belongs.

Later behaviorists argued that whenever we give our infants and children attention, we are in effect rewarding them. If we attend to them every time they cry, they will cry for attention whenever they want it. But Watson is making a different point here. He believes infants get spoiled not because mothers and nurses reward children by responding to their crying but because they do so by hugging and kissing them.

And therein lies the danger:

> The mother knows the infant can smile and gurgle and chuckle with glee. She knows it can coo and hold out its chubby arms. What more touching and sweet, more thrilling to a young mother! And the mother to get these thrills goes to extreme lengths. She picks the infant up, kisses and hugs it, rocks it, pets it and calls it "mother's little lamb," until the child is unhappy and miserable whenever away from actual physical contact with the mother.

The real problem, according to Watson, is that that this "physical contact with the mother" is so exciting and pleasurable that the child simply cannot get enough. It is no accident, according to Watson, that "unscrupulous nurses" through the ages have resorted to direct genital stimulation to quiet fussy babies (a practice common, in fact, in cultures as varied as the Kogi and the Havasu). Children so pampered grow into adults who search for this level of love and stimulation for the rest of their lives, and since adults can never find such enveloping love or such sexual pleasure, Watson reasoned, they become frustrated and unhappy. The best thing a parent can do for his or her child is to put it out in the backyard, from the age of a few months on, and dig some holes that it can fall into and scramble out of, thus developing its problem-solving skills. All alone and falling into holes, Watson argued, the baby will develop into a self-reliant individual.

In his proscriptions against coddling and soothing, Watson, although he was an active enemy of psychoanalysis, seems to have relied heavily on Freudian ideas, such as this discussion in *Three Essays on Sexuality* (1905) of the typical mother's behavior with her infant:

> She strokes him, kisses him, rocks him and quite clearly treats him as a substitute for a complete sexual object. A mother would probably be horrified if she were made aware that all her marks of affection were rousing her child's sexual instinct and preparing for its later intensity. She regards what she does as asexual, as "pure" love, since, after all, she carefully avoids applying more excitations to the child's genitals than are unavoidable in nursery care.

Although Freud believes that the mother does excite the child sexually, in other words, he doesn't think she should necessarily feel bad about it. Only the "excess of parental affection" needs to be watched. The average mother, he writes,

> is only fulfilling her task in teaching the child to love. After all, he is meant to grow up into a strong and capable person with vigorous sexual needs and to accomplish during his life all the things that human beings are urged to do by their instincts. It is true that an excess of parental affection does harm by causing precocious sexual maturity and also because, by spoiling the child, it makes him incapable in later life of temporarily doing without love or of being content with a smaller amount of it.

While such excess is a problem, it is not the rule for Freud as it is for Watson. Normal motherly nurturance, Freud feels, however sexualized, is necessary for normal development.

Watson, however, is adamant that "normal" nurturing is always harmful. The ideas of both Freud and Watson were debated and discussed in newspapers and magazines across the country in the 1920s, at a time when people were fearful of emotional excess. The Great War was seen as an indulgence of the uncivilized passions, and the rapid social and cultural transformations of the 1920s were interpreted by some as an attack against civilization by immature flappers and sheiks spoiled by the new affluence. The function of the endocrine system was coming to light, and ideas regarding primitive, biologically based emotions that needed to be held in check were also being disseminated by the intellectual and popular press. One popular magazine article warned, for instance, that (as the headline had it) "Your Emotions Will Get You If You Don't Watch Out!" When it came to infant crying, this meant that by comforting their infant's tears, "overprotective" or "indulgent" mothers were producing weepy, mopey adults enslaved by their own primitive feelings. The U.S. Children's Bureau in 1924 warned mothers not to pick up their babies at all between feedings because they would end up with "a spoiled fussy baby and a household tyrant whose continual demands make a slave of the mother."

The rejection of physical affection in favor of more scientific approaches, in other words, was not confined to behaviorism. And given Watson's notoriety, it is not surprising that a number of offshoots of behaviorism, or at least new names for it, appeared. Albert P. Weiss, blaming popularizations of behaviorism for diluting its scientific rigor, renamed his own brand of behaviorism "biosocial psychology" in 1928. For Weiss, the superiority of biosocial psychology and behaviorism lay in the fact that they are scientific, while the majority of the psychology that preceded them was "literary." Behaviorists refused to make unsupported generalizations and unwarranted forays into other people's consciousnesses. This leads Weiss to conclude that "what has traditionally been included under the term feeling may be regarded as a literary description of the biological factors of facilitation and interference." Facilitation occurs when we have pleasant feelings that facilitate our actions. Unpleasant feelings interfere with our actions. Other behaviorists had similarly pared-down understandings of emotion. Harvey A. Carr wrote in 1925 that "an emotion may thus be provisionally defined as a somatic readjustment which is instinctively aroused by a stimulating situation and which in turn promotes more effective adaptive response to that situation." B. F. Skinner, in 1938, would say that "emotion is not primarily a response at all but rather a state of strength comparable in many ways to a drive," again suggesting that emotion is significant only in terms of its effects on action or behavior.

The old woman in Albee's play, from this behaviorist perspective, could not possibly have a good cry. Either the cry is a facilitator, or it is simply a way of summoning the nurse, in which case it is clearly unnecessary. Or it is an interference, and given Albee's stage directions, that is a good guess. Like self-loathing itself, crying simply interferes with one's practical and social desires. That, from the behaviorist perspective, is what a bad cry does. The early behaviorists' principle contribution to the study of tears was their insistence on an examination of crying as a behavior for which an investigator needs no knowledge of the crier's cognition. The weakness of their method was its inability to account for the differences cognition makes.

All experimenters and most clinicians are now, at least to some degree, behaviorists; that is, they all give credence to experimental results that do not require the description by subjects of their thoughts and feelings but instead rely on measurable physical changes, movements, actions, and more focused physiological measurements. The original ban against the study of consciousness has been abandoned, and most psychologists assume (and therefore study) a combination of many factors, the totality of which do not fit neatly into a single school's main tenets. Silvan Tomkins, one of the most important American psychologists of emotion in the 1960s, rejoiced when he saw that the more rigid, archetypal forms of behaviorism were losing their hold on the discipline. "Since psychology committed itself to behavior without benefit of consciousness it has been walking in an untroubled, dreamless sleep now for over half a century," he wrote in 1964. "It is being aroused from this state and slowly regaining consciousness."

Cognition

On October 19, 1927, at Wittenberg College in Springfield, Ohio, a remarkable gathering of psychologists took place. Alfred Adler came in from Vienna, Pierre Janet from Paris, William Stern from Hamburg, Carl Jörgenson from Copenhagen, and Walter Cannon, Harvey Carr, Carl Seashore, Robert Woodworth, Joseph Jastrow, Morton Prince, William McDougall, Knight Dunlap, James Catell, Edwin Slosson, and two dozen other psychologists from around the country and the world came together for a symposium on emotion. E. B. Titchener, the Cornell professor of psychology who was a major force in establishing experimental psychology in the U.S., was to be chairman, but he died a couple of months before the conference, and the few internationally famous researchers into the emotions who were unable to attend—Dewey, Koffka, Thorndike, Yerkes, and others—sent "their sincere regrets and best wishes for the success of the meeting."

The various methodologies of the day were represented by behaviorists, functionalists, physiologists, psychoanalysts, and statisticians. And in essays like Jastrow's "The Place of Emotion in Modern Psychology," Aveling's "Emotion, Conation, and Will," and Margaret Washburn's "Emotion and Thought," a new approach to emotion was beginning to emerge. It came to be called the cognitive approach. Jastrow predicted that the evolution of psychological thinking about the emotions would lead researchers to an understanding of "motives" as encompassing both thinking and feeling. Aveling described experiments demonstrating the effects that feelings have on cognition, and Washburn gave theoretical arguments for the same, basing her work on "the motor hypothesis," or physiology. All of the participants were aware of behaviorism—several took jabs at it and its disgraced founder—but the effect of behaviorist thinking could be seen in a perceived necessity to remain attentive to bodily processes even while investigating what earlier would have been isolated as purely mental processes.

This double focus remained central to the development of the cognitive psychology of the emotions from the late 1920s on. Throughout the discipline, the convergence of quasi-physiological Freudian thinking, rabidly physiological behaviorist thinking, laboratory-trained experimentalism, and a thorough distrust of "literary" theorizing resulted in a variety of attempts to articulate a synthesis of cognition, sensation, perception, conditioning, and biology. Paul Young in 1943, for instance, gave the following definition of emotion: "an acute disturbance of the individual as a whole, psychological in origin, involving behavior, conscious experience, and visceral functioning." Cognitive psychology gained favor over the years until it gradually displaced behaviorism, while incorporating the majority of behaviorist methods. With the rise of information theories, themselves the result of computer research, cognition was thought of less and less as an object for introspection, and more in terms of circuits, appraisals, and calculations. The body retained its importance, but the center of somatic interest shifted from endocrinology to neurophysiology.

Michael Nichols and Melvin Zax, reviewing the wave of cathartic therapies in the late 1970s, made a distinction between somatic-emotional and cognitive-emotional catharsis. The first is a purely bodily experience, and the second, as in Freud's theory of abreaction, is primarily an affair of the psyche, however much somatic changes accompany the process. Somatic-emotional theories such as those of Reich, Janov, and Rolf rely on a notion of stored emotions, a notion that, in the late twentieth century, finally becomes insupportable. In cognitive-emotional therapies, patients are encouraged not simply to reexperience traumatic emotions. They are asked to call up memories they have tried to avoid because of the negative emotions they would evoke, and reexperience them for the sole purpose of cognitively recontextualizing them in therapy.

The distinction Nichols and Zax make between somatic and cognitive catharsis may be tied to what Joseph LeDoux has found to be the different functions of the amygdala and the hippocampus (see chapter 1). As LeDoux demonstrated, the ability to feel an emotion and the ability to construct or remember the meaning of an emotional event require different parts of the brain and can function separately or in coordination. This may explain why some appeals to emotional understanding have no effect on feeling and why feeling has no necessary effect on understanding. Hence an actor in the throes of emotion can weep while remembering some past trauma and at the same time calculate the effect his weeping is having on an audience. We nonactors are often able to weep in full sincerity and yet carefully modulate it in order to maximize its effect. And we can cry in therapy over and over again without ever altering, and perhaps without ever consciously accessing, the memories that have us in tears.

In cognitive theories, it is memories that are stored, not feelings.

According to the cognitive psychologists, to believe that feelings can remain inside of us, unfelt, and that tears can wash such repressed feelings away, is to be duped by our own metaphors. Instead, according to Antonio Damasio, memories are "marked" in such a way as to set off the physiological reactions the original events set off. Every time we cry about a past event, we do so because the memory is marked by tears, and in so doing we mark it once again with tears. The next time we recall it, we will cry again unless we revise our understanding of the memory and remark it with different emotions. Remembering a betrayal or insult can elicit different memories year to year, decade to decade, as we reconsider the nature of betrayal or become more immune to insult. The memory retains many of the same images, but each time we revisit it, we can revise the emotional associations linked to it.

According to Barry Guinagh, a professor of educational psychology at the University of Florida, somatic-emotional theories of catharsis employ a "container" model, arguing that unexpressed emotions accumulate and need to be discharged in order for the person to function properly. Freud's container model in *Studies in Hysteria* followed on his research into the (recently discovered) neuron, which, when filled with energy, upsets the optimal equilibrium of the nervous system. The neuron then needs to fire in order for equilibrium to be restored. Most cathartic theories employ container or "hydraulic" models, as when Janov writes of the necessity to drain the "primal pool of pain." Fritz Perls, the most popular avatar of Gestalt therapy in the 1960s, came to employ a different model, that of "unfinished business," calling the container model "the defecation theory of Aristotle and Freud." To the extent that he avoids cathartic thinking, he does so as Freud did, by thinking in terms of desire. Emotions, according to Perls, are urges for closure: fear is an unfinished desire to flee; longing is an unfinished desire to be close to someone. If the unfinished business remains unfinished—that is, if the social or psychological needs or pressures which led to the need for action continue to exist—then the sense of urgency, the feelings which the frustrated action first incited, will continue to reappear. Emotions are thus urges to action.

Perls's theory is similar to that of his contemporary Magda Arnold, whose "appraisal theory" of emotion was extremely influential in academic psychology, and whose *Emotion and Personality* (1960) is often considered by psychologists to be the beginning of a cognitive theory of the emotions. (But then psychology has perhaps the least accurate and sophisticated sense of its own history of any discipline; as we have seen, ideas similar to Arnold's began to be propagated in the 1920s.) Arnold argued that emotion is "a felt tendency toward anything appraised as good, and away from anything appraised as bad." Thus fear is felt as a tendency away from a stimulus, love as a tendency toward an object. Arnold's view was itself part of a long tradition, including the work of the Dutch philosopher Baruch Spinoza, who

Copies of the drawings of Le Brun and Chodowiecki included in Lavater's compendium of physiognomy. Johann Caspar Lavater, *Essays on Physiognomy, designed to promote the knowledge and the love of mankind* (London, 1792). Getty Research Institute, Research Library.

argued in the seventeenth century that emotions functioned to impede or facilitate action, and the English philosopher David Hume, who in the eighteenth century expanded Spinoza's argument to include mental action, or cognition: for Hume, emotions determine cognition and thereby action. Arnold makes a further distinction, between expressive and distressful emotions. Distressful emotions are frustrated impulses to action (sadness without crying, fear without running), and therefore the opposite of expressive emotions (sadness with crying, fear with screaming), in which the expression substitutes for some other action. Since emotions are action tendencies, acting on them can bring relief from their arousal. The child's crying and the man's are both based on appraisals, Arnold argues: the child's that it is hungry and that someone might offer it food, the man's that he has cause to be angry but not the ability to express it due to social pressure, fear, or what have you.

Such appraisals, Arnold notes, can take place with very little cognition—the very sight of a bear in the woods can cause fear—but these quick recognitions are just that: the fear of the bear is a re-cognizing of understandings that had been arrived at earlier. Early stimulus-response experiments demonstrated that infants will play with a snake or a rabbit unafraid, but that either can become a source of immediate fear through conditioning. In its most instinctual examples, Arnold's theory is not remarkably different from those of many of the physiologists she drew upon. But the appraisals that result in emotions can also be the result of more conscious, complicated thought processes.

Arnold's cognitive theory of emotion was elaborated upon by a number of other psychologists in the 1960s, most notably Stanley Schachter and Jerome Singer, who in 1962 introduced what would become known as the Schachter-Singer or "cognitive arousal" theory of emotion. They followed up on the experiment conducted in 1924 by Marañon, who had injected 210 patients with adrenaline and asked them to describe what they were feeling, and which Cannon had used as evidence for his theories. (This look back to the 1920s is further evidence that the cognitive study of emotion starts there rather than in 1960.) Adrenaline is known as a "sympathomimetic" drug since it mimics the activity of the sympathetic nervous system. It induces an increase in blood pressure, heart rate, respiration, and blood flow to muscles and the brain, among other things. Over two thirds of Marañon's subjects simply reported their physical sensations with no emotional overtones, and a little less than a third described quasi-emotional reactions. But the great majority of these reported that they felt not happy or afraid but only "as if" they were happy or afraid. With a few of his subjects, Marañon suggested emotional topics, and these then described genuine emotional experiences. He speculated that it was the emotional thoughts that made these subjects interpret the blood coursing in their veins as emotion.

Schachter and Singer decided to follow this up and designed an experiment in which subjects were told they would receive a vitamin shot and then have their vision checked in order to test the effects of vitamin supplements on visual skills. Some received adrenaline and some a placebo. As the design of this experiment suggests, cognitive psychology remained closely tied to study of the limbic system, but the purpose of the experiment was to determine how important cognition was in people's interpretations of their stimulated limbic systems. Therefore, the adrenalized group was given different instructions. Some were told that they should expect side effects from the vitamin, including increased heart rate, shaking hands, and a warm and flushed face. Some were told nothing about side effects. And some were told to expect their feet to get numb, itching sensations, and a slight headache. Thus one group was informed, one uninformed, and one misinformed.

Schachter and Singer then paired some subjects from each group with a "stooge," a confederate who modeled emotional behavior. Some people in each group were paired with a stooge who had been trained to act euphoric, and some in each group with a stooge who had been trained to act angry. The subjects who were told what side effects to expect, or who received the placebo, were relatively immune to the stooges, but those who were uninformed or misinformed characterized their excitement as anger or euphoria. Thus, Schachter and Singer concluded, appraisals do not only affect the onset of emotional experience, they effect how that experience is interpreted. The arousal alone does not make an emotion what it is. It is arousal combined with a cognitive appraisal of the feeling that makes an emotional experience. By this logic, crying only means what it means when we decide what it means.

Silvan Tomkins, who wrote his most important works in the 1960s and 1970s, also developed a theory of the relation of cognition to the autonomous nervous system and specifically to crying. Tomkins was one of many psychologists who found the Schachter-Singer experiment, as he wrote, "seriously flawed, both empirically and theoretically." Although the study had an undeniable impact on the field in focusing attention on cognitive factors in emotional experience, some of its results contradicted the authors' conclusions, almost a third of the original subjects were discarded from the analysis for various reasons, and attempts (most notably by Christina Maslach in 1978) to replicate their findings have failed. Tomkins also notes that Schachter and Singer failed to take into consideration findings in neurophysiology that would have accounted for the discrepancies in their data, including the discovery of the relative functional independence of the limbic-midbrain system and the autonomous system. "Why," Tomkins then asks, "was it so hugged to the bosom of social psychologists for almost twenty years?" He suggests that the battle lines between cognitive psychologists and behaviorists were well drawn, and that the cognitive psychologists latched onto Schachter and Singer's conclusions as a manifesto. Schachter and Singer had a biological base in their arousal mechanism and a cognitive conclusion. Their theory was one that "offered a neurophysiologically respectable id, tamed and led by the cognitive soul," Tomkins wrote in 1980, "in the Platonic image of horse and rider." As a consequence, cognitive psychologists were "able to maintain the fiction that thinking makes it so—even manufacturing our feelings."

And so Tomkins hardly seems like he should be included in this discussion of cognitive psychology. But as Robert Plutchik, another early critic of Schachter and Singer, notes, "Strictly speaking, there is no cognitive psychology, any more than there is an autonomic nervous system psychology or a feeling state psychology." All, Plutchik and others argued, enter into any full discussion. Tomkins devoted his career to attempting such a synthesis. He believed that emotions were the primary stimulators of human action, and that even drives like hunger and sexual desire used emotions to motivate people. Like Magda Arnold, then, Tomkins sees emotions as action tendencies, and like Arnold he saw that appraisals were often important to the onset of emotion. But Tomkins also recognized that not all emotions were activated by cognitive appraisals.

Tomkins took issue with one of the central pieties of cognitive psychology and of psychotherapeutics: that something about the cognitive or personality structure must change for a person to return to mental health. He argued that if two people with identical personality structures entered treatment and one experienced a significant reduction in negative emotions, that person would show marked improvement without any other change of heart or mind whatsoever. The lowering of tension alone allows greater clarity of thought, more attention to life beyond the body, and therefore allows the person's adaptive skills, whatever they may be, to kick in. This is the great value of pharmacological advances, Tomkins thought. The forerunners of drugs like Prozac or Zoloft that were available in the 1970s reduced negative affect "without altering in any way the basic personality structure." But they nonetheless allowed patients to react to the world around them less hampered by emotional distress.

Tomkins's physiological base was the homeostatic theory, in which the organism is always seeking to return to a state of rest after distress or some other arousal. Distress can have cognitive and social origins: a hungry man who does not reach for something to eat at a counter because he doesn't have the money to pay for it, a sexually aroused man who stops himself from having sex, an angry woman who does not hit her provoker—all of these inhibited actions are determined by a person's appraisal of the situation in relation to his or her socialization. The inhibited actions generate muscle tonus, or tension in the muscles. The high tonus in the muscles sends messages to the brain which keep it in a high degree of stimulation, and this can activate distress reactions, which add to the general state of uncomfortable arousal. Crying, which we may decide to commence in an attempt to be comforted or otherwise helped, but which can also be set off involuntarily by the parasympathetic nervous system during its attempt to bring the body back to rest, is something that we may come to associate, over time and habitually, with relief. The body has returned to a state of relative rest, so that when the crying stops the crier is in fact relieved.

Crying can be initiated, then, by an appraisal of one's inner state, an appraisal of one's environment, or by a physiological process. Tomkins therefore berates those who assume that all crying requires cognition, and ridicules theories that "imply a foetus in its passage down the birth canal collecting its thoughts, and upon being born emitting a birth cry after having appraised the extrauterine world as a vale of tears." Any theory of tears must account for both learned and innate "activations of affect," both emotions that are the result of appraisals and those that are the result of unappraised physical or perceptual stimuli. For instance, Tomkins writes, "the birth cry is a cry of distress. It is a response of distress at the excessive level of stimulation to which the neonate is suddenly exposed upon being born." Infant crying in general, Tomkins said, is a response to a "toxic" level of stimulation, whether caused by hunger, a diaper pin, or fear. But this simple stimulus-response activity does not fully explain tears. Crying is also communicative, an attempt to "negatively motivate" the self and others to "do something to reduce the crying." And as such crying is quickly socialized. If crying is responded to with sympathy, as it most often is with a newborn, the child learns to expect help, and can decide to cry to get the help. Over time, "the attempt to control the parent through crying is recognized" by the parent and sympathy can be replaced by indifference, contempt, or anger. As Tomkins notes, a large number of other responses can be elicited by tears: crying can be rejected as a violation of parental authority, as an indulgence, or as a loss of control, for instance, or, on the other hand, it can be received as "cute" or as confirmation of the universality of suffering or of the unfairness of authority (as when a sibling comforts a scolded sibling). Tomkins believed that such responses were not only determined by culture but helped create it. Negative responses to infant tears based on the ideas of authority or indulgence, he thought, come from and encourage what he called a "right ideology" of emotions, in which a person is expected to strive toward self-sufficiency and adaptation to existing authorities. Responding to crying with sympathy and comfort comes from and results in a "left ideology" of emotions, in which a person deserves and should expect the help and support of the community.

In recent years, less synthetic theories have continued to be proposed and reinvented, claiming, for instance, to take account of cultural difference for the first time, or making new arguments for a return to the James-Lange theory. But the best work in psychology is that which, like that of Tomkins, assumes that emotions have numerous possible relations to cognition; that not all of the neural circuits or physiological systems or cognitive processes that *can* be part of an emotional experience are necessary to all emotions; and that an adequate theory is one that includes rather than excludes the full range of perspectives rather than one that seeks to explain all emotion once and for all.

Aletha Solter, writing in the *Pre- and Peri-Natal Journal* in 1995, for instance, argues that the parasympathetic stimulation of tears explains some infant crying. As Tomkins suggested, the infant, since it is incapable of following up on many of its action tendencies, necessarily builds up stress, and crying occurs as that tension is released. A communication theory, she writes, can explain why infants cry out, but as all parents know, communicative crying only accounts for a portion of infant's tears. Distress due to pain can cause other infant tears. But some tears are, she goes on to show, the result of parasympathetic stimulation as the infant is in the process—because its needs have been met, its pain eased, or its distress otherwise lowered—of returning to homeostasis.

Examples of studies with similarly synthetic theoretical backing are now quite common, and later I will discuss several in the sections on men and women and on childrearing. But there is another strand in cognitive psychology which I have strategically ignored until now, and that is social psychology. The Schachter-Singer experiment and those it spawned are obviously based on cognition that is instigated by, directed, and monitored through social interaction, and when Tomkins complained about those conducting such experiments, he called them "social psychologists," as distinct from those practicing his own brand of cognitive psychology. The next wave of psychological thinking about tears has been, in fact, a very sociological approach, in which psychological researchers have been joined by sociologists.

4

Men and Women, Infants and Children

In a conversation about Albert Camus's *The Stranger,* a student told me that neither she nor her brother ever cried. Well, she said, perhaps when we were very young, but neither could remember having cried in the last fifteen years. They were therefore anxious about going to their grandmother's funeral, afraid that if they didn't cry there they would be seen as cold-blooded and uncaring. Although both had long felt awkward about their lack of tears, the woman had been censured for it, had been called a cold fish and heartless, while her brother had been congratulated for his self-control. Much to her relief, she managed to cry at the funeral after all, but continues to feel unfairly spurned by a culture that criticizes her for her lack of ready tears.

In every society, whatever the historical era, the meanings assigned to tears are always compounded by the age and sex of the crier. In a famous experiment by John and Sandra Condry, two groups (each 50 percent male and 50 percent female) were shown the same video of an infant bursting into tears at the sudden pop of a jack-in-the-box. One group was told the baby in the video was a girl, the other that it

A series of photographs commissioned by Darwin of infants crying. From Charles Darwin, *The Expression of Emotions in Man and Animals* (1872). Courtesy University of Iowa Libraries.

was a boy. The vast majority of respondents (of both sexes) assumed that the "girl" baby was crying out of fear and that the "boy" baby was crying out of anger. Similar experiments have replicated these findings. The very same cry means one thing if the crier is female, another if the crier is male.

Sociologists, social psychologists, and anthropologists have all studied such differences and noted that they vary depending on time and place. They also realized that tears seemed to be caused by rituals. Rather than funerals and weddings being places where, because of the intense emotions involved, the participants were more likely to cry, the rituals actually seemed to produce the tears. Mary Edith Durham, an anthropologist who studied Montenegrin culture in the first part of the century, reported that men were the primary weepers at a funeral and were expected to cry even if they didn't know the deceased: "The . . . men mostly did not know the poor boy's name and had to be coached in the details before beginning to wail, but within a minute or two they were sobbing bitterly. Coming home people compared notes as to who had cried best." Martin Gusinde reported in 1931 that on Tierra del Fuego, the male Fireland Indians are "much more reserved about pouring out their feelings than is the female part of the population." Both men and women are expected to weep during funeral preparations and rituals, but at different specific times, and the women much more often. When the men do cry during the funeral, Gusinde reported, "a stream of tears sometimes rolls down even their weather-beaten cheeks, and their hearts can become as soft as that of a sensitive girl."

Several things emerge in looking at such anthropological reports. One is that tears cannot be understood without taking into consideration the demands for emotional performance placed upon men and women: that is, the Montenegrin men cry at the death of an unknown villager not because they are particularly sensitive but because it is their social responsibility to do so. Another is that the researchers' cultural presuppositions can and usually do restrict their understanding— Gusinde likens the men to sensitive girls, denigrates emotion in general, and gives the lie to his own characterization of the men as "reserved." This kind of researcher bias is individual as well as cultural, as the disagreements among anthropologists demonstrate. One anthropologist's observation, for instance, that Samoan men can cry because of fear while Samoan women do not, but that both men and women cry in anger, has been disputed by other anthropologists. Such disputes about the specific meanings of emotional display tend to arise whenever they are studied by more than one field-worker.

Most anthropologists and sociologists agree, however, that in most if not all cultures, emotional "labor" is divided unequally between men and women. Sometimes this is very obvious, as in the case of the Tiv, an African tribe in which men do not take part in mourning except in rare cases. Tiv women are solely responsible for formal mourning, which is elaborate. Women write and sing funeral songs, for instance, an important form of cultural expression with its own rules, classics, and changing fashions. Tiv women, in other words, seem to be largely responsible for managing the communal emotions surrounding death, though one could argue that men's reticence also helps guide the emotional life of the group. In a few cultures' funerary rituals, men take the lead role in emotional expression, and in others the chores are divided, with men responsible for all of the physical arrangements and ritual acts, and women responsible for weeping and ululating.

The sociologist Arlie Hochschild is the writer who dubbed these kinds of responsibilities "emotion work." Beginning with her study of flight attendants in the 1970s, she and others using her basic concept have shown the ways in which American women are responsible for managing the emotional lives of the people around them, in both private and public life. Bronislaw Malinowski argued (long before Hochschild) that this kind of work is part of a general cultural economy. Malinowski found that it was a wife's duty in Melanesia to mourn her husband by carrying his jawbone for some years after his death. "Nor is this obligation without reciprocity," Malinowski noted in the 1920s. "At the first big ceremonial distribution, some three days after her husband's death, she will receive from his kinsmen a ritual payment, and a substantial one, for her tears; and at later ceremonial feasts she is given more payments for the subsequent services of mourning."

Hochschild's notion of emotional labor, like Malinowski's, is based on the idea that emotional work has a very real value, and that it is rewarded in various ways. In service professions, the reward—a paycheck—is tangible. Fear of flying, claustrophobia, and other anxieties need to be managed by flight attendants (along with the odd belligerent or drunken passenger) in an artificial community thrown together for hours at a time with no hope of escape. Hochschild found that passengers expected male and female flight attendants to perform different kinds of emotional labor, with women more likely to be asked to soothe and express care and concern than men. In other words, women in such jobs are called upon to do the kind of work they perform in the culture generally, in families and communities.

In many cultures, when the job calls for crying, women tend to do it. Among the tribes of the Gran Chaco, the lowlands where Paraguay, Argentina, and Bolivia meet, only women and children perform the weeping and wailing that are central parts of the funeral rites. Only the women of the household lament at Hopi burials. Arandan women weep and cry out loudly at funerals while men sit with their heads bent, shedding tears silently. Tzeltal men and women both weep, but while the men go home to sleep during the two days and nights of observance, the women continue to watch over the corpse, weeping. The Bara people of Madagascar use two different huts for men and women after a death, one the Tranadahy, or "male house," the other the Trano Be Ranomaso, or "house of many tears."

According to Tom Golden, a psychotherapist in Maryland, these two different mourning huts allow the Bara "to be healed by their same-sex community members" and "also honors the difference in grieving styles between men and women by allowing the opportunity for each to be near those who grieve as they do." This nicely relativist reading, with its New Age, self-help aura, may have a certain validity. But in most cases, the sexual division of labor in mourning simply follows that in the rest of the culture. As Irving Goldman says of the Cubeo, "The women are weepers and have, in the main, a passive ritual role. Stimulated by masculine-initiated activity, the women burst into fits of ritualized weeping, their only active ritual role." The men's job is to conduct the ceremonies at which the women cry. The men do the ceremonial work, the women do the emotional work.

Women in America, says Hochschild, are asked to do "emotion work that affirms, enhances, and celebrates the well-being and status of others." While this has the ring of truth, it also misses the full range of emotional interaction in our society. The average high school football coach does an enormous amount of emotion work affirming and celebrating the well-being and status of his team, even though he often does so by expressing anger, disdain, and disgust rather than through nurturing behaviors. The female flight attendant's expressions of caring concern and the coach's bluster are both masks assumed in order to accomplish other tasks. The slugs on the back and friendly insults of men in bars are forms of emotion work, as is the public holding back of tears. The young boy who comforts his mother's tears and the father who reprimands his son's are both doing emotion work: they are fulfilling role-specific chores in which emotions are managed on both sides of the interaction.

Emotion work is always more complicated than it appears because its rules and boundaries are forever shifting as the culture changes and individuals misapprehend them, disobey them, and improvise with them. Societies sometimes condemn and sometimes reward those who flout these rules. In Camus's novel, set in Algeria, the antihero Mersault shoots and kills a man, perhaps in self-defense, perhaps accidentally. During the trial, the prosecutor brings a number of witnesses to the stand who testify that Mersault did not shed a single tear at his own mother's funeral the week before. This detail seals his fate, and his apparent cold-bloodedness earns him the death penalty. Compare this fictional scenario with a real one—such as when Jackie Kennedy became a heroine of almost mythic proportions by not crying at her husband's funeral—and we can see that to map the rules for emotional expression through tears is an endless and ever-changing task. In *The Stranger,* a man is condemned to death for the emotional reticence his role requires; in life, the First Lady is celebrated for what we might otherwise be expected to consider a failure of femininity.

And yet defining these rules is exactly what sociologists and anthropologists attempt to do. From its beginnings as a discipline, sociology has been interested in emotions not just as a set of customs but as forms of knowledge. One of the founders of sociology, Emile Durkheim, was already arguing in 1895 that emotions were *représentations collectives,* or fundamental ways in which people represent their world to themselves. Like many disciplines, sociology has a history of issuing manifestos announcing new methodologies, the promotion of and attacks on which form the stuff of theoretical discussion. Presently, the theoretical arguments center on whether it is most useful to think of emotional rules as a "cognitive structure," a vocabulary, a grammar, a script, a discourse, a set of values, or a "framework of meaning." Different sociological camps also disagree as to the best way to model the process of emotional socialization, differ in their willingness to account for things like physiology and biology more generally, and disagree as to the relative weight to give the variables involved—the relative importance of power, gender, ethnicity, kinship, and the like. From a nonspecialist's perspective these are largely quibbles, since most sociologists agree that emotions are determined by social interactions rather than being fundamentally innate and universal. They also agree that once emotions have been socially constructed, they "feel" natural, and thus what feels natural can be said to be based on one's social position. And they agree that the sociology of tears can best be studied by looking at infant tears and at the difference between men and women.

Infants and Children

In one of the more famous poetic passages about babies crying, Tennyson writes of "An infant crying in the night:/An infant crying for the light:/And with no language but a cry." Tennyson is not just describing a scene here, he is evoking a particular attitude toward the crying infant. Crying signals the infant's distress and impotence, and can evoke our own worst feelings of insufficiency, our moments of abject alienation, our fears of helplessness and inadequacy. And at the same time it can be an image of our most profound desires, as in Tennyson's poem: an image of our desire for the light of understanding, our sometimes strangulated desires to communicate and share, our desire for an audience that will not only answer us but transport us from darkness into the light.

The Victorian laureate was neither the first nor the last to ask an infant's cry to carry such metaphorical weight. The French new-wave feminist theorist Catherine Clément, for instance, offers a related image in her book *Syncope*: "Think of the infant who often has only tears at first to let it be known what he needs; then the infuriated sob that ends in a sniffling hiccup, before ceasing abruptly in a satisfied sleep," she writes. "The emerging individual, deprived of words, often uses . . . the water of tears to escape." Tennyson believed, like most Victorians, that children were simply small, innocent, uninformed versions of adults, while Clément is writing after Piaget and thus accepts the fact that the infant goes through stages of biological maturation in which functions like language develop over time. But both Tennyson and Clément assume an inborn desire on the part of infants to communicate, who thus feel frustration at not being able to express themselves. And both take this to be emblematic of adult emotional states as well. Another French feminist, Luce Irigaray, makes this clear in her injunction to women to learn to speak rather than weep: "Don't weep. One day we will learn to say ourselves. And what we say will be far more beautiful than our tears."

But clearly to presume that an infant wants to speak endows that baby with much more knowledge about communication than it could possibly have. It implies that an infant's cry is not, in itself, a form of expression but an expression of the infant's inability to express itself, a self-contradictory notion. And it implies that the impetus to formal language is not learned but inherent, an idea contradicted by, if nothing else, the few studies we have of "feral" children. It is very hard, of course, to get reports from this front, since the infants cannot tell us. But theories of infant consciousness and preconsciousness abound, from Freud's talk of the oral stage to Karen Horney's and Melanie Klein's psychoanalytic arguments about infant aggression and alienation to Hélène Cixous's romanticization of the prepatriarchal, prelinguistic communitarian world of the infant who cries not as a demand but as a "song."

That parents and other adults routinely project complex emotions and desires onto their babies undoubtedly serves an important function, for such projection is central to the emotional education of the child. As we pretend that the child feels love, we bring its love into being. As we pretend that the child feels ashamed rather than angry at a reprimand, we instill shame—that is, we can condition the child away from anger and toward shame by repeatedly interpreting it as such. And in this process we also teach the infant what situations warrant tears and which don't, by teaching it what tears warrant comfort and which don't.

And it is clear that the infant, "with no language but a cry," has a specific kind of persuasive and sublime eloquence. The main effect of infant crying is to draw parental attention, which fulfills more than simply practical needs. John Bowlby and a number of other social psychologists, most notably Mary Ainsworth and Silvia Bell, have developed what is known as attachment theory, and they understand crying on the part of infants as the thing that not only triggers the appropriate caretaking activities of an adult but also creates the bond between infant and parent. The evolutionary anatomist Paul MacLean's suggestion that crying is a mammalian response to parent-infant separation makes sense here as well: crying is the tool humans use to stay attached to each other. The tears help create and sustain the attachment that is the salient fact of the parent-child relationship, and once the feeding is done, the attachment behaviors continue to be important. Some of Ainsworth and Bell's studies suggest that attachment follows a fairly routine developmental timetable. In one study of infants and their mothers over the course of a year, for instance, they found that there were two peak times for separation crying when mothers left the room, one at thirty-three weeks and one at forty-five weeks. This suggests that there is a biological clock as well as a socialization process at work.

Some researchers have argued that a "biobehavioral shift" occurs at between two and three months in which the infant moves from involuntary to voluntary control of crying. This occurs, in other words, as the infant develops other interactive abilities, such as responsive smiling and eye-to-eye contact, and begins to express a wide range of emotional states with its cries, including boredom and the desire for attention.

Daniel N. Stern has shown that parent-child communication begins with a kind of musical call and response—imitation through responses in the same modality or register. The parent responds by imitating each of the child's gurgles with words and coos, and in turn the infant imitates the parent's speech. This process, which Stern calls "affect attunement," also includes parental vocalization as a response to the baby's gestures, and gestures that answer many vocalizations. The infant thus learns what kind of impact expressions and actions have, and becomes acquainted with the complicated business of emotional relationships.

At one level, crying can be seen as a fairly mechanical device—the infant cries when it needs the parent, the parent responds and fulfills those needs. But every parent knows that infant cries mean much more than any on-off switch. The way in which we attend to its cries gives a child one of its most important images of human relation and possibility. In the tears of the infant and the answer of the parent lies that which is most instinctual and primitive in human nature and the image of love's most developed compass.

But good parents, bad parents, or no parents, crying is a fact of infancy and childhood. If a baby enters the world not crying, it is whacked on the buttocks or otherwise prodded until it starts. Crying peaks somewhere between six and ten weeks but continues to be a very regular activity for years—one study estimates an average of four thousand crying sessions by the age of two. An enormous amount of advice in child-rearing manuals, research in social psychology and medicine, and parental agonizing has been devoted to answering the perennial question of how often and how fast parents should respond to infant tears. The poles range from John B. Watson's recommendation to never respond for fear of spoiling the baby, to the suggestion, in a significant number of today's parenting manuals, that tears should always be comforted in order to give the infant a sense of security and attachment. One possibility, although rarely advanced, is that the reduced quantity of tears people cry as they mature is a simple biological fact, akin to the reduction from ten to three feedings a day. Perhaps as our bodies mature, we quite naturally eat less often and cry less often. If this is true, it would render an enormous amount of parental energy, as well as a lot of freelance social stigmatizing, an atrocious waste of time. On the other hand, one psychologist in the 1950s went so far as to suggest that, contrary to the common view that infants cry naturally and are gradually socialized into controlling their tears, we in fact teach our babies to cry through rewarding them with the breast or the bottle, lullabies and other diversions. In other words, the four thousand crying sessions in the first two years are not nature but culture at work. This would render parental attempts to stem the flow of tears through nurturance a sad comedy.

Researchers in many disciplines have focused on infant tears. A mass of spectrographic analyses have been performed to see if cross-cultural norms might be established for "normal" crying, or if irregular acoustic patterns in an infant's cry indicate specific diseases. Within cultures, infants cry in very similar ways if they are healthy. One early American study found that most cry at a C or C-sharp at birth, with a range of only a halftone, or the difference between adjacent keys on a piano. As they grow, babies cry at different pitches, and with different intensities, durations, and qualities. The amount of crying increases steadily until about two months, according to another American study, and decreases until about four months, after which it remains fairly constant through the first year. In a Japanese study, the amount of crying rose from birth to peak on the third day and leveled off at eight weeks, and again the variation in cries increased, with more short cries and more expressive fluctuation. Another American survey, however, found that the duration of the cry and the fundamental frequency were stable over the first twelve weeks of life. Still another found that at eight weeks the range had grown from a half step in pitch to a quarter of an octave—from do to mi. (Yawning rather than crying first ranges across an entire octave.)

And even these slightly contradictory averages can be deceiving. Infants with compromised fetal growth cry at a higher pitch and with more variation than normal infants, researchers found, perhaps because they need more help, giving their cries more urgency. But some babies cry if they are laid on their stomach, some if they are laid on their back; some cry at loud noises that others would barely notice. One study monitored the level of nervous activity in the brains of thirteen infants, half of whom cried when their mother left the room and half of whom didn't. The criers had more right-brain activity before the separation and the dry-eyed babies had more left-brain activity. It is not clear what these differences mean, finally, but clearly the nature of the baby's patterns of mental activity while calm—which may be hereditary or at any rate congenital—influences the times and duration of the baby's cry.

Sociologists have made their greatest contributions to the study of infant tears by carefully measuring crying and its effects in a number of simulated social situations. It can sometimes seem that sociology does little beyond translating common sense into an arcane academic language. When Donald Barthelme, in his novel *Snow White*, portrayed a professor who is doing a sociological study of "incidents of weeping in the bedrooms of the faculty of the University of Bridgeport," he implied that such studies are bound to be trite, myopic, and puerile, unable to add to our understanding of human pain and sorrow. And while all academic disciplines are occasionally mocked by laypeople for highfalutin jargon, sociologists receive an extra dose precisely because when translated back into everyday speech, their findings are so readily understandable. The columnist Dave Barry offered a credible parody of the way sociologists talks about tears: "Methodological observation of the sociometrical behavior tendencies of prematurated isolates indicates that a casual relationship exists between groundward tropism and lachrimatory, or 'crying,' behavior forms." In other words, children tend to cry if they fall down.

And some actual sociological studies of tears do seem to speak a Barry-like language. One study's major finding "supports the hypothesis that acoustic features of the infant cry may be a benchmark of the biological integrity of the infant." In other words, babies cry plaintively when they are sick. Another argues that "the nature and selectivity of social interaction in the first year of the infant's life appear to be precursors of the elaborate, comprehensive and sophisticated social skills which the individual develops throughout his life-span." Crying, it seems, is an early form of communication. In the jargon of another study, the fact that crying is a form of communication is rendered as: "Cry responsiveness is not a function of infant behavior alone but is inherently an expression of the dynamics of the mother-infant interactional system."

But as sociologists and social psychologists have worked toward a more comprehensive understanding of crying, they have also discovered some important, counterintuitive functions of tears, and in all cases, the results of their careful experimentation have provided a useful counterpoint to everyday reports and to psychological thinking that ignores differences of history and culture. These studies hold out the promise of answering some of the most common yet perplexing issues of child care, among other things

Many of these studies contradict each other. A study by U. A. Hunziker and R. G. Barr in Quebec found that babies who were held twice as much during the first twelve weeks of life (four hours a day rather than two) cried less frequently while the less-carried cried more. A team of Korean pediatricians also found that more maternal handling led to less crying. But Australian pediatricians found that carrying a baby in a soft sling—much touted in the touchy-feely child-rearing manuals from the 1970s on—had no effect on the total amount of crying it did. The babies carried in slings, in fact, shed no fewer tears and experienced slightly longer periods of fussiness than the control group. Child development researchers at the University of London's Institute of Education compared mothers in Manali, India, with those in London, England. The Manali mothers left their babies to cry much less frequently, took them into their own beds much more often, and were much more likely to breast-feed (and to do so up to an older age) than mothers in London. But in both places, the researchers found, the babies not only cried the same amount, they did so at the same times, peaking in the early evening. In both groups, the evening crying peak was most pronounced at six weeks of age, after which it diminished. Extra handling, on-demand feeding, and other "nurturant" behaviors seem to make little difference to the amount of crying a baby does, they decided, or even the specific times that it cries.

When pushed for more practical advice by parents afraid that their babies were still crying too much at six months, parenting guru Magda Gerber suggested that parents relax: "The child will learn to give better cues." And of course this is what happens. Eventually, children can ask for something to eat rather than crying for it. "Instrumental" crying, crying to get attention rather than from other, more "real" forms of distress, begins as early as three weeks, and by the age of ten months the big shift has occurred. Instead of crying primarily when they are alone, infants begin to cry primarily when their caregiver is present, suggesting that the majority of crying had become, at least at some level, instrumental.

But the emphasis on crying frequency and attachment as the sole measures for understanding the meaning and purpose of infant crying may be misplaced. Ruth H. and Robert L. Munroe conducted a longitudinal study of children in Kenya in the 1980s and found that some mothers practiced "distancing" treatments, refusing to pick up the babies when they cried and taking a long time to respond when they did. This distancing was seen as a way to promote heightened awareness of the surroundings. The more distancing the parent, the Munroes found, the more likely that the child would demonstrate superior cognitive performance (on standardized tests) at the age of five. And other studies, such as one that found that children given zinc supplements in their diet in Guatemala cried less often, or that regulatory problems of various kinds increase the frequency of crying, suggest that the frequency of crying may be a very unreliable measure of parent-child relations or of social and psychological maturation.

Nonetheless, getting an infant to stop crying is seen in most places to be one of the necessary goals of day-to-day living, if for no other reason than the parent's need for sleep. One day in the 1920s, as Charles Chewings was passing by the Macumba station on Macumba Creek in central Australia, he saw what he described as a "hideous sight." It was a boy with his lips cut off. Aghast, he asked the local people what had happened and was told that when the boy was young, he would not stop crying. The shamans met in council and decided that the only cure for his interminable crying was to cut off his lips.

Although few solutions have been as drastic as this one, people have perennially invented or tried to refine ways to get children to stop crying. Lullabies, bribes, threats, punishments, genital stimulation, feeding, rocking—all are used in efforts to quiet babies, and sometimes they even work. "Excessive" crying has been interpreted as the result of family tension, infant neuroticism, spoiling, regulatory disorders, inherent temperament, nervous system irregularities, and immature digestive systems.

In some cultures, infant crying is thought to be an ominous portent, a sign not just that something is wrong with the baby but that something is wrong with the world. In the mountains of Celebes, according to early Dutch anthropologists, the Toradja believed that an infant's crying could bring a curse upon its parents. A frog would be tied up and placed in a pan of water, and some of the water sprinkled on the baby to transfer the crying to the frog, which would then cry (or croak) all night. This would, they were told, "bring the child to itself so that it will stop crying," suggesting the fundamental alienation that crying is thought to cause. In some cultures, infant crying is thought to cause rain, in others to keep the rains away, whichever is worse for the planters in the region.

For these and other reasons, in some cultures the crying of children is barely tolerated. Carlos R. Gallardo, a statesman and scientist who spent time with the indigenous tribes of Tierra del Fuego at the turn of the century, found that the young rarely cried, and that when they did so it was in response to sickness or bodily pain. Martin Gusinde, a German anthropologist who studied the same people in the early 1920s, was immediately struck by the remarkable stillness in the Indian's huts:

> After my first tour through the camp on Rio del Fuego I squatted down at a hut fire. Scarcely had the Indians satisfied their curiosity about my having appeared when a few of the women repeated to me most emphatically: "That child over there is crying!" From a neighboring hut one could hear persistent crying. It was not until the following day that it was explained to me what people were trying to tell me, namely, that the crying of children is a rarity here.

The child, it turned out, was suffering from a serious intestinal ailment and died a few weeks later. The adults claimed that hearing crying is the equivalent of having a terrible earache. If a child does cry, its parent screams and shouts into its ear so loudly that it immediately becomes quiet, or shakes it violently and angrily until it stops. As a result, babies cry very little.

In other cultures, crying has been similarly discouraged. Marion Pearsall, after visiting the Klamath in 1875, reported that children were warned that "Owl will come to pluck out your eyes or carry you off to a cave." If that didn't work, Bear and Coyote were invoked. Among the Dogon of the Sudan, according to Denise Paulme, terror takes a middleman, as parents beat the older sister in charge of the baby if the baby cries. A standard Dogon lullaby ends:

stop crying,
do not cry, otherwise father will beat me,
do not cry, otherwise mother will beat me.

And in some cultures crying is discouraged by ignoring it. Among the Kurds in Turkey and Iran and the Kogi in Colombia, babies are left to cry unnoticed for great lengths of time. Margery Wolf, studying Taiwanese mothers and children in the 1960s, reported that children were ignored or scolded if they cried. According to Norma Joyce Diamond, who also wrote about Taiwan in the 1960s, children were sometimes slapped or scolded, and sometimes coaxed and bribed. She felt that the prevalence of bribery meant that children learned that they could earn money or favors by whining.

These cultures explain their relation to crying in different ways. The Kurds say that "crying develops the voice." The Taiwanese mothers Wolf studied told her that crying was beneficial to the child, that it was a form of infant exercise. Some believed that crying made children's intestines grow large ("apparently a desirable trait"), or quoted a proverb that "a child must cry to grow." Others explained that if the mouth stays open too long in crying, the children could catch cold or swallow air and vomit. Too much crying could also make a boy's testicles swell (apparently an undesirable trait), Wolf was told.

And if parents sometimes do not know how to respond to children's tears, the same is true for children confronted with adult tears. While children sometimes mimic the comforting behavior that parents have modeled for them, they can be bewildered and frightened by the sight of adults sobbing. The Mexican folk figure "La Llorona" is a woman who haunts the woods and other places at night, snatching young children like many another bogeyman. The most horrifying thing about La Llorona, whose name literally means "weeping woman," is that she weeps eternally.

A short piece in *Parenting* magazine recently told women that "motherhood is an emotional time," and so they should expect to cry, and that such crying would be good for them. Although there is no scientific evidence that crying has any physiological benefits, the article admits, "85 percent of women report feeling better after crying." Since children may worry about their mother crying, the magazine passes on the advice of Dr. Mardi Horowitz, director of the Center on Stress and Personality at the University of California, San Francisco, who suggests that mothers say something like "Mommy's sad right now, but she's not upset with you. Sometimes when parents are sad, they cry and then they feel better." Such advice is echoed by many experts and represents the current consensus on dealing with children's fears of adult crying, and it is probably perfectly good advice.

Two Dutch anthropologists, N. Adriani and Albert Kruyt, recorded a mother in the mountains of Celebes singing to her child this song, which attempts to explain adult tears and is without a doubt a more complex and demanding response to the problem:

> My tears are dripping down,
> I alternate them with laughter.
> The dripping of my tears
> I alternate with talking.
> Do not let your desire speak, my child,
> now your father has gone away.
> Do not entertain homesickness,
> now your father has disappeared.

Here the mother does not suggest that crying is simply a technique for feeling better. She examines her own tears, explains her ability to "alternate" them with laughter and talking, and gives her child instruction on the relation between tears and desire. Although one can imagine a child being somewhat confused by the complexity of this lyric, it certainly offers a more haunting response than "It's OK that Mommy's sad."

In any case, the parent's tears tend to be short-lived, much closer to the six-minute average found by contemporary researchers than the eternal tears of La Llorona. What frightens the child is the child's own impotence in the face of adult tears, somewhat like the impotence parents feel with a colicky baby. And of course more frightening than a parent's tears is a parent's anger, and nothing, it turns out, makes many parents angrier than a child's crying.

The frustration, anger, and even hostility that can arise in the classic struggle for sleep pops out in one of the most famous lullabies: "When the bough breaks, the cradle will fall, and down will come cradle, baby and all." Crying can cause fantasies of harm. Infants with colic, wailing inconsolably at the top of their lungs for hours at a time, can drive the most patient parent nutty. And even moderate crying as infants are put down for naps or the night is a frequent cause of strain and stress, or an aggravation of preexisting stresses. One study of high-risk care-takers (those who had been abused themselves and thus had higher than average "abuse potential") reported increased feelings of hostility and distress when presented with a crying baby. They reported no increase in empathetic feelings. Other studies confirmed that frequent or unrelieved crying was among the most common triggers of abuse.

In a related study, both high- and low-risk male undergraduates found infant crying disturbing. The subjects were told that they were involved in a taste test of alcoholic beverages, and their alcohol consumption was monitored as they were presented with either the sounds of an infant cry or a smoke alarm. Both groups consumed significantly more alcohol in response to the infant cry than they did when the smoke alarm went off. "Regardless of risk group," the researchers wrote, subjects "who heard the infant cry reported feeling more aversion, arousal, and distress than those who heard the smoke alarm. The infant cry is a stressful and aversive event, capable of eliciting increased drinking." And the stress and aversion were equally prevalent for high- and low-risk men. The implication here is that regardless of "abuse potential," babies' crying can drive one to drink. And several studies have shown that women are just as likely to feel hostile. One in New Zealand found that 80 percent of the women in the study at least sometimes felt like smacking their babies when they cried.

Some gender differences are apparent, as one would expect. John Furedy and his colleagues at the University of Toronto measured the heart rate of male and female students while they watched segments of video representing emotional scenes. True to cultural stereotypes, the men's heart rate accelerated more during erotic segments and the women's more in response to segments showing babies crying. But Ann Frodi conducted a similar experiment with different results. She had men and women, all of whom were parents, watch a film of a smiling baby and of a crying baby. The smiling infant triggered positive emotions but negligible physiological response, while the crying infant raised the subjects' diastolic blood pressure and skin conductance. Frodi makes this interesting comment: "Mothers and fathers did not differ either in their responses to the stimulus baby or in their perception of their own baby although mothers gave more extreme descriptions of their moods and feelings than did fathers." The reports of the parents, in other words, would lead one to believe that the mothers were much more strongly affected than the fathers, but the physiological measures were the same.

In another study, Lawrence Stein and Stanley Brodsky at the University of Alabama studied one hundred female and one hundred male students and measured their willingness to express their feelings by exposing them to a bawling baby. The women won; men were in general less willing to disclose their emotions to the investigators than women. Half the men and half the women were shown a tape of an infant crying, which was selected for its frustrating and "noxious" quality. The men who were shown the tape were even less likely to disclose their emotions after seeing the tape than men in the control group. There was no difference among the women, and so the conclusion was that men had more trouble dealing with crying infants than women did. While the laboratory setting obviously does not replicate normal experience—men may be willing to tell their wives, lovers, or friends how they feel about the baby crying but still be unwilling to share it with researchers, for instance—these studies do nonetheless confirm what we already know, that on average women are more comfortable around strange crying babies than men are.

This, too, is true in many cultures. Gerardo Reichel-Dolmatoff studied the Kogi, a tribe in the Sierra Nevada of Colombia, in the 1940s, for instance, and found that a Kogi father will pick up a baby for a brief time only in emergencies, and even then he indicates "by gestures and by the look on his face that this task is not at all pleasant for him." Still, gender is not the only divide, and other studies demonstrate that adolescent and adult mothers have different responses to crying (adolescent mothers are less likely to notice pitch differences associated with certain birth defects, for instance); that women with their first baby are more prone to experience distress than women who have had more than one; that women with babies who cry excessively experience extreme stress; and so on. And the gender variable can mean many different things as well. One study, for instance, found that crying led mothers to rate their infants more negatively while increasing their own sense of adequacy, whereas it led fathers to feel that both they and the mother were inadequate, but did not increase negative evaluations of the infant.

As parents (and other adults and older children) find various ways to stop the child's crying—through feeding, cajoling, changing, amusing, frightening, or systematically ignoring it—a number of things are accomplished. Infants learn one of three things: either that crying leads to relief, or that it sometimes leads to relief, or that it rarely leads to relief. If tears are responded to with anger or punishment, the child often develops either a need for negative reinforcement or some form of stoicism. But in our culture today, no matter how strict a parent may be, most regularly (and all at least occasionally) respond to tears with some kind of comfort—from open displays of affection to feeding or rocking to plopping the pacifier back in the screaming mouth. Crying "negatively motivates" parents, in psychologist Silvan Tomkins's terms, to fulfill the infant's needs. Diapers eventually get changed and mouths fed, and each time such care comes in response to crying, it reinforces the idea that crying leads to comfort. We are born knowing how to cry and quickly learn its various efficacies.

The most significant change in the American culture of parent-child relations over the last several decades is a change from thinking of that relationship as one of child rearing to one of parenting. "Child rearing" (or management or care) is a set of responsibilities, techniques, and tasks, while "parenting" creates an identity, a way of being that includes a cluster of attributes, like sensitivity, intuition, nurturance.

The child-rearing or technological approach has been the more widespread through human history. Paul and Laura Bohannan provide one example in their description of the Tiv (from northern Nigeria), who, when a baby starts to cry, immediately tell it to "stop shouting."

"A surprising number of infants, at a very early age, obey this command, the meaning of which has been taught them by the mother's placing her hand loosely over the baby's mouth while she pinches his nostrils." And there are other techniques as well:

> If a man is holding an infant that starts to cry, he at once tries to get rid of him by summoning his nurse, mother or any woman available. If the man is alone with the child, he bounces him gently and tells him that his mother will soon return and feed him. A very few men say that the only way to keep a baby quiet under such circumstances is to slap him. A mother offers her crying infant the breast, and sometimes may even give the breast to a child already weaned to quiet it momentarily. . . . Another technique, frequently used for shushing a crying baby, is for the mother or nurse to outshout the child, and then break into loud laughter. This works with some babies, but makes others furious; in the latter case, Tiv laugh even louder and much more genuinely. Nurses . . . dangle fronds of grass before his nose, place bits of thatch on his head so that the ends are visible to the child, jounce him or gently nip his face with their lips.

The Tiv do not identify themselves as good or bad child rearers based on these techniques. Children are shushed because their crying is aggravating, not because parents feel a responsibility to fulfill their roles—witness the father handing off, slapping, or bouncing the child on his knee, as the case demands. One takes care of children using the available techniques, and that is all there is to the job.

Parenting is different, less common, but still widespread. For instance, according to anthropologist E. A. Dry, among the Hausa (neighbors of the Tiv in northern Africa) there are no "good" or "bad" children, only good or bad parents. The emphasis is on the adult's ability to keep the child happy. If a baby cries, it "is a grave reflection on the mother," and at the slightest whimper, the baby is offered the breast. Responding to, and bringing an end to, the baby's cry is the appropriate thing for a parent to do, and only someone who was an inadequate parent would want to do any different.

The American culture of parenting is very similar in that the emphasis is less on the behavior of the child and more on the adequate role-performance of the parents. If parents perform their roles properly, children will in effect raise themselves; if children behave badly, it is because they have been badly parented. William Sears, M.D., advises parents to respond to their children's crying because it will make them better parents: "Promptly responding to your baby's cries increases your sensitivity to your baby. Sensitivity helps develop your parental intuition." Being sensitive to your baby's tears is an important part of what being a parent is all about—because it is about being the kind of person who has parental intuition.

The shift to parenting in American culture is fairly recent, overturning what had been a long tradition of ignoring infant cries. Throughout the nineteenth century, child-rearing manuals warned against overcoddling of infants, and it wasn't until Dr. Benjamin Spock's *The Common Sense Book of Baby and Child Care* was published in 1946 that the idea that children should be comforted when they cried, and that people should be less afraid of spoiling their children, began to take hold. Spock's recommendations were attacked at various times for encouraging permissiveness, but the pendulum has swung well past what Spock had in mind in the intervening decades.

Baby and Child Care has sold over 40 million copies, has been translated into thirty-nine languages, and is the obvious touchstone for the second half of the century. In his advice, Spock is clearly reacting against the stricter admonitions of John B. Watson and company. He reassures parents that they will not ruin their child if they pick it up sometimes when it is screaming in the middle of the night, nor will they spoil a child by holding it between feedings. Spock is hardly a simple coddler, though. He warns parents that they will ruin their own lives if they don't teach the child how to cry itself out on occasion, and he counsels a golden mean between comfort and its withholding. From Spock's ascendance in the 1950s on, this notion of balance became the rule. Two examples of the call for balance will suffice: Dr. Grace Ketterman, author of child-rearing guides and a speaker on the Christian lecture circuit, argues that "a baby needs to cry a bit to exercise both his lungs and his healthy soul." Parents should try for a balanced approach because "the child whose parent ignores crying or hovers over protectively suffers." And Penelope Leach, author of the best-selling *Your Baby and Child from Birth to Age Five* (1986), warns parents not to be afraid of spoiling their children. It is important to teach your children how to rationally present their case if they want something, and to accept rational arguments that run counter to their desires. But it is also important for them to learn how to charm or manipulate other people, and therefore important for parents to allow them to exercise these other forms of interpersonal power. Children also need to know that their parents love them enough to answer their cries of distress and frustration. If a baby cries at bedtime, Leach argues, you should come back into the room but not pick the baby up. That way, you balance the child's need for attention with your need to have the baby stay in bed.

And the second thing Spock urged on parents was consistency. As this idea took hold, even anthropologists were bothered by the arbitrariness with which parents in other cultures approached the task of parenting. Thomas Gladwin and Seymour Sarason, writing in the 1950s about Truk, an atoll in the South Pacific, described how children were sometimes reprimanded and sometimes rewarded for crying. The decision seemed to the anthropologists to be at the adult's whim:

> When [the infant] can toddle about he . . . of course falls down on occasion and may be picked up, but on the other hand he may be completely ignored and left to scream in rage and pain in the dust. If his mother or whoever is tending him is preoccupied but thinks he may have really injured himself, she may rush up, see that he is not actually hurt, and leave again without any attempt to console him. The child cannot predict, either from the nature of his mishap or of his response to it, whether he will be fussed over and comforted or simply ignored; this is almost entirely a function of the parent's momentary inclination and preoccupation.

Young children were told, according to Gladwin and Sarason, that if they cried the Americans would eat them, which made interviewing the children difficult: "For months the small children would flee in terror if they found themselves without a phalanx of adult bodies between them and a voracious American." Other forms of subterfuge were used as well. If a very young child cried for its mother, for instance, an adult might say, Stop crying, here she comes now. When the child looked up, it would see that the mother wasn't coming and perhaps start crying again, but sometimes, having stopped, it would remain quiet. Alternately, children of all ages were beaten or slapped for crying, according to the parent's "momentary inclination."

Among the Kogi, according to Reichel-Dolmatoff, arbitrariness also ruled. The majority of the time, infants are ignored. "The babies cry desperately, but since no action is taken by the adults to satisfy their desire for food or warmth, since nobody gives them any, their crying soon ceases, and rare are the babies who cry after having completed one month. From then on cold, hunger and physical effort are stoically endured. Nobody complains about them because it would be completely futile." Mothers carrying heavy loads along arduous mountain paths and working in the fields have little time to attend to their infants' cries, but even when the mother is not busy she tends to ignore the baby's tears. The problem is that sometimes mothers do respond to tears with nurturing, comforting, or food, and so young children can never know whether their tears will bring parental displeasure, neglect, or affection.

Reichel-Dolmatoff, Gladwin and Sarason, Wolf, and the other anthropologists of the 1950s and 1960s who noticed this kind of inconsistency got their cue from Spock and other child-rearing experts who had been arguing that parents needed to be more methodical and consistent in response to their children's crying. Garry Cleveland Myers, author of the popular *The Modern Family* (1934), to take just one example, emphasized "the value of strict routine" and "habit building," asking parents to be consistent with the child and with each other; otherwise the child will learn "to gain his way by crying." More than half a century later, William Homan, M.D., wrote in *Child Sense: A Pediatrician's Guide for Today's Families* (1969) that the first rule of disciplining a child was "Be consistent."

Recently some parenting experts have argued, as Leach does, that consistency means never ignoring tears. Magda Gerber, the force behind the *RIE Manual for Parents and Professionals*, which was in its eighth printing in 1994, argues that since crying is natural, parents should always respond to their children's cries with attention and respect: "Respect the child's right to express feelings, or moods, whether crying or smiling." William Sears agrees that to comfort a crying child is always a good idea, and that a good parent is one who understands the infant's tearful language. These recommendations suggest that we have changed not only our notions of coddling but our understanding of what it means to be a parent as well.

Eventually, parents are no longer the most important deterrent. Children do, as Gerber suggests, learn better cues, in part because they begin to grasp the costs of crying and figure out how to avoid those costs by using other communicative tactics. Even in cases where crying is not actively discouraged, occasional parental disapproval or withholding has its effect, and children learn that crying can backfire. And parents are much more apt to fall for manipulative crying than friends or classmates. As Marie Faust Evitt writes, "Kids know all too well that crying isn't cool, not even at the tender age of six or seven. Once children are past preschool, they tend to see weepers as losers." After being humiliated by their classmates, they learn what adults know, that it is only safe, and only worthwhile, to cry in private or with their intimates. And of course by that time boys and girls have also learned that their islands of safety are different.

Some studies have suggested that families continue to be important in determining the crying habits of adolescents and young adults. One long-term study of the socialization of emotion, for instance, followed forty-three adolescents in New England and found that those whose families had been "more emotionally expressive and accepting of emotions" when they were ten years old were more likely to break from traditional "emotion rules": the males were more likely to cry and the women more likely to express anger. Greater emotional expressiveness was in general associated, the researchers found, with social and psychological adjustment, with one notable exception: while crying was correlated with better adjustment for the males, it was associated with poorer adjustment for the women.

But since male expressiveness, in these changing times, has been shown to be correlated with income level in a number of studies, it may be that general, class-based cultural determinants are at least as important as specific, family-based training, especially in adolescence. The figures indicating when boys and girls diverge in their crying habits—the frequency of boys' crying begins to taper off to adult levels several years earlier than that of girls—suggests again that social pressures beyond the family have more impact than families once children are in school. Given the constant change in gender ideology, we can expect the sociological data to continue to change.

Men and Women

The differences in men's and women's emotional styles and makeup have been studied by many different people through the ages, and from many different perspectives, some scientific and some otherwise. In the history of this inquiry, the same questions arise over and over: Why do men and women cry, and why do they cry at different times? How do these differences develop? How do they feel? History provides one set of answers to these questions, sociology another.

The earliest scientific attempt to analyze the different emotional behavior of men and women is Aristotle's discussion in the *History of Animals*:

> Woman is more compassionate than man, more easily moved to tears, at the same time is more jealous, more querulous, more apt to scold or strike. She is, furthermore, more prone to despondency and less hopeful than the man, more void of shame or self-respect, more false of speech, more deceptive, and of more retentive memory. She is also more wakeful, more shrinking, more difficult to rouse to action, and requires smaller quantity of nutriment.

Aristotle's text may not sound particularly scientific, but it is the most detailed text of descriptive biology the world had seen at that time, and remained so until the Renaissance. Much of it is concerned with specific species' traits, as when he describes the number of teeth a horse has or the mode of reproduction in snakes. But Aristotle also does comparative ethology, studying traits across many species. He finds many of what he considers the emotional tendencies of women, such as shamelessness and cowardice, replicated throughout the animal kingdom: "When the [female] cuttle-fish is struck with the trident the male stands by to help the female," Aristotle writes in support of a basic, cross-species difference between male and female, "but when the male is struck the female runs away." Since weeping is exclusively human (Aristotle doesn't suggest otherwise), his opinion that women are "more easily moved to tears" is clearly not based in a study of comparative behavior but an argument from his own observation, a kind of amateur qualitative sociology.

Even if Aristotle had had hard data about the frequency, duration, and intensity of his contemporaries' crying habits, though, he still would have been wrong to conclude that women are "more easily moved to tears." Because of their caretaking roles, women may simply be in positions that more often demand tears than men are. Since the

Hagar, the Egyptian slave who bore Abraham a son, was a popular subject in the seventeenth through nineteenth centuries. Hagar wept after being banished into the wilderness by Abraham with God's blessing; God then hears her tears and saves her. Gerbrand van den Eeckhout, *Hagar Weeping* (early 1640s). Oil on canvas, 30 x 27 in. Gift of Martin J. Zimet, The J. Paul Getty Museum, Los Angeles.

occasions for men's and women's tears varies from culture to culture, both are more or less "easily moved" at different times. But Aristotle nonetheless began the attempt to isolate the differences between men and women based on their emotional expression.

Such differences are notoriously difficult to pin down. Johan Huizinga, the author of *The Waning of the Middle Ages*, has said that the fourteenth century was a time of incredibly boisterous emotionality, in which people wept, screamed, sobbed, and caterwauled in the streets at what seems to modern ears to have been slight provocation. When the Franciscan friar Richard told his audience in Paris that he was preaching his last sermon, "great and small wept as touchingly and bitterly as if they were watching their friends being buried, and so did he." At funerals, "lamentations uttered throughout the town." At the same time, Giannozzo Manetti, a fifteenth-century humanist, in describing his own grief at his son's death, did not feel that he could assume that his readers would accept his tears as justified. He felt compelled to argue against stoicism, and to defend his tears using biblical and classical examples of weeping, such as Jesus weeping at the grave of Lazarus. He didn't need to justify his tears vis-à-vis what men as a whole were expected to do, as Huizinga's description of the everyday world around him shows. As a philosopher, Manetti felt a need to justify weeping in grief because of the discourse on the passions that was central to the tradition within which he worked, from the Stoics and Plato on. Manetti has any number of identities—as a man, an Italian, a humanist, a philosopher, a father, a husband, a citizen, and so on. Each of these positions, identities, or selves carries emotional demands and responsibilities, and they don't always overlap. Historians and sociologists have suggested that this kind of multiplicity is part of the emotional life of men and women in the modern age, which has increasingly asked people to develop both private and public identities, and which has "identified" people in a number of other ways as well—in terms of their class, status, profession, job, politics, ethnicity, and so on. The rowdy bawlers in the street whom Huizinga describes perhaps also had times when they felt the need to justify themselves. But there is no question that modernity has proliferated the identities we assume when navigating our social lives, and with that proliferation comes a complex set of emotional protocols.

Scientists in the sixteenth and seventeenth centuries had a much simpler explanation for why some people cried more than others: "Weeping is easier for those who by their very constitution and nature, or by reason of their age, sex, or culture, are weaker and moister," the physiologist Joubert wrote in 1579, in line with the humoral theory of the body, "which is why we see phlegmatic people tear promptly, along with children, elderly people, and women." Since women and children are more "moist" than men, their brains are closer to a weeping state at all times. As the literary historian Marjory E. Lange has noted, when more modern medical ideas replaced the humoral theory, "moistness" lost its explanatory power but weakness did not. In 1658 the philosopher Thomas Hobbes wrote, "Those that weep the greatest amount are those, such as women and children, who have the least hope in themselves and the most in friends." For Hobbes, a sense of our powerlessness is what makes us weep, which is why children weep when they realize they can't have what they want. "For the same cause women are more apt to weep than men," Hobbes wrote elsewhere. And since women are "more accustomed to have their wills," He explains, their disappointment when they are thwarted has the secondary impact of reminding them of their actual powerlessness.

Humoral moistness is no longer taken to offer a reasonable physiological account for the difference in crying rates, of course. But powerlessness still frames our own cultural understanding of tears. The psychoanalyst Robert Sadoff, for instance, sums up one school of thought when he argues that "weeping is a regressive phenomenon, recapturing the feeling of weakness and helplessness of the child as it calls out for aid and support." And it is fair to say that the reigning popular myth at the end of the twentieth century is this: men are crippled by their social training, which has taught them that crying is a sign of weakness. Because men don't cry, they are too aggressive, they don't know how to be intimate or nurturing, they don't know how to get in touch with their feelings. And because women do their emotional work for them, they haven't had to learn to do their own. Women are socialized into a more expressive mode, and hence cry more. For many this is simply a good thing and should be imitated by men. But since crying is taken as a form of weakness, some have argued that women's tears are complicit with women's oppression.

Given what we know about the long history of male weeping, however, it is hard to accept either of these two arguments—that men should cry more or that women should cry less as a way to somehow address the power imbalance between men and women. Being "manly" undoubtedly has something to do with the way men exercise control over women, but being manly has, historically, required many different levels of tearfulness. At the height of the eighteenth century's celebration of sensibility, Rousseau was asked what was needed of a heroic man. He answered "Manliness!" and by this he meant not just the adventuring spirit of explorers and the like but the ability to feel and express, through tears, the strongest possible emotions. As an anonymous eighteenth-century writer put it,

> Moral weeping is the sign of so noble a passion, that it may be questioned whether those are properly men, who never weep upon any occasion. They may pretend to be as heroical as they please, and pride themselves in a stoical insensibility; but this will never pass for virtue with the true judges of human nature.

Over the next two centuries, men were encouraged to be manly in many ways, some of which Rousseau (or Laclos or Goethe) might not have recognized. In America, standards for male behavior were changing in clear relation to changing economic realities.

The new style of manliness can be said to have been inaugurated in 1829, along with the rough-hewn, populist soldier Andrew Jackson, after he defeated John Quincy Adams, with his periwigs, tights, and aristocratic manners. Primarily as a result of the industrial revolution, new roles for men were emerging in America and Europe—the entrepreneur, the manager, the professional, the financier, and the like—creating among other things new forms of and anxieties about male identity. The new manliness encouraged men to curb their emotional expression, at least at certain times. One businessman and reformer, John Kirk, wrote to his mother in 1852 to say that her lessons and admonitions followed him "and caused the tears of penitential sorrows and affection to flow from my weeping eyes." As the historian Anthony Rotundo noticed, no such weepiness appeared in his letter to his father in the same year. In his letter to his mother, he represented himself as a traditional gentleman; in that to his father, as a modern businessman. And while the gentleman might still weep, the new businessman did not.

But this emerging stoicism, as Kirk's two letters suggest, was context-specific. In the middle of the nineteenth century, during the great age of American political oratory, politicians were still expected to weep at appropriate times during the delivery of a speech. Daniel Webster, one of the best of them, was described by a newspaper reporter crying at his own speech: "A burning tear drop that gathered in his eye, and trickled down his pale cheek, showed how deeply the orator himself was moved." Weeping was considered a necessary part of the orator's art, and thought perfectly manly in this and many other forums—the phrase "manly tears" was used regularly. Men continued to weep in literature and at literature, in the theater, and in other traditional places. But in the new roles and public spaces created by indus-

Laurel and Hardy displaying the poles of male emotion—anger and tears.
From *A Haunting We Will Go* (1942) © Metro-Goldwyn-Mayer.

trial capitalism and its rationally organized relations and routines, crying—and all emotional expressivity—was by and large forbidden.

This is obviously an oversimplification of the full range of ways in
which men and women actually lived and felt. I have run through it
quickly in order to point out that the "traditional" gender division that
people (and social scientists) refer to doesn't really exist as a tradition,
but as a constantly shifting and evolving set of arguments and as a very
diverse collection of ways of living. Even in the mid-twentieth century, when the manly man as we know him had supposedly emerged
as an ideal—the stoic who could endure any injury without tears—
there were competing ideals embodied by the movie stars and crooners who welled up and wept in their performances. And some of the
images of stoicism that have stood for that tradition—like Hemingway's shell-shocked characters—are so ambiguous morally and sexually that they seem more like exceptions than exemplars. Women, too,
were often confounded by conflicting cultural messages about their
crying: was it ennobling or hysterical? Did it prove or disprove their
feminine fortitude? But in both cases tears could be used to announce
a person's defiance or compliance with their gender roles. Tears could
be "women's weapons," as Shakespeare called them, or could help
uphold the fiction that she was weak and reliant on men. A man could
let a tear fall, sometimes, in order to show that he was not going to
give in and cry.

"Crying, in our day," Gretta Palmer wrote in the *Ladies' Home Journal*
in the 1940s, "is a woman's monopoly." She cites a credit manager at
one of New York's largest department stores who found that "one
third of all women customers who are in arrears will cry when they sit
down at his desk; he keeps a box of facial tissue in his top drawer,
silently peels one off and hands it to the tearful customer." (Usually, he
says, "it makes her stop. I don't know why.") American men of the
1940s cry less than women, Palmer says, and this, she argues, is for two
reasons: "(1) open tears are no longer allowed men by the stern code
of our day; and (2) modern women cry much oftener than honest
emotion alone demands." Young boys are abjured to "be a man" while
young girls are comforted when they cry.

Palmer assumes a golden age of balanced emotional expression and control at some point before the stern code of her own day, and expects that one day we will find a new and better balance again as well. The main problem Palmer sees is that the current code teaches a woman to use tears "as a useful racket for getting her own way," and she bemoans the weakness and dishonesty such stratagems encourage in women. Women should be ashamed, Palmer says, and men should be ashamed of their stoicism as well, since both psychiatrists and physiologists agree that the American man "would improve his health if he would himself indulge in an occasional good cry (as Latin men sometimes do)."

While the lesson people took from the endocrinologists of the 1920s was one of strict emotional control, the physiologists the 1940s were arguing that certain forms of emotional expression were necessary. They discovered that lysozyme, an enzyme that is a powerful antiseptic, and therefore important to the eye's self-cleaning, was also found in abnormally high concentrations in ulcer patients. Excess lysozyme produced in times of emotional upset eats away at the lining of the stomach, they concluded, and four out of five people afflicted with such ulcers are male. Crying, therefore, might let off both steam and lysozyme. Men who didn't cry were polluting themselves, and, Palmer wrote, they therefore clearly needed to express themselves, to learn once again how to cry.

Some writers in the late thirties and forties continued to exhort men and women to control themselves. *Reader's Digest* ran "How to Gain Emotional Poise" in 1945, for example, a piece that counseled readers who are "easily thrown into a turmoil" on the fine points of "self-mastery." The ultraserious *North American Review* ran an article in 1939 on how to "educate the emotions" so that one might experience them while always keeping them under rational control. But a growing number of experts were suggesting that people needed not more control but what a writer for the health magazine *Hygeia* in 1941 called "emotional outlets," a phrase that gained immediate currency. An article by Louisa Church for *American Home* magazine in 1945, "No Time for Tears," suggested that women who suffered from "uneasiness, uncertainty, fear, timidity, hesitancy and other undesirable traits" needed to discover an "emotional outlet," in particular by developing their talents and skills in the real world. An article in *Newsweek* in 1948 made an argument similar to Gretta Palmer's, warning against the "cumulative effect of festering emotions on the physical health of the frustrated adult." Men have to worry about the ulcers that result from such festering more than women because of the greater pressure on men to "inhibit overt emotional expression."

But journalistic advisers notwithstanding, American men were not devoid of tears in the 1930s, 1940s, and 1950s. At a time when butch masculinity was at more of a premium than at any time since the heyday of Theodore Roosevelt, men cried in public on many occasions. Lou Gehrig cried at his farewell speech in 1939, and Babe Ruth cried at Yankee Stadium in 1948 when it was announced that he had cancer. Mickey Mantle sobbed in the locker room when injuries kept him out of a World Series game in 1951. The country-and-western star Roy Acuff was famous for singing with tears running down his cheeks. One of the originators of "blue-eyed soul," Johnnie Ray, "the Crying Crooner," became one of the biggest singing stars of his day with the release of "Cry" in 1951, the first single to have its A and B sides numbers one and two on Billboard's charts (the B side was "The Little White Cloud That Cried"). "The Nabob of Sob" continued to head the charts until Elvis Presley hit the scene. If his ironic nicknames—he was also called the Cry Guy, the Prince of Wails, the Golden Tearjerker, the Cheerful Tearful, Squirt-Gun Eyes, and America's Number One Public Weeper—display a certain amount of sniggering at Ray's sobbing, the American record-buying public was clearly enamored of his tearfulness. In the era when women supposedly held a monopoly on tears, men who cried were highly revered and handsomely rewarded.

In the meantime, "manly tears" have regained a certain amount of cultural currency, and to be called a "sensitive male" is in many contexts a compliment. Crying by men can now be interpreted as strength rather than weakness. Crying by women can be seen as instability, rather than the moral responsiveness it implied a century ago. In the late 1960s, the idea that women were more "emotional" and men more "rational" came under explicit attack as sexist ideology, as some argued that identifying women with emotionalism was necessarily demeaning and debilitating in a culture that prized rationality. But at the same time, an opposite argument was afloat—the idea that women's emotionalism constitutes a kind of moral superiority: cold rationality promulgated war and oppression, while an emotional approach to life encouraged empathy and harmony. The "patriarchal tradition" had seen emotion as a kind of degraded thinking, a kind of polluted cognition, and some feminists turned this argument on its head, claiming instead that emotion was the full human response, of which rational thought was only part. To insist on rationality, according to this way of thinking, was to limit oneself to a fraction of one's equipment for understanding oneself and others.

In this context, two complimentary arguments about crying gained currency. Women had been socialized into crying instead of expressing their anger, and men, socialized into a fear of tears, tended to express anger when they should be crying. Women needed to stop crying and get angry, and men needed to stop being angry and start crying. That these two arguments might be at loggerheads did not seem to bother anyone. Never before had there been such a clamor for change in people's basic emotional makeup. The biological and social sciences were called on to establish both the nature of gender difference and its cultural contingency, and thus the malleability of those differences.

The first detailed research into American crying habits was not done until the late 1970s and the early 1980s. Surveys then suggested that women do in fact cry more often and longer than men. A study by Hastrup, Baker, Kraemer, and Bornstein claimed that women cried an average of thirty times a year, men somewhat less than six. Women, in other words, cried more than five times as often as men. William Frey's study claimed that women averaged sixty-four episodes a year, and men seventeen, or a bit more than four times as often.

Frey gave his subjects a questionnaire about their crying habits and asked them to record their crying in a diary. He found that the men cried for an average of four minutes per episode, while women cried for about six. The most significant gender differences showed up at the extremes: one woman cried twenty-nine times a month, and only 6 percent of the women never cried, while 45 percent of the men reported no crying at all. But a number of other statistics show much more similarity: 40 percent of the women's crying episodes and 36 percent of the men's were due to close personal relationships; 14 percent of the women's crying episodes and 10 percent of the men's included sobbing; 47 percent of the women's episodes involved running tears, compared with 29 percent of the men's; 27 percent of the women's episodes and 36 percent of the men's were in response to movies or television.

One of the problems with Frey's data is that his questionnaire asked a somewhat flawed basic question: "How many times a month, on the average, do you shed tears," he asked, "because of emotional stress?" Not everyone would include welling up at a movie, for instance, to be crying or a response to stress, but some might—the question presupposes what "crying" is. In a British survey of responses to films in 1950, several men claimed that they never cried in response to a film but admitted to lumps in their throats, moist eyes, and the like. "I have on occasion been moved to a wet eye," a twenty-eight-year-old civil servant said, "but never to tears." A thirty-five-year-old man said, "I would never admit to crying in the pictures though I have often had to stifle back what were suspiciously like tears." A thirty-two-year-old journalist said flatly and yet enigmatically, "I do not cry as a woman does." Frey's diary instructions left other possibilities alive—asking the subjects to record emotional tears, irritant tears, and "other tears." But even so, as we know from the experience of sex researchers, self-reporting tends to be skewed toward cultural expectations. While there is no obvious checkpoint (as in the case of sex research, when the total number of sexual experiences men report having with women is twice the number women report having with men), we can nonetheless assume that the data is somewhat faulty. Experimenters using audiotape recordings have helped correct some of the inaccuracies in mothers' reporting of the frequency and duration of their babies' crying, but no audio recordings have been made (much less video recordings) to monitor the daily crying habits of adults.

James R. Averill, Randolph R. Cornelius, and T. R. Sarbin all argued from slightly different theoretical perspectives in the 1980s that adults weep in order to transform their social environment. In particular, we weep in an attempt to change other people's negativity into support by weeping, and it often works: observers tend to offer comfort, especially when the weeper is female. Other studies have reinforced this argument, finding that both men and women are more likely to help and empathize with women who are weeping, and that women are more likely to help and empathize with a weeping man. The studies of Hoover-Dempsey, Plas, and Wallston found that in work environments crying, whether men or by women, was frowned upon, which indicates that these studies are context-specific in ways the experimenters have not addressed.

In order to get at some of the contextual variables, Susan Labott, Randall B. Martin, Patricia S. Eason, and Elaine Y. Berkey performed a number of experiments monitoring people's responses to films in the company of a confederate of the experimenters. Both men and women displayed more stereotypical behavior—that is, the women cried more, the men less—when they watched a film with a person of the opposite sex than when they watched with someone of their own sex, showing that men and women both respond to very complexly gendered expectations in the context of the experiment. This suggests, on the one hand, that none of the other surveys have adequate controls, and that, again, cultural expectations of gender difference will skew any findings. But another experiment by this same team in 1993 suggested that these contexts are changing rapidly. In this experiment, 168 undergraduates watching a film were paired with a man or a woman who either laughed, cried, or remained neutral. The majority agreed that they liked the men better when they cried and the women when they did not, and the criers were considered more emotional but not more feminine than the laughers or the neutral confederates. Labott's conclusion was that gender-role expectations are changing.

And obviously they are. Already in 1984, a survey of 1,360 men and women by Catherine Ross and John Mirowsky found that men who adhered to traditional sex roles were less likely to cry than men who didn't. In the early 1980s, Cretser, Lombardo, Lombardo, and Mathis published a number of survey-based studies that suggested similar changes. They asked almost 600 students about their reactions to men and women crying, and also asked how they thought other people would react. The students agreed that women cried more often and more easily than men, to an extent that was not backed up by their own self-reported behavior. And most of the respondents thought "people" would have more trouble with male crying than they did. This group clearly saw their acceptance of male crying as nontraditional.

Catherine Kohler Riessman has argued that the very standards of measurement sociologists use also skew their results. She did extensive interviews with divorcing men and women and at the same time evaluated them using standard sociological tests. The women's standardized scores showed that they suffered much more depression and distress than the men. But in their interviews the men described behavior that suggested serious distress—heavy drinking, overwork, restlessness, loss of control—and that was not reflected in their scores. "Besides making females look 'sicker,' customary measurement approaches systematically skew understanding about the patterning of emotions by gender," Riessman writes, "and underestimate males' emotions in the face of life events."

Muriel Egerton, using social psychologist James R. Averill's theory of emotional schemas, found that men and women tended to use the concept of "passion" in different ways. Men interpreted anger as the result of passion, that is, as externally caused and uncontrollable, while women did not. Women interpreted crying as the result of external, uncontrollable forces. In other words, even if notions of the acceptability of crying are changing, many of the underlying understandings may remain very much the same.

Some of this literature assumes that emotional expressivity is a good thing and repression bad, and that crying is expressive and not crying repressive. Some studies make political claims that are far from warranted by their research. The studies of office crying by Hoover-Dempsey et al., for instance, argued that if women were in charge of offices, more nurturing and accepting responses to crying would become the norm. Studies of the management styles of women do not back this up. And some social theorists have suggested that in learning to cry, men are just changing their style rather than their substance, that their crying is simply a new mask. "Men would like to stop paying the 'costs' of masculinity," as Michael Messner, who does not include himself in this group, wrote in the academic journal *Theory and Society*, and so they exchange macho styles for sensitive ones while maintaining all the other trappings of power. This seems like a somewhat paranoid reading—are men all over the country learning to cry and express their feelings as some kind of massive ploy to retain their traditional prerogatives?

Certainly some of the most pervasive and some of the ugliest forms of male power are still central to our society. Sarah E. Ullman and Raymond A. Knight studied police reports and court records in 274 rape cases and found that crying by the woman during an attack significantly increased the amount of physical injury she sustained. Clearly no simple notion of the place of tears in the gender system can account for that gruesome fact. And as we saw, crying can be extremely dangerous for infants and children as well, a trigger for abuse by both men and women. If men learn to cry, it will not, of course, automatically change the social system. The sociologist Norbert Elias has argued that the taming of emotions has been at the center of what he calls "the civilizing process," and that children repeat this process by learning the regulative rules for the expression of emotion as they mature. As James Averill has observed, this idea can be extended to include not just regulative but consitutive rules. That is, "as women move from the home into the workplace," as men "assume greater domestic responsibilities," and the like, the "transitions require fundamental changes in values and beliefs," and these changes evoke "radically different emotions." In other words, crying will not change social arrangements, but as social arrangements for both men and women change, so will the meaning of tears for both.

And things do continue to change. Male crying is everywhere. We need only point to the use of tears by male movie stars over the last five years—not just Leonardo DiCaprio, Brad Pitt, and Tom Hanks but even action stars like Mel Gibson, Sylvester Stallone, and Bruce Willis—to see that the desired male is once again becoming the man who cries. Michael Jordan wept freely when the Chicago Bulls won their first NBA title, and it passed uncommented upon; he wept again—falling into a fetal position on the floor and sobbing as soon as the game ended—when they won the title in 1996. The television announcers explained that Jordan's father had been murdered a year and a half earlier, that the game was on Father's Day, and that he had made a miraculous comeback after two years of retirement. This coincidence of circumstances, they seemed to say, made his otherwise excessive crying understandable. In figure skating, men and women alike get teary-eyed as they hear the announcement of the judges' scores while sitting on the benches known as the "kiss and cry" box. Baseball players can cry when they win the World Series, even if they are expected to do so at few other times. Boxers who are acknowledged underdogs can show tears when they win, while favorites who win an easy match may not, and neither vanquished underdogs nor favorites can cry without losing face. Each sport, in effect, has its own rules of expression, and of course there are exceptions to every rule, and ways to tell any story of crying so that it somehow fits the rules.

Floyd Patterson, for instance, famously cried at losing the title bout to Muhammad Ali in 1965. Ali had called Patterson an "Uncle Tom" and had humiliated him in the ring: one reporter likened Ali's performance in the fight to a boy taking the wings off a butterfly, and Ali's own corner pleaded with him to knock Patterson down so that the fight would end. When Patterson cried, it was cast in mythic terms, with Patterson seen as the great, fallen hero slain by a new, even greater warrior. Now an athlete's tears can just be a character trait. Derek Loville, a running back for the San Francisco 49ers, cries before his games, not every week but often, and has ever since he was on his high school team. His teammate Adam Walker says that "it was strange at first," but figures that "it's the way he deals with his emotions because he loves playing so much." This may not strike us as deep insight, but it does point out how easy it is to make sense out of seeming breaches in male etiquette. The *San Francisco Examiner* ran a story about Loville's crying that was headlined "49ers Loville Cries Tears of Strength." But the most obvious example of the new freedom for male tears was the Olympic wrestler Kurt Angle, who cried for a solid half hour after winning the gold medal in 1996. Although there was a lot of talk about this most unabashed display of crying in the history of modern sport, news accounts interpreted the event without ridicule or humor.

A 1994 article in *Glamour* magazine by Cindy Chupak does find humor in male tears. Chupak assumes that male crying is not only possible now but required as part of the rituals of courtship. And so if a young man has not learned to cry in the bosom of his family, he is very likely to learn how in the process of dating. But, Chupak writes, not just any crying will do. A man may cry at how beautiful his girl-friend is, but if he cries about balancing the checkbook, all bets are off. Of course we want to know that our men *can* cry, writes Chupak, but we don't want them crying "out of fear, frustration or weakness." The ideal is for men to cry exactly once, jokes Chupak, at the beginning of a relationship. After that they should never, ever cry again.

When one of the women on Tom Hanks's baseball team in *A League of Their Own* (1992) begins to cry in the dugout, he yells at her: "What is this? This can't be crying? You know why? *There's no cry-ing in baseball!*" This is a laugh line because we accept tears in sports. We are clearly reapproaching, in fact, the kind of cross-gender weepi-ness that the eighteenth century knew. The young boys who are going to see *Titanic* a dozen times and coming out with their shirts sopping wet are often the sons of men who have rarely cried, much less consid-ered it a pleasure. We can't know for how long, but the mingling of male and female tears has returned.

Elisabeth Badinter, a French historian, interviewed in the Italian magazine *L'Espresso*, was asked why men are now crying more than they used to: "They cry because of the malaise of masculinity, because they do not know how to behave with these new women. Above all they cry because they no longer know who they are." One can imagine a man for whom this is true, but as sociology it obviously falls short. Nora Ephron, in her novel *Heartburn*, took issue with the crying man from another angle:

> There has been a lot written in recent years about the fact that men don't cry enough. Crying is thought to be a desirable thing, a sign of a mature male sensibility, and it is generally believed that when little

boys are taught that it is unmanly to cry, they grow up unable to deal with pain and grief and disappointment and feelings in general. I would like to say two things about this. The first is that I have always believed that crying is a highly overrated activity: women do entirely too much of it, and the last thing we ought to want is for it to become a universal excess. The second thing I want to say is this: beware of men who cry. It's true that men who cry are sensitive and in touch with feelings, but the only feelings they tend to be sensitive to and in touch with are their own.

What Ephron, Badinter, and Chupak all rely on is a knowledge that the social world has changed. All assume that men are weeping, and weeping a lot, so much so that it has become the center of a social diagnosis for Badinter and comic fodder for Chupak and Ephron. All three assume, in ways the sociological studies have not quite caught up with yet, that there has been a reevaluation of male emotional expressiveness, that the revolution is under way. And all three suggest, with varying degrees of seriousness, that it is time for some social pressure in the opposite direction, something to keep male tears from becoming a "universal excess." The splashy return of weeping movie stars and politicians' tears in the last decade are further evidence, as we'll see, that all sociological conclusions about crying habits are doomed to a quick obsolescence.

5

Cultures of Mourning

Early in this century, anthropologists observed a very curious custom among both Andaman Islanders, who live off the coast of Thailand and Malaysia, and the Maori of New Zealand. In both cultures, when two friends or relatives have been separated, they greet each other in an odd way. The two sit down, one in the other's lap, arms around each other's necks, and weep or wail together for several minutes. According to E. H. Man, who was in the Andaman Islands in the 1870s, relatives who have been separated by as little as a few weeks weep and howl so violently when they see each other again that "there is no difference observable between their demonstrations of joy on these occasions and those of grief at the death" of a close relative. A. R. Radcliffe-Brown, who wrote about this in his 1922 study, *The Andaman Islanders*, thought at first that the friends or relatives must simply be experiencing what we call tears of joy, set off by their profound pleasure in being reunited. The islanders corrected him, though, saying they were instead mourning for the people who had died since their last meeting.

Radcliffe-Brown soon noticed that the same interlocked weeping

happened even if no one had died and the two weepers had been separated for as little as a week. He then hypothesized that when the
natives claimed that their communal crying was a form of mourning,
they were accounting for its origin, not for its current purpose or
meaning. Like the handshake or the two-cheek kiss of the European
greeting, whose origins are also lost in the dimness of history, this form
of meeting had originally been meant to honor the dead but had
become purely conventional, customary.

This explanation is eminently plausible, and yet nonetheless at odds
with what the Andamans and Maori say—that is, at odds with the
understanding of the people for whom the event has its primary
meaning. We, after all, would find it amusing but wrong if Maori or
Andaman social scientists told us that when we weep at the movies,
we are really just repeating a ritualized ceremony whose origins we
had forgotten. Whenever we try to understand the emotional life of
our own or other cultures, we encounter similar problems. To what
extent is an emotional display purely conventional, a performance of
etiquette rather than an expression of feeling, or do these two things
simply merge? Do we take the testimony of the participants at face
value, or do we get closer to the truth when we ignore their testimony
and offer our own explanations? Is the way individuals view their tears
central to what their weeping actually means?

There is ample evidence that even in the extremity of mourning,
some tears are largely "performative," a word linguists use to describe
an utterance, like "I apologize," which is itself an action rather than a
proposition. Other tears are just a simple performance of a duty: "Our
tears—they are for the kinsmen of our father to see," one Trobriand
Island mourner told Bronislaw Malinowski. And yet another told him
that when someone dies, the whole subclan suffers, and therefore
cries, because it has been maimed by the loss of one of its members,
"as if a limb were cut off, or a branch lopped from a tree." The sense of
communal loss, felt as a purely natural fact, and the sense of communal obligation, felt as a fundamentally social fact, combine in the Trobriand's tears. Some groups alternate, as Alcionilio Bruzzi Alves da
Silva suggests in his description of the Uaupes in Brazil: "In front of
their own dead brother they will burst out in a desperate cry, and with

the same aptness they will pass to the noisiest and most indecent laughter." According to Hans Becher, the Yanoama of Brazil intermingle loud sobs of loss and "sustained, shrill" cries of joy that the deceased's soul has "found entry into the moon." Loss, joy, mourning, ceremony: all hover around, and yet fail to comprehend, the full meaning of funeral emotion.

Death may be universal, but the human response to it is not. All cultures work to express, contain, celebrate, and manage death's inexorable personal and social havoc, and all do so somewhat differently. Ceremonies of mourning ritualize tears in different ways, channeling grief into a variety of funereal forms. The finality of death has generated practices and symbols that can look elaborate, intense, beautiful, inappropriate, strange, indecent, or inadequate in the eye of the beholder, whether they are the customs of a distant culture or our own. Crying, nonetheless, takes place during funeral practices in all but one of the cultures discussed in the Human Relations Area Files, the U.S. State Department's attempt to collect all of the available writing about world cultures. (The odd man out, as I mentioned in the Introduction, is Bali, where weeping takes place at death but not at the funeral, which is held several years later.) The tendency to cry at death is a human universal.

But the ceremonies are very particular. The British sociologist Geoffrey Gorer wrote an article in 1955 describing what he called "the pornography of death" in mid-twentieth-century British culture. The death of friends or relatives was avoided in polite conversation, he noted, never talked about around children, and only referred to with euphemisms. Death was talked about behind closed doors and furtively, Gorer wrote, just as sex was in the nineteenth century—a time when, conversely, death was discussed openly. And a half century later, it is still true that most funeral practices around the world include more sobbing and wailing than our own. And yet we do, after all, cry.

Today's anthropologists insist that most descriptions of emotion are necessarily contaminated by the values, customs, and understandings of observers, and that imperfect relativism has made for a long history of error in our descriptions of other cultures' emotional lives. Such

errors of flawed translation infect the work, they say, not just of travelers, colonialists, and missionaries but of past generations of anthropologists as well. And in surveying the literature on mourning in other
cultures over the last hundred years, one sees various forms of patron-
ization, sexism, infantilization, and the like. Earlier visitors from the
West to the far reaches of the globe were in fact willing to evaluate the
cultures they studied, rather than simply describe them.

Margaret Mead, for instance, in her *Coming of Age in Samoa* (1928),
makes it clear that she thinks the Samoans have some attitudes worth
emulating, some ways of understanding emotional life that it would
behoove us to imitate. Learning about other cultures, she wrote, "should
sharpen our ability to scrutinize more steadily, to appreciate more lov-
ingly, our own." The anthropological assumption (or argument) was that
emotional differences were the result of cultural training, that they were
not natural but learned, and could therefore be unlearned or relearned.
Mead's colleague at Columbia University, Ruth Benedict, in her 1934
classic *Patterns of Culture*, expressed what was by then an anthropologi-

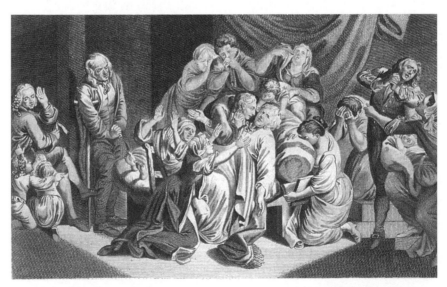

*Lavater, a friend and sometime collaborator of Goethe's, included this etching of
the varieties of mourning in his four-volume work on physiognomy.* Johann Caspar
Lavater, *Essays on Physiognomy, designed to promote the knowledge and the love of
mankind* (London, 1792). Getty Research Institute, Research Library.

cal truism, that cultures developed different emotional styles in accordance with the other demands of their culture. According to Benedict, there is a vast array of human possibility and each human group only makes use of part of that array in any field. She uses the example of linguistic difference to make her point: humans have the capacity to make an infinite number of vowel sounds, for instance, but each language only uses of a limited number of them. And all humans can make clicking noises with their tongues, but only a few cultures use that clicking noise in of their language. The same is true with emotions—of the vast possible array, cultures make do with a delimited few.

This does not mean that emotional styles are therefore thoroughly relative or "arbitrary," as some have argued since, but simply that they vary significantly from culture to culture. Benedict argues that the Zuni emotional culture makes sense given their desert living conditions, that Japanese emotional culture makes sense given their "vertical" social structure, and so on. What the anthropologists (and their Enlightenment forebears) were arguing against was the idea that feelings simply reside in people's bodies as part of their natural equipment, waiting for situations to stimulate or activate them. Emotions are, instead, learned in interaction. Charles Darwin assumed as much in the 1860s when he argued that the Sandwich Islanders acquired the habit of crying as a sign of happiness.

Weston Labarre told a story of going to a peyote meeting in the 1940s at which "a great burly Wichita Indian . . . suddenly burst out blubbering with an abandon which no Occidental male adult would permit himself in public. In time I learned that this was a stereotyped approach to the supernatural powers, enthusiastic weeping to indicate that he was as powerless as a child, to invoke their pity, and to beseech their gift of medicine power." Labarre, with his "burly," "blubbering" Indian bursting out inappropriately, hardly seems the relativist we expect anthropologists to be, but his work was received as new evidence of the cultural construction of the emotions. The real object of Labarre's criticism is his audience's preconceptions about what tears mean. If tears are just culturally constructed actions, like bowing or shaking hands, then they are relative, socially acquired forms, not the unfettered outpouring of pure feeling.

Whatever cultural blinders they may have worn, in other words, early anthropologists, travelers, and missionaries discovering new emotional styles succeeded in showing an emotion to be a piece of culture rather than simply a natural reaction. Like today's anthropologists, they understood that emotions vary from culture to culture and are integral parts of those cultures. Some saw that people have different understandings of the body, mind, and group—so different, in fact, that the very categories "body," "mind," and "group" are often untranslatable. And most understood that the different vocabularies for describing emotions are likewise impossible to translate directly.

The occasional incomprehension with which some early anthropologists and travelers viewed different customs of mourning is itself instructive, helping us to map the pertinent differences in this most fundamental human activity. The rituals these travelers describe, however imbued with their own values, collectively represent an incredibly diverse world of human responses to death. At a Taiwanese Taoist funeral, for instance, the priests act out, with musical accompaniment, the slapstick voyage of a messenger to the spirit world, including scenes of bribing the gods with wine, getting drunk, acrobatic and tumbling feats, and Keystone-Cops–like chase scenes, as part of a three- or four-hour series of ceremonies replete with weeping and exhortations. More perplexing are rituals of self-mutilation: how can the infliction of pain be an antidote to the pain of loss? Do people weep to remember or weep to forget? Anthropologists also wonder at the practice of crying at weddings: what have weddings and funerals in common? Do people weep simply because the customs and rituals of their society encourage them to weep? Do people weep as a mark of resisting change or as a mark of acceptance? And even if anthropologists could provide us with an adequate answer to these questions, we would still be left with our central query: Why tears?

Professionals and Other Mourners

In the 1740s, the French explorer Antoine Edmé Pruneau de Pommegorge encountered the Wolof tribe in what is now Senegal and was

intrigued by their practice of using hired mourners. He published an
account of his journeys in Amsterdam in 1789, in which he describes,
with a somewhat skeptical eye, the work Wolof women do during the
traditional eight days of funeral rituals:

> These are hired women, who most often do not know the deceased.
> Those who in this capacity show the greatest sorrow by their cries
> and their lamentations are the best; they are at the head of the pro-
> cession and of the family. When the deceased is taken to be put in
> the ground, the ceremony concluded, these women return to wail at
> the door of the hut, and in the presence of the woman who has just
> lost her husband. They interrupt their tears and their cries only to
> eulogize the deceased and his widow, after which they enter the hut
> to receive the compliments of the family and the company, for
> whom they have played their role well, and they drink as much
> brandy as one is willing to give them.

His countryman L. J. B. Berenger-Feraud, in a book on the Senegalese
published in Paris ninety years later, wrote that the wealthy hid their
heartlessness behind such services: "In default of real grief," he concludes, "wealthy people have the tears and cries by means of hiring
certain women for the role."

Missionaries, from whom we get many of the earliest descriptions
of cultural difference, also viewed professional mourners with disdain. When missionary Edwin Gomes wrote his *Seventeen Years
Among the Sea Dyaks of Borneo* in 1911, he described with some contempt the sleight of hand used by hired criers. The custom in Borneo
was to throw food and trinkets into the jungle as offerings to the
gods and the dead. But "among tribes where professional wailers
exist it is not enough to throw the offering of food out of the window at the back of the house. The wailer must help to send that food
to Hades" by placing it in the beak of an effigy of a bird supplied by
the professional mourner. Gomes suggests that the bird stops off
first at the professional's place and leaves the gifts there. The Rev-
erend William Howell, as a missionary to Borneo who emphasized
the general lack of civilized dignity in such proceedings, notes that
"whilst the women are attentively listening to the fascinating poetry

of the wailer, which composition is sometimes heart-rending and sometimes soothing, the men are busily engaged in setting cocks to fight."

Professional mourners have often come under attack in their own cultures for insincerity and profiteering as well. Like the funeral directors in Evelyn Waugh's *The Loved One* (1948) and other spoofs, or as in the stock comic figure of the priest or minister eulogizing a person he has never met, they can seem more driven by business considerations than empathy. Professional mourners continue to work, where they do, because they fulfill an important role in people's adjustment to loss. They are paid advocates, called upon to help bolster the bereaved's case, however futile that may be. They amplify and attempt to dignify the tearful demands of the bereaved, first among which is the demand that the dead not be dead. Like infants crying out of earshot, bereft relatives and friends weep and lament their impossible desire to reclaim the dead, crying out to no one, and the professionals make a living by claiming that they can intercede in this imaginary transaction.

Professional mourners flourished and were criticized throughout the classical ages of Greece, Rome, and the Middle East, and later in the Islamic world. They are often found in lists of the degraded professions along with criminals and moneylenders. Solon legislated curbs against the use of professional mourners early in the sixth century B.C. St. Paul argued against them. St. John Chrysostom, patriarch of Constantinople at the end of the fourth century, railed against using "hired women . . . as mourners to make the mourning more intense, to fan the fires of grief," and threatened to excommunicate anyone who hired professional weepers. The word "placebo" was used to describe both servile flatterers and the laments sung at funerals by professional mourners; only in the eighteenth century did the word take on its current medical sense. "Placebo" is derived from the Latin for "I shall please," and the tears of the professional mourners were clearly found to be pleasurable for someone at some level, even if the profession was seen as a fairly debased way to earn a living.

In the twelfth century, professional mourners were so ubiquitous that El Cid, hero of the epic of the same name and mythic hero of the

Christian Reconquista of Spain, felt compelled to brag that he needed only his wife, Jimena, to cry for him:

When I die, heed my advice:
Hire no mourners to weep for me.
There is no need of buying tears;
Those of Jimena will suffice.

By the late Middle Ages, El Cid's ethic of personalized mourning held sway and professional mourners of the old stamp had become much rarer in Europe.

They were replaced by a new group of professional mourners: the priests who, as Philippe Ariès has shown, took over the business of organizing and directing funeral rites. The church and its wards, in effect, came to have a monopoly on the mourning market, which perhaps helps explain the missionaries' abhorrence of competing professionals in Africa. It became customary for rich people to leave money in their wills for orphanages and monasteries, and in exchange the orphans and monks took part in the funeral processions and masses. The larger the bequest, the bigger the funeral.

Islamic clerics, too, attempted to enter the trade and attacked their competition. In discussions of Islamic law, professional mourners were regarded as on par with thieves and prostitutes. The rules governing the custody of children, for instance, dictated that if a mother was to be granted custody, "she must be of good character for if it was proven that she is corrupted by illicit sex, or theft, or has a low trade such as a professional mourner, or a dancer, she loses her right to custody." Under the priests and imams of today, the weeping is left to family and friends while the clerics perform processions and rituals full of quiet, somber intonations. Professional mourners have not so much disappeared over the last millennium; they have simply donned robes and stopped crying.

Explorers, anthropologists, and missionaries were fascinated not just by professional mourners but with all aspects of other cultures' response to death, which was second only to their fascination with sexual mores. Travelers and missionaries to Korea in the nineteenth century, for instance, wrote about the elaborate mourning clothes, mourning rituals, and proper times and places for shedding tears that were regulated not just by custom, but by law. Several were amazed that an official "Guide to Mourners" was published by Korean officials, prescribing the specific number of belts and sashes to be worn by each of the mourners and requiring that the corpse be put in a coffin that had stood for several months in a special room prepared and ornamented for this purpose. "It is proper to weep only in this death-chamber," related one William Elliot Griffis, who was in Korea in the 1880s, "but this must be done three or four times daily." Before entering the death chamber, moreover,

> the mourner must don a special weed, which consists of a gray cotton frock coat, torn, patched, and as much soiled as possible. The girdle must be of twisted straw and silk, made into a rope of the thickness of the wrist. Another cord, the thickness of the thumb, is wound round the head, which is covered with dirty linen, each of the rope's ends falling upon the cheek. A special kind of sandal is worn, and a big knotty stick completes the costume of woe. In the prescribed weeds the mourner enters the death-chamber in the morning on rising, and before each meal. He carries a little table filled with food, which he places upon a tray at the side of the coffin. The person who is master of the mourners presides at the ceremonies. Prostrate, and struck by the stick, he utters dolorous groans, sounding "ai-ko" if for a parent. For other relatives he groans out "oi, oi."

Other Western writers have gone into even greater detail, fascinated by the baroque complexities of dress and occasion.

Many found a certain amount of disingenuousness in such ritual elaborations, just as they did with professional mourners, and Griffis goes on to suggest that Korean funeral crying tends to be mendacious: "According to the noise and length of the groans and weeping," he writes with some skepticism, "so will the good opinion of the public be." Writing in a British anthropological journal in 1896, E. B. Landis, after outlining the standard Korean funeral liturgy—seven stakes put in the ground, ritual wailing accompanying the placement of gifts to spirits over each stake, a series of ritual prostrations, prescribed clothing and accessories for all involved—describes the first of many "libations":

> The mourner will kneel opposite the censer. The attendant will then take empty cups and pour wine therein, and kneeling will hand it to the mourner, who will pour thrice on the sand, and will then return the cups to the attendant, who will refill them and place them before the tablet. The chief mourner will then retire a little back and the master of ceremonies will then kneel and recite the above prayer for the descent of the spirit. During this time the mourner ceases wailing. After all is finished he will wail and all present will prostrate themselves twice.

The mourner will then retire to his hut and, leaning on his staff, wail. The ability of the mourners to turn theirs tears on and off, their very fluency in the languages of grief, is exactly what made them suspect to outsiders.

Walter Baldwin Spencer and Francis James Gillen, studying the Aranda people of Oceania in the 1910s, decided that this control of mourning was in fact a childish lack of control: "It is not for a moment to be supposed that the self-inflicted pain and the loud lamentings are to be taken as a measure of the grief actually felt," they wrote. While the Arandan "is certainly capable of genuine grief and of real affection for his children . . . the mind of the Australian native is like that of a child amongst ourselves. One moment he will be in a passion of grief or rage, and the next, if anything attracts his fancy, his humour will rapidly change and tears will give place to laughter."

Francis Lambrecht, reporting to the Catholic Anthropological Conference in the 1920s on his stay with the Ifugao in the Philippines, doubted the sincerity of the women who returned to the corpse every few minutes to weep because, he wrote, they overdid it, wildly "gesticulating and out-crying all the others," trying to prove their expertise in lamenting. "Indeed it seems as if all their lamentations are done upon command. They mourn and lament and a little later they stop all their cries abruptly and go to sit with the others, chew betelnuts, and laugh and chat with them just as they would if they were attending a feast;

and when the funeral meal is ready their faces show fairly well that they came for this purpose." The rituals of death, which should have displayed the depths of natural grief, looked to the anthropologists and missionaries like artificial, unfelt exercises, in which ersatz crying covered for ersatz sorrow.

Otto Klineberg, of Columbia University, and Beatrice Blackwood, of Oxford University, provide typical examples of the way in which the arbitrariness of emotional response was depicted by anthropologists at mid-century. "Among the Huichol Indians of Mexico," Klineberg reports, "it was possible for a man who wept [at a religious ceremonial] to stop at will; . . . as soon as it was over he returned to his usual cheerfulness." Blackwood, in *Both Sides of Buka Passage: An Ethnographic Study of Social, Sexual and Economic Questions in the North-Western Solomon Islands* (1935), tells the story of a girl in the Solomon Islands who had to be dragged away from a coffin because she was mourning so strenuously, but who within minutes was laughing with the other girls. The anthropologists' point is not just to show how artificial, even trivial, the expressions of grief are in other cultures, but that weeping is purely conventional, and that our own pieties about crying are therefore suspect as well.

J. Robert Moose, a missionary writing from Korea in 1911, explained one of the relationships between custom and insincerity: "When a father dies, all the members of the family gather about the boy *[sic]* and begin to wail. . . . This wailing is done according to fixed rules, and cannot be looked on as an outburst of grief and sorrow." The very fact that there were rules for emotional expression, in other words, made it impossible for true feeling to be expressed. This is, of course, a view dictated by the missionary's own belief that emotion was a spontaneous, natural outpouring, unfettered by cultural constraints. Spencer and Gillen, too, assume that Arandan insincerity is due to the fact that their "every action is bound and limited by custom."

That nineteenth-century missionaries were not very accomplished relativists is hardly news, and they were not alone in having this deficiency, of course. The Mbuti Pygmies, for instance, in what has been a widespread custom around the globe, use two words to describe their nearest neighbors, the Bantu: "savage" and "animal"; the Bantu use the equivalents in their language to describe the Mbuti. Anthropologists may attempt to conquer this sense of unreconcilable difference, but they remain outsiders nonetheless. The Zuni word for "human" is *zuñi*, and the anthropologists who studied the Zuni were not. Renato Rosaldo, one of the most respected anthropologists in the country, has addressed this question in terms of emotion. Rosaldo traveled regularly to the Philippines, where he and his wife, the anthropologist Michelle Rosaldo, did extensive fieldwork. Renato Rosaldo studied the Ilongot, a tribe famous as headhunters, and analyzed the emotional and social functions of headhunting as a form of revenge. On one trip in 1981, Michelle Rosaldo slipped on a mountain trail and plummeted sixty-five feet down a precipice; she died from her injuries. Some years later, Renato wrote an essay in which he described the anger he felt when his wife died, and how that anger gave him a new understanding of the mourning rage that led Ilongot men to headhunt in retribution for a death. Rosaldo's argument in this essay is primarily about what it means to practice ethnography, about the mixture of "blindness and insight" (he borrows the phrase from Paul de Man) that is part of anthropologists' and natives' understanding of the social processes in which they take part. He did not come to appreciate the final truth of headhunting rituals all of a sudden, he writes. He just understood for the first time the real force of the desire for revenge. His position had changed from that of one outside the process of mourning to that of one inside.

But these fundamental issues of ethnography aside, it is clear that some missionaries and anthropologists seriously misapprehended the relation between ritual and emotion. They often failed to take account of the ways in which rituals can produce, rather than simply be a forum for, emotional reactions. They therefore regularly mistook as insincere people who were caught up in the communal emotions of an important ritual. People who cry at weddings do not always do so because of their specific feelings about the bride or groom, but because of what the ceremony itself means. People who cry at funerals often do so despite, rather than because of, their relationship to the deceased. Important rituals are designed to elicit strong emotions, which always seem natural and right to the participants.

The early interpreters had the most trouble understanding funeral ceremonies in which people were joyful. Moose notes that not everyone at a Korean funeral is adequately solemn. "Many in the procession are neither relatives nor friends, but are bent on having a good time and drinking all the free wine they want. Often the men that carry the bier are so full of bad wine that they can hardly walk, and so swing from side to side as they go," he writes. Nonetheless, they weep and wail as much as the family. "These bearers and the mourners keep up a sort of wail that cannot be described, but will never be forgotten if

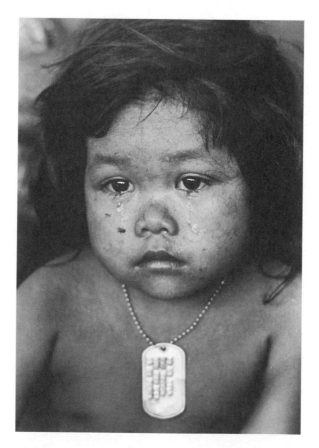

Cambodian girl crying, Phnom Penh, March 1975. David Hume Kennerly, *Cambodian Girl* (1975). Courtesy David Hume Kennerly.

once heard. It can be easily heard for a half mile, and nothing more weird in the way of a noise can be imagined."

In addition to such questionable crying, according to anthropologist Eugene Knez, at large costly funerals in Korea, "professional mourners of Fang-shang would expel evil spirits, and other professional 'weeping maids,' would participate," allowing superstition and questionable commerce to sully the proceedings. Laurentius Bollig, in Micronesia in the early part of this century, found a similar combination of calculation and bad manners among the Kanakas of the Truk atoll:

> Wailing Truk women look like hyenas, they are so dirty, disheveled, and swollen with tears. But it is regarded as cold-blooded to be reserved and not to let oneself be disturbed by the sight. True pity is rare among the Kanakas. The lamenting of the dead is more traditional, bound up with striving to furnish proof that they were fond of the deceased. The same women who now wail in a way that would melt stone can be seen sitting together, laughing and smoking, two minutes later. I myself once tested the seriousness of such a situation, and I was able to spirit away all grief in an instant with a little piece of tobacco.

The Koreans and Trukese are faulted not so much for their "weird" display as for their insincerity. Stopping and starting on cue, alternating between observance and everyday pleasures, these mourners break a seemingly fundamental rule of Western weeping: they appear to have ulterior motives; they appear to be less than overwhelmed.

Not all Western visitors took such a jaundiced or cynical view, of course, and some found a way to recast foreign rituals in Western emotional terms. In his study of the Tlinget, natives of Alaska, Livingston F. Jones argued that they made the same kinds of discriminations between true and false grief as he and his readers did, however much the surrounding customs and rituals might vary. "Widows painted their faces black as a sign of mourning," he explained. "If a widow's face was streaked from flowing tears, people pitied her, as they believed she truly missed her husband. But if no such streaks were visible they disliked her and talked about her, believing that she did not care for her husband." And although we might find it an odd practice to shave our heads or paint our faces black as signs of mourning, Jones writes, "we should remember that this was an expression of their grief. No people in the world have keener anguish over the loss of loved ones than the natives of Alaska. We have heard wailings from them that would melt the hardest heart to tears."

R. S. Rattray, writing about the Ashanti in the 1910s, makes the obvious point that not everyone at a funeral carries the same load of grief. At a typical Ashanti funeral, he writes, "the firing of guns, the weeping and lamentations, the half-drunken jollity of the crowds, the songs, the dancing, the drumming, the nauseating stench of the body, the heat and the dust, all combine to drive away the European spectator of such scenes." But although

> every one generally becomes very drunk . . . we should not pass a very severe judgment on this account. Grief and sorrow are very real where the clan (blood) relations are concerned, for the tears demanded by social custom are none the less a token of genuine grief. For others, not clansmen and women, such occasions are perhaps not so tragic, and on this account these rites may seem to the uninstructed to be somewhat heartless shows, as mirth and jollity are not altogether absent.

Many anthropologists have recognized that just as the presence of mirth at a funeral does not mean that a people is heartless, neither does ritualized weeping necessarily mean that the tears are false. Clyde Harrell, writing about funeral rites in Taiwan in the 1970s, for instance, makes the obvious distinction: "The loud, almost melodious wailing is a required part of the ritual for some mourners, and when an old person dies at the end of a full life, it is often merely perfunctory. But for someone . . . who died in what should have been the prime of life, the grief is real and so are the tears." The Dogon of the Sudan make a similar distinction. At the funeral of a child, sadness and tears are the norm, and the whole community joins the family in weeping and wailing. The death of an old person, however, "is the occasion for a gathering including dances and rejoicing; the young men who have come from neighboring villages think more about courting the girls than about weeping for the deceased, the dances last all night."

Mourning rituals are often determined by a culture's view of the hereafter. In the Chinese countryside, according to Emily Ahern, people also cry to ensure the passage from this world to the next. They believe that on the seventh day after the funeral the deceased

> is allowed one last glimpse of his living relatives. In anticipation of the terrible grief and sorrow the ancestor must feel on that day, the descendants rise very early to make offerings and to weep for him. They say, "If we get up early enough to wail before the ancestor finds out he is really dead, then his own sorrow will be lessened. The more we weep, the less he must."

Here weeping is performed *for* the dead, quite literally.

The Aymara of Peru, much as the Victorians did, believe that the souls of children, since they are innocent, necessarily go to heaven. Funerals for children are therefore more joyous than those for older people. "In fact," writes anthropologist Harry Tschopik, Jr., "it is imperative that the parents of a dead child do not weep for it, for this prevents its soul from going to heaven." Many people in Brazil also believe that the deceased child is a "little angel" and should not be wept over: Euclides da Cunha wrote in 1944 that "the death of a child is a holiday. In the hut the poor parents' guitars twang joyfully amid the tears. . . ." Landis reports that in Korea if a child dies under the age of eight, no mourning is worn. "For an infant under three months," he writes, "there is not even wailing."

A woman who worked as a health care volunteer in Mali for several years told me she had been severely reprimanded for crying at the death of a child in the Fulani family she was living with. It was acceptable to cry at the death of an older person, but to cry at the death of a child was to question the wisdom of Allah, who had decided to take the child away. The volunteer reinterpreted this explanation—or more precisely, she denied it—and concluded that the ban on crying was a way to maintain some sort of equilibrium under such harsh circumstances. In a culture in which infant mortality is high, to indulge in one's grief would be too emotionally expensive.

Nancy Scheper-Hughes, in *Death Without Weeping* (1992), a study of death and violence in rural Brazil, discusses this same issue, as her title suggests. She found that the joyful funerals for children that da Cunha, Gilberto Freyre, and others had described a half century earlier had been replaced by very muted ceremonies, with little joy or grief. Scheper-Hughes interprets women's lack of grief in various ways, including as a gesture of defiance by women who are often impregnated against their will. She notes that none of the American arguments about the necessity of grief, the stages of normal grieving, or repression make sense in this context. The women's lack of grief is a culturally appropriate response, and therefore has no psychological repercussions. And the question of sincerity is beside the point. The decision not to cry, whether it be individual or communal, is as multiply determined as the decision to weep.

The anthropologists Paul and Laura Bohannan provided a neat parable of this point in the 1950s. They described a scene in a Nigerian village where it is customary for the men to dig the grave while the women wail formalized dirges and ululations. As they were preparing the grave for one man, however, "one of the women drew the attention of the others to the fact that the youngest daughter was actually crying, whereupon the women turned to her and told her to shut up this real crying, that she could not do this, and that she must wail in the same way as the others, with songs and ululation." What is important in the culture of emotional expression is not individual feeling but the expectations of the group, which may or may not coincide with what is most important to the individual.

Many cultures attempt to limit the amount of crying people do. In central Thailand, it is believed to be "inauspicious" to let teardrops fall on a dead body. Anyone who succumbs to tears is taken away from the corpse. People believe that the soul of the dead person may be having trouble separating from the body, according to one anthropologist, and crying relatives "make it difficult for the soul of the deceased to depart from this existence."

The Zuni, according to Ruth Benedict, cry for four days, after which the chief says that the death happened four years ago, and that since it happened so long ago it is now time to stop mourning and forget. Benedict takes this to be typical of Zuni culture, which prized rationality and control over emotional experience and display at all times. But many cultures with no fear of emotional display in general are nonetheless intent on stopping the tears of mourners. The Sahih Bukhari, an Islamic holy text, states that "it is not legal for a woman who believes in Allah and the Last Day to mourn for more than three days for any dead person except her husband, for whom she should mourn for four months and ten days." Prince Maximilian, in his 1833 expedition up the Missouri River heard a chief reprimanding people who were weeping over a dead warrior, saying, "Why do you lament and cry?—see, I do not cry: he is gone into the other country, and we cannot awaken him." The chief of Santal groups, after the first day of weeping, tells the family: "Do not be constantly grieving; he is gone, he is happy; we shall also one day in the future have to go. If we should be continually crying, our body would suffer, our work would also be neglected; . . . from to-day keep your soul down with a stone-rock." Chippewa were taught not to weep at death, not even at the death of nearest relatives; if they wept at the loss of a child, they would be more likely to lose another. Turnbull writes that the Pygmies tried to conceal their regret and avoid any excessive show of grief: "The uncomfortable fact of death has to be obliterated from the memory as quickly and effectively as possible, and the band, which has received a blow at its strength, must be rejuvenated in an exaggerated display of all the things pleasing to the forest—good hunting, singing, dancing, [and] feasting." In central Celebes, if someone cries after the corpse has been placed in the coffin, "a chicken is immediately slaughtered in order to undo the crying." The Bororo customarily burst into lamentations whenever they are reminded of the deceased, and so to curtail weeping they burn all of the dead person's belongings. This has the added benefit of keeping the soul from returning to try to get his or her things.

In all of these cases, crying is prohibited by beliefs that override the culture's understanding that the loss of a loved one prompts tears, and in all cases neither "heartlessness" nor "genuine emotion" is the issue, but a culturally determined agreement, sometimes vague, sometimes precise, about what constitutes sufficient mourning. Euripides expressed the Greek view when he wrote that one should "waste not fresh tears over old griefs." Dr. Bruce D. Perry of the Texas Children's Hospital and Baylor Medical School, expresses the current medical consensus in saying that grieving after six months is a sign of pathology.

But few attempts to curb the desire to cry in bereavement are ever fully successful, and in cultures where it is outlawed, weeping relatives must often be forcibly removed from the scene. In cultures like those of northern Europe, in which public weeping is frowned upon and wailing is rare, funerals are most often the scene of quiet tears and sniffling, but occasional sobs and "breakdowns" occur. Missionaries from Europe, as they attempted to replace native funeral rites with Christian ones, wrote of having to quiet the wailing in their congregations in order to get on with the liturgy, and mixed rituals of various kinds have sprung up around the globe. Mourning can encompass sorrow, despondency, gloom, melancholy, and despair complemented by relief, release, disengagement, fear, guilt, and other emotions for which English has no names. These emotions can come in waves or coexist, and each is emphasized in different rituals and practices in different cultures. Sometimes these rituals demand crying; sometimes they demand that the crying cease. In all cultures, such ritual performance can feel adequate or inadequate to any individual, but by and large they tend to do the work that they are meant to do.

If our culture expects us to sniffle and have the experience of holding back most of our tears (or even bravely not cry at all, like Jackie Kennedy), most of us will comply. If our culture expected us to weep with abandonment for weeks at a time, or for twenty-four hours straight, or to perform other such feats of emotional stamina, most of us would be able to manage. The performance of the ritual is obviously not enough in itself to generate the right response—belief is necessary as well. Peter Buck has written that young Maori who have been educated in English schools lose their ability to cry at will, and find it difficult to weep at the proper time in ceremonies. But when the general tenets of the culture are accepted, the ritual produces the appropriateness of feeling the missionaries and early anthropologists so often found lacking. The young woman who was afraid of becoming a Camus character in her own life by not crying at her grandmother's funeral did in fact cry. The power of the ritual to evoke the proper response had worked its mundane magic.

Matrimony, Masochism, and Melancholia

In the late nineteenth century in the Andaman Islands, Edward Horace Man described how "the bridegroom . . . allows himself to be led slowly, sometimes almost dragged, towards his fiancée, who, if she be young, generally indulges in a great display of modesty, weeping and hiding her face." Diamond Jenness, writing of the Copper Eskimos in the 1920s, assumed that the bride wept "because she is leaving her familiar surroundings and going out into a new and unknown world." Martin Gusinde, also in the 1920s, suggested the same was true for the Fireland Indians of Tierra del Fuego: "In the heart of the [bride] the bitterness of the parting outweighs the happiness of now being able to establish her own home. Sometimes silent tears roll down her cheeks when she feels a certain loneliness in her own hut with the family group of her husband."

As with funerals, weddings often require crying. According to Lucy Mair, writing in the 1930s, among the Ganda people of Africa the bride was expected to weep loudly, and although in the past this weeping had been done publicly and by the 1930s was done in private, it was nonetheless expected. Among the Hausa of North Africa, the expectation of weeping was so strong, one informant told Mary Smith in the 1940s, that "if the tears wouldn't flow they put spit on their eyes instead!" The exclamation point serves to underline how unthinkable it would be to have a wedding without tears and, again, their artifice.

According to Bernard Gallin, writing about Taiwan in the 1960s, brides cry to satisfy their parents. The departure of the bride in Taiwan

is accompanied by a good deal of crying by the girl, her mother, and other women of the immediate family. These tears, of course, reflect

sincere regret at parting as well as the girl's fear at leaving the famil-
iarity of her home and family. There is no doubt, however, that
much of the girl's weeping is a conventional display of filial piety to
show that she regrets leaving the home where she has been brought
up and treated so well all her life. To smile on this occasion or not to
weep for all to see would be extremely disrespectful toward her parents.

Again the tears are not just the spontaneous overflow of upwelling
emotion but a response to societal expectations. The brides cry, at least
in part, because brides expect to and are expected to cry. In Radcliffe-
Brown's functionalist description, "In all instances we may say that the
purpose of the rite is to bring about a new state of the affective dispositions that regulate the conduct of persons to one another, either by
reviving sentiments that have lain dormant, or producing a recognition
of a change in the condition of personal relations." We cry, in a slightly
circular formulation, in order to "recognize" a change that is significant
enough to demand tears.

And as with funeral tears, these tears have a kind of contagious efficacy. Younghill Kang, in his autobiography *The Grass Roof* (1931),
wrote of watching his aunt prepare for marriage in Korea:

> My new aunt wept and wept at the parting and used up all the long
> silk kerchiefs which were laid out ready for her use. Two dozen
> there were—for a bride is supposed to cry hard at this time, whether
> she is sincere or not. But my new aunt wept so hard that my cousin
> Ok-Dong-Ya wept too with sympathy, and came out of the bride's
> room weeping, where I found her on the porch, behind a pillar,
> shaken with sobs.

Tears mark the impossible desire to go and remain, to celebrate and
mourn, to embrace the new and hold on to the old. And watching
someone else cry can make us realize our own conflicted desires, our
own embeddedness in and uneasiness with our place in the social
world.

Marriage is a ceremony honoring the taking on of new roles, and
tears always accompany ceremonies and representations of role fulfill-

ment. Funerals mark such role changes—from husband to widower, from child to adult, sometimes from being a parent to being childless. Rites of passage—bar mitzvahs, graduations, confirmations, initiation rites—are also great occasions for tears. The adolescents involved are not just being reaffirmed as members of society, they are inhabiting new roles within it, and the tears they shed mark their ritual enactment of these new roles. The tears their relatives and neighbors shed show their recognition that these people are no longer boys but men, no longer girls but women, or, at least, no longer children but adolescents. And weddings, of course, mark the initiation into new roles not only for the bride and groom but for their mothers, fathers, siblings, and friends, who also cry. The fact that such ceremonial tears might have social functions does not in any way diminish the dread, perturbation, and anxiety that is expressed by bridal tears, or the very real power of grief.

Mair suggests yet another reason for bridal tears. The bride cries not just from "modesty," or at the thought of leaving her parents, but "at losing her freedom and passing into the power of a man who could treat her just as he liked." As Vera St. Erlich wrote, remembering her own marriage in Yugoslavia in the 1930s, "It is no joke to renounce everything, your life, your freedom, and go away into a strange home, where you know nobody and nobody knows you, to call a strange mother your own, a strange house your own, make an alien world your own. . . . I cried and cried and would have cried a long time, had [my sister] not come." For many women, the change in status from daughter to wife can mean more work and less freedom than they had as girls. Even if the bride doesn't feel that loss heavily, and even if the ceremonies have become private rather than public, as Simon Messing writes of the Amhara of Ethiopia, still "men like to believe that, though there are no tears in public, brides weep silently, out of fear;— the 'vanquished sex.'"

Wedding tears can thus share with funeral tears a mixture of acting or posing and sincerity, of grief and relief, of fear and resolution, of self-congratulation and self-loathing. And as in the case of death, marriage can bring on not only tears at the occasion but melancholy afterward. In his 1917 article "Mourning and Melancholia," Freud offered a theory of the relationship of mourning to self-hatred. Mourning, Freud writes, is a normal reaction to grief, to the loss of a loved object, whether a person or an ideal, or, we might add, a former self. A loved object has been powerfully "cathected," or invested with psychic energy, and whenever this energy is fixed on an object, its removal is a source of pain and distress. Each time one of the memories and hopes associated with the former loved one or former self comes to mind, the mourner must painfully remove and redirect these cathexes, and mourning is the name we give to this protracted process.

Melancholia (or depression, we would now say) is also a reaction to the loss of a loved object. Instead of mourning the lost object, the melancholic seems to be mourning his or her own lost ego. In both mourning and depression there is a feeling of dejection, a loss of interest in the outside world, and inhibitions of feeling and activity. The difference is that in depression there is also "a lowering of the self-regarding feelings to a degree that finds utterance in self-reproaches and self-revilings," Freud writes, as well as "an extraordinary fall in self-esteem, an impoverishment of the ego on a grand scale." The ego turns on itself, in effect, as if it were responsible for the loss.

Depression, in Freud's understanding, then, is simply mourning gone bad. In successful mourning, one remembers the dead, and each time, although it is painful, reinvests elsewhere the energy that had been bound up with the dead person. This means, in effect, that one stops loving the dead person and begins to think of them as someone to fondly remember. Melancholia includes refusing to give up the dead, and the only way to do this, Freud suggests, is by some form of self-denial or masochism. The melancholic bride (or the postpartum depressed mother), Freudian theory suggests, may turn against herself, blaming herself for the loss of freedom and promise her new role implies. Unwilling to give up her former self, she falls into masochistic melancholia.

This is obviously more metaphor than science at work, but it may help explain some ritualized forms of masochism in the mourning rituals of many cultures. Among the Bororo of Brazil, the Ona of Tierra del Fuego, the Mbuti in Africa, and several groups of Native Americans and Australian aborigines, mourners make cuts on their arms and legs as a standard part of the mourning process. Karl von den Steinen described a man named Coquiero in Brazil who alternately cut himself and cried after his wife died: "Coquerio in his hut, made cuts on his arms and legs, which became covered with scabs of coagulated blood. . . . He sat down silently at the side, he sobbed and wept. He did not have any adornment besides the black rope around his body, which he had spun and interwoven out of his wife's hair. His cheeks were wet with tears; he pressed his eyes as if the weeping were painful." Another anthropologist describes a Bororo mother "weeping, wailing and jibbering in a low, squeaky voice which was almost gone, her body emaciated, covered with gashes and besmeared with blood," while the other "relatives . . . cry[ied] and gash[ed] themselves with stones and bamboo knives." Self-mutilation and tears are always part of the same process in the beginning; in Tierra del Fuego, for instance, "the women always inflict these scratches on themselves amidst whimpering, groaning wails, or constant weeping." But as the death recedes, self-torture can almost completely replace weeping.

Martin Gusinde described a man named Saipoten who repeatedly cut his legs in mourning, two years after the death of his child:

With a sharp stone splinter, he cuts a shallow wound 20 millimeters long and 5 millimeters high directly below the kneecap by horizontal back-and-forth motions. With the splinter, by superficial guidance on the skin, he gives the blood, only slowly gushing out, the direction now to be taken toward the foot. From the wound, by slowly guiding onward the thin thread of blood, he first draws a long line 2 to 4 millimeters wide over the upper edge of the shinbone, down almost to the tarsal bone. This may use up 15 minutes. Now he must either again scratch in the wound anew at the surface or knead its immediate surroundings with the fingers so that more blood flows. . . . He was occupied with this for 90 minutes, during which time he never turned his eyes away from his wound, did not utter a sound, and, with a sad expression on his face, shed a few tears. He drew seven lines of blood. Finally he raised his head again and stared in front of him, deep in thought. He kept both legs drawn in, bent at the knee, so that every visitor or occupant of the hut could see his work of self-torture on his lower right leg. . . . Saipoten spent the time from eight o'clock in the morning until four in the afternoon in his hut, demonstrating his grief.

This is one of the calmer rituals of self-immolation. Among the Australians studied by Herbert Basedow in the 1920s, the ritual was more frenzied:

> Then, as the blood pours down over their faces and bodies, the wailing is accentuated with additional vehemence. At times some terrible wounds are inflicted during this part of the obsequies. The widow often cuts a long, median gash right along the scalp. The men, on the other hand, flourish their big stone knives, with which they hack their bodies in a revolting manner. In the Katherine River district, the nearest relatives on the male side not infrequently cut their thighs in such a way that almost the entire mass of muscles on the extensor side is severed, and the man makes himself hors de combat. A general melee now ensues, during which women deface themselves and each other without restraint, the places of predilection being the head and back. Each mourner submits to the mutilation voluntarily and without flinching. The women, too, make free use of their nulla-nullas, with which they crack each other over the head. But a short while after they will seat themselves in groups about the body, with their arms tenderly thrown around each other, crying bitterly.

And such physical violence sometimes goes even further. Ojibwa men "stuck knives, and needles, and thorns through their skin and flesh, and principally through the fattest parts of the chest and the muscles of the arm." At the death of a husband or son (but not a daughter), Blackfeet Indian women were known to go so far as to remove one or more joints from a finger.

These excruciatingly painful rituals are an explicit expression of the pain of loss. The desire to die is another. Colin Turnbull tells of a Pygmy woman who tried to hang herself when her mother died, to cite just one instance, and numerous cultures have semiritualized practices in which mourners symbolically throw themselves, sobbing, into the grave. And the desire to inflict pain is a third. The Aranda inflict wounds on themselves and each other. One woman, after having beaten herself with a digging stick and dragged herself through brambles, came to the grave where she

> threw herself upon it, tearing up the earth with her hands and being literally danced upon by the other women. Then all the [female relatives] threw themselves on the grave, [some] cutting and hitting each other about the body until they were streaming with blood. Each of them carried a digging-stick, which was used unsparingly on its owner's head and on those of the others, no one attempting to ward off the blows, which they even invited. . . . The weeping and wailing of the women who were standing round seemed to drive them almost frenzied, and the blood, streaming down their bodies over the white pipeclay, gave them a ghastly appearance. At last only the old mother was left crouching alone, utterly exhausted and moaning weakly on the grave.

And this infliction of wounds is mirrored in the various ceremonies of privation, in which, despite the needs, say, of a dead man's wife and children, his house is burned to the ground, or his llamas sacrificed, or his possessions buried. Among the Blackfeet of the northwestern Plains, for instance, the weeping and wailing of the relatives was taken as a signal to the others to make a run for the dead person's property, taking his horses, weapons, and other wealth. Anything the deceased owned was up for grabs, even if that meant that a man's widow and children were thereby impoverished. The widow could claim these things, but doesn't, preferring privation in the same way that self-mutilators prefer pain.

And such actions are found in some form or other in many other cultures. In *The Iliad*, Priam besmears himself with dung in his grief. Achilles covers himself with dirt, tears his hair, and wallows in dust on hearing of Patroklos's death. Hecuba lacerates her cheeks. Ernest Hemingway, doing a bit of amateur anthropology, tells the story of an Indian in Michigan who sliced open his own stomach when his wife died in childbirth, and of course Romeo and Juliet are simply the best known of the innumerable literary characters who kill themselves in grief.

This leaves open the obvious question: if tears express pain, why do it so inadequately that one must also slice off one's fingers or stab oneself in the belly? Self-mutilation, from Freud's perspective, is a ritual enactment of melancholia, a maladaptive turning against the self. But in these cultures, it is not maladaptive but normal. Just as funeral crying is a ritualized intensification of feeling—people most often walk in and out of funeral services dry-eyed and cry while there—so are the rituals of mutilation and privation meant to intensify the pain.

In his introduction to a recent collection of essays, Dennis Klass writes that "the dominant twentieth-century model holds that the function of grief and mourning is to cut bonds with the deceased." The essays in his collection argue instead that maintaining a continuing bond with the deceased is the best way to experience the healthy resolution of grief: not de-cathecting but re-cathecting, in Freud's terms. Slicing and stabbing at one's body maintains a state of pain and thereby a living, felt connection with the dead, and reverses the physiological process by which tears help return the body to a state of rest. This is in one sense an escape from a world in which the dead person is irretrievably gone, but it is also a refusal to allow oneself to escape from one's pain, and thereby an attempt to live constantly in the presence of the loss.

The lifelong mourning of widows in Italy and elsewhere is meant to do the same thing, the black dress and veil being a constant reminder to the self and others of the dead husband. George Bird Grinnell, crossing the American prairies in the 1880s, recounts coming across a grieving woman on the trail. She was "an old wrinkled woman, who was crouched in the sage brush, crying and lamenting for some one, as if her heart would break," Grinnell writes. "On inquiring if any one had lately died, I was told she was mourning for a son she had lost more than twenty years before."

Communities

Perhaps the polar opposite of this attempt to eternalize mourning is represented by those cultures in which funeral rituals and crying are meant to sever all relations with the dead. When a husband dies among the Tarahumara, an Indian tribe of northern Mexico, the weeping widow pleads with her husband, now that he has died and left, to stay away for good. A mother wails at her dead infant: "Now go away! Don't come back anymore, now that you are dead. Don't come at night to nurse at my breast. Go away, and do not come back!" A father says to his buried child: "Don't come back to ask me to hold your hand, or to do things for you. I shall not know you anymore. Don't come walking around here, but stay away." Similar weeping protestations in the Chaco of Argentina and Bolivia use a slightly different tack. In order to keep the dead away, elaborate weeping is offered as a

Grief and religious exultation mix in this painting of the artist's wife. Charles Wilson Peale, *Rachel Weeping* (1772). Philadelphia Museum of Art: Given by the Barra Foundation, Inc.

tribute, a sign of the community's great love and respect for the dead, and this tribute is supposed to keep the deceased spirit from returning and wreaking havoc.

Our own relation to mourning might be said to fall somewhere in the middle: we seek to remember the dead, hence memorial services. But we also have a fairly clear sense of what "normal" grief is: that for it to be normal it needs to follow a process and come to an end. An enormous body of self-help literature, starting with Elizabeth Kübler-Ross's books on mourning, has argued that we, as a culture, have inadequate rituals and fail to mourn properly without a little help. A fact sheet developed by the National Resource Center for Crisis Nurseries and Respite Care Services, funded by the U.S. Department of Health and Human Services, describes the difference between grief and mourning: "Grief is one's own personal experience of loss. Mourning, on the other hand is 'grief gone public.'" Grief, the fact sheet says, can involve shock, denial, anger, guilt, fear, exhaustion, depression, confusion, and many other emotions. "All of these emotions are a normal part of the grief and mourning process." And if we go through the appropriate mourning rituals but still have trouble with our grief, we need to go through the correct "process." According to Kübler-Ross, this means passing through five stages: denial, anger, bargaining, depression, and acceptance. Rather than seeing these emotional attitudes as overdetermined, as layered upon each other, she sees them as stages through which one passes on the way from the shock of mortality to mental health. Making a narrative out of the jumble of competing emotions in grief makes therapeutic sense—it is a way for people to name, give shape to, and help manipulate their own experience. The process is also, in relative terms, extremely individualistic. The process is entirely one of grief rather than of mourning, completely private rather than public.

Some anthropologists have suggested that the more communal the society, the more weeping is part of the funeral ritual. The relative quiet of funerals in England, Scandinavia, and the U.S., for instance, has been explained as the result of an individualist culture in which emotion is largely seen as a private fact of life. The cultures in which professionals are hired with the idea that the more mourning the merrier, goes this line of reasoning, are cultures in which the community comes together to heal what it sees as a communal wound. The Chinese belief that mourners' tears comfort the dead, too, suggests that crying at a funeral is something done not out of an individual's sense of loss but because of a community's sense of what must be done. Our lack of weeping is a mark of how little we value the community. At the same time, we also believe in the necessity of and the right to emotional expression. Since our fairly staid funeral rites have very little if any accommodation for wailing and screaming, the rites are very inadequate as a form of communal recognition of individual grief. Our communal grieving does not answer our individual need to experience and express our grief.

But in both individualist and communal societies, the community norms determine the duration and intensity of weeping, and following the rules ensures the continuance of the community. Radcliffe-Brown noticed that in the Andaman Islands there were four main ceremonial occasions when people wept—at funerals, rites of passage, marriage, and ceremonies of reconciliation. When two people or two groups who had been enemies are reconciled, there is weeping on both sides. At the climax of initiation ceremonies for boys and girls, there is communal weeping. And as in many cultures, there are tears at weddings. Radcliffe-Brown, influenced by Arnold van Gennep's work on rites of passage, decided that tears were always present at times of the reinvigoration of social bonds, of the "affirmation of solidarity." Weddings, initiations, and reconciliations all involve an affirmation of social bonds, in most cases after some kind of forced separation. Likewise, Radcliffe-Brown notes, during funeral rites the mourners are separated from the rest of Andaman society: there are special rules for what kinds of paint and ornaments they may wear, what they can eat, and where they can go. At the end of the series of rituals, there is a ceremony called "the shedding of tears," after which the mourners resume their daily lives. Radcliffe-Brown argues that as in the case of the other crying rituals, this one expresses the "return" of the mourners to the full community.

This idea, that tears mark the return of the community from a time of exceptional activity to one of normal interchange, is analogous to the way tears mark the body's return to normal functioning after periods of exceptional arousal. Just as the sympathetic nervous system arouses the individual and prepares it for action, and the parasympathetic system returns the body to its normal state, often accompanied by tears, so the social group is thrown into exceptional activity by marriages and deaths, after which the community, weeping together, returns to its everyday, normal functioning, taking account of the changes that have occurred. Both individuals and communities cry as they return to a normal state following this period of arousal and adaptation. And the social return to normal community life after a ceremony may very well entail, as a matter of course, the return to homeostasis of the bodies of the participants. The portentous time, with its rare activities and demands, is over, and the parasympathetic nervous systems of all the participants kicks in at roughly the same time. This return does not require any "working through" of grief or guilt in order to be accomplished, and the crying means nothing for the future well-being of the individuals or the group. All it means is that the ceremony has done its work. In most places, that means that both some kind of real adaptation and quite a bit of crying have taken place.

6

Tears of Revenge, Seduction, Escape, and Empathy

And so the brides weep and the Tierra del Fuegans mingle their tears with blood from self-inflicted wounds, refusing to accept the loss of love, freedom, or their own sense of what the future should hold. The participants in these ceremonies of resistance can seem infantile, like a baby who screams at having its diaper changed. Or they can seem heroic, if we view them as social protesters, as Kay Carmichael suggests we should in her *Ceremony of Innocence: Tears, Power and Protest* (1991). A few cultures have found the tears of its victims to be such a significant form of protest, in fact, that they have had the audacity to outlaw them.

Tears may come involuntarily, but they are always a goad to action as well. In public life, they are frequently forms of emotional blackmail, as in the case of Sally Struthers's blandishments on late night TV, in which her tears are meant to elicit contributions to Save the Children, or when Jim Bakker or Jimmy Swaggart shed penitential tears in an attempt to keep their ministries afloat. The assumption here is that tears will spur others to pity or empathy and then to action.

Tears have power precisely because they can "change the environment" in which the crier finds himself or herself. Sometimes that means simply altering the attitude of the person or group to whom the tears are addressed—Struthers's or Swaggart's potential contributors, one's lover, one's creditors, one's therapist. Such transactions can be thought of as forms of seduction on the part of the crier, or of empathy on the part of the audience: the person who sends the weeping evangelist money feels sorry for him. Sometimes tears change the environment around the crier in a more imaginative sense, as Jean-Paul Sartre described in his examination of emotion: Sartre believed that some emotions had the ability to effect a "magical transformation" of the world, and he saw emotion as an escape hatch for unacceptable situations. And sometimes tears are meant to change the environment by motivating others, as in the case of funeral tears that are meant to bring a community's desire for revenge to a boil. Empathy, seduction, escape, and revenge are far from the only uses of tears, as should be clear already. But they are common ones, and worth a closer look.

Revenge

On February 10, 1996, a thirty-four-year-old woman named Demetria Nyirabahutu gave birth to her sixth child in a tent at the Kibumba refugee camp near Goma, Zaire. Her other five children had been lost when a Tutsi rebel group attacked the refugee camp in Rwanda where she had been living in 1994. When James C. McKinley, Jr., of the *New York Times* asked her if she missed her children, she averted her eyes and, with a hard face and voice, said yes. "I want to replace these children," she told the reporter. "Crying has no meaning to me. It is useless to cry." Appearing on the front page of the *Times* under the title "Anguish of Rwanda Echoed in a Baby's Cry," McKinley's piece reported the birth of twenty-eight hundred babies each month in the five refugee camps around Goma.

Despite its headline, the story never mentions a baby crying and the only reference to tears is Nyirabahutu's denial of their efficacy. The editor who wrote the headline drew a message about tears from a story in which there were none. Perhaps the editor saw the theoretical baby's tears as a symbolic stand-in for the dry-eyed mother, or as a fit-ting tribute to the story of deadly retribution between the Hutu and the Tutsi. Whether Nyirabahutu herself wanted the cycle of retribu-tion to end, the story doesn't say. After losing five children, she may not have had the energy to mourn, or the will for revenge, and this may be why she feels tears are useless.

Weeping and wailing at funerals have often been spurs to revenge. Among the Ifugao in the Philippines, for instance, a first set of funeral rituals honored the dead, while a second set, which followed immedi-ately and also included tears, were traditionally intended to gird the warriors in their quest for vengeance, as Renato Rosaldo has explained. The tears in this second ritual are goads to retributive head-hunting. This is why, in Sophocles' *Antigone*, Creon forbids mourning over the corpse of Antigone's brother. He worries that there is a "fatal purpose" in Antigone's grief—that is, he worries that her mourning will spur some kind of vengeance.

Antigone mourns anyway, and Creon has her imprisoned. Antigone dies while in prison for the crime of mourning, and Creon's son Haemon commits suicide when his beloved Antigone dies. Now Creon has further mourning worries on his hands. The chorus warns that Creon's wife Eurydice will kill herself if she does not cry at the news of her son's suicide: "There is danger in unnatural silence / No less than in excess of lamentation." Eurydice does indeed commit sui-cide, and by the end of the play Creon is pleading for his own swift death. Creon's edict against mourning brings about his own downfall.

In *Dangerous Voices: Women's Laments and Greek Literature*, Gail Holst-Warhaft has argued that in ancient Greece lamentation was one of women's main forms of public expression and therefore one of the areas in which they exercised public power. Beginning with Solon in the sixth century B.C., Holst-Warhaft claims, a series of laws were passed limiting public lamentation in order to contain the subversive potential of women's mourning, which was perceived as a direct threat to the Athenian state.

Other classicists—Margaret Alexiou in the 1970s, and S. C. Humphries more recently—suggest that the laws against mourning were aimed not at women but at the rich, whose use of professional mourners and other ostentatious displays were seen as divisive, and that however they may have affected women in particular, their primary goal was to squelch blood feuding. Prohibitions against funeral weeping and wailing show up in many classic plays besides *Antigone*, demonstrating that it was a live issue for at least half a century after Solon's reforms. Aeschylus's *Seven Against Thebes* and *Persians*, Sophocles' *Antigone*, and Euripides' *Medea* and *The Suppliants* all include scenes in which excessive mourning is castigated. In Sophocles' *Ajax*, the hero orders his wife Tecmessa into the house and forbids her any further public mourning, saying in disgust: "Truly woman is fond of lamentation." On the other hand, in Aeschylus's *Oresteia*, Electra condemns Clytemnestra for the sin of not mourning her husband.

Much more recently, in 1994, only a few hundred miles from the site where Creon and Solon outlawed excessive mourning, the military junta that ruled Ethiopia declared it a crime for mothers of "disappeared" sons to cry. By outlawing public tears, the junta denied these women an essential forum for demanding revenge and justice. The junta clearly feared that the crying of these grieving women might contain a "fatal purpose." The tears of women are thought to be dangerous in themselves, with special demands on our sympathies. As the producers of Struthers's commercials know, they can also be contagious.

Mark Twain gives us an indelible image of the relationship between mourning and revenge in *Huckleberry Finn*. He describes the thirty-year feud between the Grangerfords and the Sheperdsons with his usual mix of humor and horror at the human animal, but one of his main points is that the bloody feud had become customary. The participants no longer feel the enmity between the families very strongly, they just go about mindlessly gunning for each other. One of the Grangerford daughters, fourteen-year-old Emmeline, writes funereal doggerel such as the "Ode to Stephen Dowling Bots, Dec'd." ("Then list with tearful eye,/ Whilst I his fate do tell./ His soul did from this cold world fly,/ By falling down a well"). Emmeline writes her weepy elegies not for the people dying in her family but for people she reads about in obituaries. She draws crayon pictures of women weeping over their dead lovers, dead friends, dead pet birds. Twain uses Emmeline to make fun of the saccharine funerary art and poetry of his day, of sentimental culture in general, and of the inadequacy of this brand of art to respond to the violence of his society. He echoes the classic Greek tragedians in damning both blood feuds and the "excess of lamentation" that spurs them on. The title of Thomas Reed Turner's book on the assassination of Abraham Lincoln, *Beware the People Weeping*, also suggests how common classical images of revenge were for nineteenth-century American writers: it refers to the fact that when an effigy of Julius Caesar, complete with all of his knife wounds, was put on public display after his death, the crowd rioted and burned down the Senate.

A medieval Chinese folktale provides a metaphor for tears as a literal instrument of revenge. When a cruel emperor forces peasants to work day and night building the Great Wall, large numbers die from the cruel conditions. A young wife comes looking for her husband, who had been pressed into service, had died, and was buried under the Great Wall. Hearing the news, the wife bursts into a flood of tears, for several days on end, and many of the toilers weep with her. The resulting flood of tears washes away a length of over two hundred miles of the Great Wall. The woman's tears are her revenge. The relationship between mourning and vengeance has stayed alive in our culture in part through the long line of Mafia films by Francis Ford Coppola, Martin Scorcese, and a host of lesser filmmakers. Allison Anders's film *Mi vida loca* (1994), in its depiction of gunplay and revenge in East L.A. gang life deals with the same issues of gang-based blood feuding. The film depicts the culture of revenge that fuels the cycle of violence between gangs, and Anders suggests that both personal and cultural growth is needed to stop the cycle. Here she parts company with the Mafia film, in which tears are a spur to revenge. Instead, at key moments in the film, the growth needed to end the violence is represented by people learning to weep. Joseph Addison argued this alternative in the eighteenth century as well, based on classical sources: "When the Romans and Sabines were at War, and just upon the point of giving Battle, the Women, who were allied to both of them, interposed with so many Tears and Intreaties, that they prevented the mutual Slaughter which threatened both Parties, and united them together in a firm and lasting Peace. I would recommend this Example to our British Ladies, at a time when their Country is torn with so many unnatural Divisions. . . ." When Robert Bly suggests, in *Iron John*, that maturing into manhood requires learning how to grieve, he is suggesting something similar: grieving can offer an alternative to violence, an end to violence, rather than a spur to revenge.

Seduction

Jeremy Bentham noted in 1788 that most people believe that "the emotions of the body" are "probable indications of the temperature of the mind." But, he went on to advise, this is not something anyone should count on.

> A man may exhibit, for instance, the exterior appearances of grief, without really grieving at all, or at least in any thing near the proportion in which he appears to grieve. Oliver Cromwell, whose conduct indicated a heart more than ordinarily callous, was as remarkably profuse in tears. . . . To have this kind of command over one's self, was the characteristic excellence of the orator of ancient times.

And in America, tearful oratory was a living art, with politicians continuing to use tears on the stump at least until the 1890s, at which point it gradually began to go out of style.

Politicians remained dry-eyed through most of this century. In 1972 Edmund Muskie was famously run out of the presidential primary race when he cried in front of the press corps. Earlier in the campaign, before the New Hampshire primary, Muskie had been under attack by William Loeb, the rabidly conservative editor of the *Manchester Union Leader*, New Hampshire's largest daily newspaper. Using information and misinformation provided by the same Nixon plumbers who later brought us Watergate, Loeb told stories about Muskie's wife, suggesting that she was "emotionally unstable." Muskie hired a platform truck and parked outside Loeb's office, where he challenged Loeb to prove his accusations. As he spoke into the microphone, he at one point "broke into tears," according to the *New York*

Times and other reports.

The *Union Leader* and some of Muskie's rivals for the nomination then charged Muskie himself with emotional instability, suggesting that no one wanted a president who would burst into tears under pressure. Bob Dole, then chairman of the Republican National Committee, agreed that the tears proved that Muskie "lacked stability." For his part, Muskie insisted that melting snow—not tears—had adorned his cheeks that day, yet he also suggested, through spokespeople, that his display of emotion made him "more human" and should therefore help him with some voters. But in 1972 American voters were much more afraid of emotional instability than they were interested in the emotional availability of their leaders, and Muskie had to drop out of the race soon after.

Since Muskie, politicians have rediscovered the persuasiveness of tears. As one sign of how much things have changed, *Time* magazine published a squib in 1994 about former president George Bush crying while in office. "Bush, though no match for our current President, is a frequent weeper," the article reported. Tailhook scandal victim Paula

Bob Dole at Nixon's funeral, 1994. David Hume Kennerly, *Nixon's Funeral* (1994). Courtesy David Hume Kennerly.

Coughlin describes how Bush started to cry when she described her ordeal to him. He cried when his dog Millie's first litter was brought to him, upon hearing Dixie Carter sing the national anthem, and while listening to the Oak Ridge Boys perform on Air Force One. According to Barbara Bush, he cries over "touching, poignant things." These ready admissions of Bush's weeping show that tears are no longer the sign of mental instability they were twenty years earlier. But the *Time* headline, "Annals of Blubbering," signals that the activity is still far from respected, still a source of cultural comedy.

Bill Clinton tears up at all of the appropriate moments, that is, at moments when it is now considered men's responsibility to be teary-eyed: during moving invocations of patriotism, for instance, or when he wants to convince us that he "feels our pain." Criticism of Clinton's tears are not, as they were for Muskie, based on questions about his manliness or stability, but about his sincerity. At Commerce Secretary Ron Brown's funeral, Clinton was filmed laughing and joking with a colleague until he realized that he was on camera; he immediately became serious and tears came to his eyes. Rush Limbaugh ran the tape in slow motion on his TV show numerous times over the next weeks, playing on the common perception of Clinton's insincerity and sending his studio audience into howls of laughter. But it is possible that Clinton, in proving his capacity for tears and his ability to control them at the same time, may have helped rather than hurt himself.

Perhaps the clearest one-man example of changing times is Bob Dole, who by the time he slammed Muskie for emotional instability in 1972 had already been in politics for over twenty years and had never been seen teary-eyed in public. He teared up in 1976 when he announced his vice-presidential run in his hometown of Russell, Kansas, thanking his friends for their support when he was recovering from his wounds after World War II. (After his defeat in the election, he told reporters that he was taking his loss in stride; afterward he simply went home and slept like a baby: "Every two hours I woke up and cried.") In 1983 he visibly cried on the Senate floor while delivering a eulogy to the surgeon who had tended his war wounds. In other words, Dole allowed himself to cry only twice in his first forty years in public life, and then only when referring to his war wounds.

But in the 1990s he was a changed man. He was filmed crying at Nixon's funeral in 1992. In 1993 he wept on camera as he related to CBS's "60 Minutes" the story of his father visiting him in the hospital in 1945. He teared up recounting his story of the war on several other occasions during his campaign for the presidency in 1996, repeating his tearful visit to Russell for the cameras twice. One of Dole's biographers, Stanley G. Hilton, argued that the instances of crying were significant lapses from a life of stoicism, bred by a typically severe Midwestern family at mid-century. Thomas Powers, reviewing two Dole biographies in the *New York Review of Books*, saw Dole's tears as proof that, despite his well-known toughness and even meanspiritedness, he is "not an unfeeling man." It would be more correct to say that Dole cried in order to prove that he was a man with feelings: his tears were produced for the cameras, in a 1990s version of kissing babies, designed to show that he had the right kind of stuff to be president.

But this may not fully explain why Dole cried at Nixon's funeral. It couldn't just have been sadness at the loss, since Dole had gotten through many funerals of friends and family dry-eyed. My guess is that in Nixon's fall, Dole had had an empathetic glimpse of how a man can bring about his own Greek tragedy. Dole, who renounced a respected career in the Senate for his doomed run at the presidency, was trapped by his own hubris in ways that recall Nixon, his old mentor. One can imagine, watching Dole cry at the funeral, that he had projected himself into Nixon's experience only to have it reflect back on his own. And therein lies the very thin line between empathy and self-pity.

If public men have been given new permission to cry—even Al Gore, known for his woodenness, can well up on occasion—women in politics now feel an equal and opposite prohibition. No women representatives, senators, or governors cry in public if they can help it. Like Muskie, Pat Schroeder was counted out of the presidential race when she cried in public in 1988. She was not attacked, as Muskie was, for being mentally unstable, but for fulfilling gender expectations, for being a weak woman. When Schroeder retired from Congress in 1996, Representative John D. Dingell said, at a roast in her honor, that Schroeder "leaves us with a rich legislative record: the Violence Against

Women Act. The Economic Equity Act. And one most of you have never heard of: the Emotional Freedom Act. That's the one that makes tearful Presidential candidates immune from ridicule." Dingell's joke might suggest that the tide is turning once again, but if so not very far. Hillary Clinton has been routinely condemned by some of her critics for being too masculine, too hard and cold, but one can imagine the criticism that would rain down on her if she were to cry on camera.

It may be that the current state of crying in politics is simply one manifestation of the general trend: politicians have been grabbing for the center, claiming to represent not a liberal or conservative fringe but the very middle of the electorate's wishes, governing by poll results. The men who cry prove that they are not too manly; the women who maintain stoic control of their emotions prove that they are not too "feminine." In any case, politics now has the distinction of being the central arena of public life in which men cry more often than women.

Similar changes in public crying are occurring elsewhere as well. Take the case of Nikolai Ryzhkov, the "Weeping Bolshevik," as he was dubbed. Ryzhkov, who was the Soviet prime minister during much of Mikhail Gorbachev's reign, got the nickname when he cried in front of the press while visiting Armenia after the devastating earthquake of 1988. His opposition treated him like a clown or an object of ridicule. In running for Parliament in 1995, he felt compelled to justify his tears and counter his opposition's insinuations that his tears meant that he was too weak and flighty to be in a position of power. "Visibly stiffening when reminded of the name 'weeping Bolshevik' which he was given after his emotional outburst," wrote Timothy Heritage of Reuter's during the campaign, "he implied others would have wept if they had seen the horrors he saw in Armenia." Ryzhkov believed that the public could be persuaded to see his tears not as weakness but as an appropriate empathetic response, and he indeed won the election.

And it is not just in politics that tears can win votes. Preliminary trial motions by attorneys for Terry L. Nichols, Timothy McVeigh's coconspirator in the bombing of the Oklahoma City Federal Building, argued that Patrick Ryan, a U.S. Attorney who helped prosecute

McVeigh, should be disqualified from prosecuting Nichols on the grounds that he cried in front of the jury. He wept while examining a witness, and the defense attorneys argued that his crying would unduly prejudice jurors. The defense drew on our understanding that tears elicit empathy, in this case for the victims and not Nichols.

Henry Peacham wrote of the persuasive power of tears in *Minerva Britanna* (1612): "Teares haue moou'd the savage fierce, / And wrested Pittie, from a Tyrants ire: / And drops in time, do hardest Marble pierce." But if the tyrant thought that the tears were being shed simply to wrest pity from his ire, they would be much less effective. No one wants to empathize with strategic tears; to do so would be to be a sucker. Harlem Renaissance novelist Wallace Thurman describes his protagonist Emma Lou reading a letter from her mother in *The Blacker the Berry* . . . (1929), and the narrator, speaking for Emma Lou, tells us that her mother "was being tearful as usual. She loved to suffer, and being tearful seemed the easiest way to let the world know that one was suffering." Tears demand empathy, in other words, but they don't always get it: "Sob stuff, thought Emma Lou, and, tearing the letter up, threw it into the waste basket."

Escape

The notion that one can be fully absorbed in the sensations of one's own crying has long been a commonplace, and in the eighteenth century, novelists and playwrights were judged by how effectively they could induce this state of self-absorption. When a certain Mademoiselle Aïssé read Abbé Prévost's new novel, *Memoirs and Adventures of a Man of Quality*, in 1728, she recommended it to a friend by saying, "One spends the hundred and eighty pages dissolved in tears." One's world can be dissolved in tears and virtually disappear. Or, in the metaphor Lewis Carroll uses in *Alice in Wonderland*, we can cry and cry until we find ourselves, like Alice, afloat in a pool of our own tears, adrift in a transformed world.

Jean-Paul Sartre argued that this transformation is what emotion is all about. Midway through his career, Sartre wrote a short book titled *The Emotions: Outline of a Theory* (1948), in which he tried to find a

Alice floating away on her own tears. Illustration by John Tenniel, from Lewis Carroll, *Alice in Wonderland* (1865). Courtesy University of Iowa Libraries.

way out of what he saw as the dead-end argument between the mentalists and the peripheralists about whether emotions originate in the brain or in the body. In his introduction, he retells a story told by Pierre Janet, the director of the laboratory of pathological psychology at Satpêtrière and later a professor at the Collège de France and the premier French psychologist at the turn of the century. A young woman was seeing Janet for treatment for a series of hysterical symptoms. She would fall on the floor, "prey to violent emotion," without warning. In the course of treatment, Janet became convinced that the woman's problem was not neurological or physiological, but was a neurosis caused by the repression of the guilt she felt at not wanting to continue the daily care of her invalid father. As Janet was informing the young woman that this was his conclusion, she burst into tears.

The patient had gone to Janet for comfort, hoping that he would pronounce her medically unfit to continue nursing her father. Instead of giving her comfort or pronouncing her unfit, Janet told her that her worst fears were true—that she was selfish, that her sense of filial duty was not enough to compensate for the strain of caring for her parent, that she wanted out. Janet assured her that all this was quite normal, but this was not enough to salve her conscience, and so she began to cry. Janet called such crying "setback" behavior. When the act of confession or self-realization becomes too difficult, the patient regresses and resorts to tears: "The tears, the hysteria, represent a setback-behavior which is substituted for the first by diversion from its proper course." The tears are a "less well adapted behavior," says Janet, "a behavior of disadaptation."

What Sartre sees in this incident is not just a case of denial or regression but a paradigmatic case of emotional "magic." Sartre argues that the crying is not simply an inferior or degraded behavior, a path of least resistance, but an active attempt to change the world. He agrees that the young woman sees the truth of Janet's remarks and can't bear it, but disagrees that the emotion represents a failure of adaptation. Her crying was instead, according to Sartre, a positive act. She was attempting to alter Janet's behavior with her tears. She was crying in order to try to elicit from him the comfort he had so far refused to give her. And she was doing so not as a simple ploy. These were not crocodile tears, Sartre assumes. She was overcome.

The idea that tears overcome our rational thought is as old as Plato and as new as recent neuroscience. Dr. Floyd E. Bloom, for instance, of the Scripps Clinic and Research Foundation in La Jolla, California, argues that emotions like stress and anxiety serve as buffers between events in the world and how we react to them. Emotional experiences, because of the release of hormones and the physiological changes they cause, radically alter our physical sensations. While we are having an emotional experience, our attention is turned not so much toward our inner selves as toward our physical selves, our inner organs, our hearts, lungs, skin, skeletal muscles, and endocrine glands. As our nerves fire and our hormones secrete and our respiration and circulation speed up, we perceive and interpret the changes, and our interpretation can then set off new nervous and physiological activity, once again experienced as bodily sensations. At times the information from the viscera and skin can so overwhelm a person's consciousness that it completely dominates the processing capacity of the brain. To be "overwhelmed by tears" is in fact to be overwhelmed by bodily sensations, and to thereby remove ourselves from the world as it existed, and as we understood it, before we began to cry.

Sartre believed that emotions are more constructive than this mora-

torium suggests. Whenever we find ourselves in an untenable situation, he argued, our natural inclination is to re-create the world with
the help of our emotions. In Aesop's fable of the fox and the grapes,
Sartre writes, we see the standard pattern of emotional life. The fox
wants the grapes and tries to get them, but when they prove to be
beyond his reach, he decides that they aren't ripe, that he didn't really
want them, that unripe grapes make him sick. Rather than live in a
world that doesn't fit his desires, the fox magically transforms the
world into one in which the grapes are not desirable.

Likewise, Sartre claims that every emotion is a "particular subterfuge, a special trick, each one of them being a different means of
eluding a difficulty." Janet's patient, rather than accept a world in
which she is a less than perfect daughter, magically re-creates (or
attempts to create) a world in which the doctor will fulfill her desire
for comfort without blame. Her crying is sincere—the woman sincerely wants her doctor's comfort, and sincerely "feels" her own distress at confession—and at the same time an escape. Her sincere desire
for comfort allows her to escape from her feelings of guilt.

And the sense of sincerity necessarily takes the upper hand,
because, as Sartre says, emotion is always accompanied by belief.
When we are angry or distraught or joyous or fearful, we do not just
have an extra mood or tinge added to our preexisting sense of the
world. We have transformed the world into one in which we are necessarily joyous or fearful. The man in the throes of a jealous rage, no
less than a man chased by a bear, feels that the world in which he lives
demands and determines his emotional state. Our anger or joy infuses
our entire world of consciousness and perception. Walking down a
dark street at night, we conceive of our paranoia as a quality of the
world as well as a state of our own bodies; we believe that our fear is
called for. To believe that it is paranoia, to consider it uncalled for, is
often enough to abolish it.

The world which emotion transforms is one that exists in time, and
so our emotions construct not just our present state but our sense of
the future as well. This is a central part of Sartre's theory, and one of
the reasons he persists in seeing emotion, if not as maladaptation in
Janet's sense, as nevertheless a degraded form of consciousness—

when he calls it "magical" he is not far from calling it childish or primitive. The real world, in Sartre's view, is largely deterministic. The laws of physics, biology, genetics, and psychology all dictate a very small arena for the exercise of free will, much less for changing the world. In an appropriately reflexive consciousness, Sartre argues, we realize this. Emotion is degraded because in the thrall of it we revert to more primitive, magical thinking, in which the world reacts to our desires. The woman in Janet's office believes she is so distraught that Janet must comfort her. If she did not believe that her tears could so change the world (from a world in which patients must do what doctors want to one in which doctors must do what patients want), she would not cry. Without the belief that she can make Janet answer her tears, Sartre suggests, she *could* not cry.

One of a series of paintings of weeping women Picasso painted in 1937. This one, with its patch of white in the middle, suggests the way tears can wash away aspects of reality. Pablo Picasso, *Weeping Woman* (1937). Tate Gallery, London. © 1999 Estate of Pablo Picasso / Artists Rights Society (ARS), New York.

For many people this is going too far altogether. Sartre's view galls people who are certain of the naturalness and involuntary quality of their own emotional responses. But Sartre is not claiming that emotional magic is the result of instrumental reason. He doesn't suggest that Janet's patient rationally concluded that tears would change Janet's behavior. If we direct our bodies at such moments, we do so only partially consciously and in desperation. "Let it be clearly understood that this is not a game," Sartre writes. "We are driven against a wall, and we throw ourselves into this new attitude with all the strength we can muster."

Some of our actions are *effective*—we can switch on a light, use a gun, hurt someone's feelings. Emotional "action" is *affective*, Sartre writes, precisely because it makes no such real change in the world. Emotive behavior seeks to change the world without requiring us to take any other action. The man who faints in fear as the bear approaches does not really make the bear disappear. The fox does not alter the grapes themselves, making them less ripe than they had been moments before, nor does he alter their proximity to his grasp. "In short," Sartre writes, "in emotion it is the body which, directed by consciousness, changes its relation to the world in order that the world may change its qualities."

We might at first suppose that the neurologist Antonio Damasio would find such a theory congenial, since in both Damasio's and Sartre's view, emotion is a necessary part of the rational choices we make—whether to bet on a card, whether to reach for the grapes. For both the neurologist and the philosopher, it is essential that the body send appropriate information to the brain if a person is to act *as if* the future might respond to his or her desires. Phineas Gage and Damasio's patients with damaged frontal lobes demonstrate what happens if these bodily sensations do not help control the decisions one makes about the future.

But Damasio sees a rational mind devoid of emotion as a degraded or damaged reasoning instrument, while Sartre argues that all emotion is a degraded form of consciousness, a mask or substitution for more rational thought. Only through purifying, nonemotional reflection, according to Sartre, can one reapproach the real, deterministic world. For Damasio, only by incorporating emotion's projective abilities can we make what we consider "rational" choices.

Both Sartre and Damasio see tears as signs of a sincere engagement with the world, however unrealistic, and as spurs to action, whether rational or imaginary. The problem with Sartre's theory is not its instrumentality, since it is clear that emotion—from the temper tantrum of an infant to the crocodile tears or seductive tears of an adult—can have instrumental designs. Nor is the problem, as his lover, Simone de Beauvoir, and others have charged, that it leaves little room for a positive view of those emotions we usually do not consider "degraded," such as love, honor, or affection. The real problem is that it posits, like Plato's theory before it, the possibility of rational thought devoid of emotion. Damasio shows what such thought looks like—it looks like brain damage. Sartre's theory brilliantly describes the ways in which emotion creates and re-creates the world of phenomena in which we live every day. It is his desire for a world free of such magical transformations that is misplaced.

Rather than changing the world (or allowing us to make better decisions within our worlds, as Damasio suggests), the physiologists who argue for the parasympathetic function of tears suggest that tears mark the temporary end of decision and change. They see tears as signs that we are seeking and finding a steady peaceful removal from the world of action. Such a temporary moratorium may be of great value in making rational decisions, but if so it is because the crier has already returned from emotional extremes. It may be that Janet's patient, contemplating her predicament in tears, understood more of its significance than she had while in the throes of anguish. It may be that she knew quite well that she needed the doctor's permission to stop caring for her father, not his semimoralistic description of that desire. Since our desires are so often social rather than material, since we want approval more often than we want grapes, it may be that the call of our tears is exactly what is needed: our magical re-creation of the universe means little unless we can get others to join us there. Our tears command empathy, we hope, and as others feel along with us, they enter our transformed world.

And it works. The television producer Norman Lear, among others, ascribes Oliver North's popularity to his ability to "get moist" at the right moment. During the televised Contragate hearings that made him a national figure, North's eyes welled up whenever he declared his patriotism to the congressional committee he was lying to. North's teary-eyed performance is instructive here, because his emotion was, we can assume, perfectly sincere; he was feeling something deeply when his eyes welled up. To those who believed he was telling the truth, his tears had a fairly straightforward meaning—he was a man announcing to the world the nature and content of his most deeply held beliefs, overwhelmed, as heroes have always been, by his own sense of honor and devotion. He was sincere in that he truly believed the patriotic clichés he mouthed, and in that he truly desired to protect his commander in chief from the political impact that telling the truth would have had.

But given what we now know, his tears also suggest another possibility—that at key moments in his testimony, when the legality of his actions and his veracity were being challenged, North escaped into a safe emotional haven, the place where duty, honor, and pride inform patriotism—a complex of ideas and feelings that was clearly authentic in North's eyes. His "moistness" was the bodily sign of his refuge, and his refuge was precisely this overwhelming of his conscious state by the feelings arising from his body, feelings he knew he could call on at critical moments. Like a child's tears when he is caught with a hand in the cookie jar, Ollie North's moist eyes—and, we assume, a series of other bodily changes in temperature, muscle contraction, respiration—accurately reflected his feelings, even if they were, from another perspective, far from honest.

And the same may be true of someone like Tammy Faye Bakker. Her tears of religious desire and exultation were her trademark in the lucrative evangelical Ponzi scheme she ran with her husband Jim Bakker until he was sentenced to forty-five years in prison for fraud. But it is the image of her face dripping with tears and mascara as she cried about her husband's arrest that etched itself on the public consciousness. In her two autobiographies, Bakker (or actually now Messner, since she divorced Jim while he was in jail and married his best friend) describes herself crying sixty times, as if in some kind of lachrymal imitation of Wilt Chamberlain's boasting. The title of one of her autobiographies announces her authenticity in pop-music vernacular: *I Gotta Be Me*.

Here the distinction Lionel Trilling made between sincerity and authenticity comes in handy. Sincerity, Trilling wrote, is when one says exactly what one feels and feels what one says. Authenticity is when one desires what one experiences and when one experiences what one desires. Tammy Faye's tears may be sincere at one level—she may feel as awful as she says she feels. But the cynical do not perceive her tears as authentic; that is, her experience of emotion is incongruent with what appears to many to be her desire to hold on to her evangelical income, to shop with the proceeds of her tear-logged persuasiveness.

But however we might feel about North or Bakker and their sincerity or authenticity, it would be wrong to assume that they were not truly feeling what they appeared to be feeling. We are only wrong to conclude, based on such a display of true feeling, that they must therefore be telling us the truth. What some of us in our jadedness reject in the emotional beliefs of the eighteenth and nineteenth centuries is not the irreducible truth of the crying body but the idea that such prayers for relief are necessarily smiled upon by God, the idea that such tears are necessarily a sign of virtue. What those who voted for North in subsequent elections and those who bailed Bakker out with contributions felt, we can assume, was empathy.

Empathy

Empathy is a fairly recent philosophical or psychological concept, so recent, in fact, that there is no entry for "empathy" in the *Oxford English Dictionary*. The German aesthetician Theodore Lipps introduced the word to the critical vocabulary in *On Einfühlung* (On empathy) in 1913. According to Lipps, when we see a representation of other people in artistic works, we project ourselves into these other lives, and we thereby experience empathy, which he took to be central to the aesthetic experience and to the value of art. Wilhelm Worringer was one of the many German intellectuals who followed Lipps's suggestions. In his classic text *Abstraction and Empathy* (1917), Worringer tried to clarify the combination of identification and distance involved in empathetic experience, setting the stage for much later debate. The word only began to acquire wider English usage in the 1920s. Robert Frost was influenced by these German aestheticians, for instance, when he gave as one of his credos: "No tears in the author, no tears in the reader."

When the nineteenth-century poet Ella Wheeler Wilcox wrote the line that was destined to become a cliché, "Laugh, and the world laughs with you," she was relying on a purely sentimental notion of how hearts harmonize with each other. In the culture of sentimentality, such affective consonance was part of the ideal harmony of the universe, and something that happened almost physically, like a contagion. But the German aestheticians were not talking about a simple case of the transfer of emotion. Theirs was a philosophy consciously different from that of the Romantics, emphasizing the distance empathy also demands. Empathy for them was a combination of affective identification and cognitive distance.

The psychologist Carl Rogers explained this in the 1970s by saying that "the state of empathy or being empathic is to perceive the internal frame of reference of another with accuracy . . . but without ever losing the 'as if' condition." This cognitive, conditional dimension of empathy has been well documented by a series of experiments which have shown that reasoning with children about the effects of their actions increases their empathetic responses. And thus it makes sense that, as studies have shown, older people tend to be more empathetic than younger people. As our cognitive skills become more developed, we have the necessary equipment to be empathetic. And undoubtedly more specific cultural training comes into play as well. Other studies have shown that, as with crying, women are more prone to empathy than men, girls more empathetic than boys.

If empathy, named as such, is a fairly new concept, the general idea is much older. Both the patristic authors Gregory and Hilary wrote that tearful prayers for others could heal them. This makes of empathetic tears not just an attitude but a remedy. And empathy is not fully empathetic until it is shared. The prayer needs to be said, the tears need to be shed, and they need to be seen being shed. Tears are one of the ways empathy is recognized, and one of the ways empathy is sought.

As the mad Captain Ahab is about to start his final and fatal chase of Moby Dick, he says good-bye to his chief mate, Starbuck. "Their hands met; their eyes fastened; Starbuck's tears the glue," the narrator tells us, suggesting that Starbuck's visible empathy is not just the result but the cause of their connection. Starbuck appeals to Ahab not to go, saying, "Oh, my captain, my captain!—noble heart—go not—go not!—see, it's a brave man that weeps; how great the agony of the persuasion then!" The feeling that Starbuck expresses with his tears, unlike a more passive empathy, is the social glue itself. It is persuasion more than attitude, Melville says, action more than feeling.

But empathetic tears can work as the opposite of social glue, as we saw in the case of tears that spurred people to revenge. When heavyweight Kurt Angle beat Iran's Abbas Jadidi in the 1996 Olympics, the wrestler took a tearful victory lap, during which he cried so profusely that it became a major news story. Angle was a close friend of wrestler Dave Schultz, who had been shot dead by his sponsor, the millionaire madman John E. du Pont, just a few months earlier, and the news reports all attributed Angle's tears to his grief. Those who empathized with his tears found them moving. But his tears were not a universal glue. For some viewers and commentators, Angle's tears elicited comic disdain, and from silver medalist Abbas Jadidi during the awards ceremony something else: "The Iranian stared up at him darkly," Reuters reported, "from the next step down on the podium."

The power of crying to elicit empathy is related to its persuasiveness, and one can imagine that Abbas Jadidi remained unconvinced that Angle's emotional state was one he should share. But most criers are careful to address their demands for empathy to people who are likely to answer them: We tend to cry only to a receptive audience. But tears can sometimes rope in an audience that otherwise wouldn't have our ear, that wouldn't be receptive to our demands if they were made in some other way. The student who asks for a reconsideration of a grade tends to get a stock recitation of why the grade was well considered and fair. The student who cries can often receive a more attentive response. If our husband or wife asks us to alter some habit, we may listen, but if he or she asks us through tears, we may listen better.

Arthur Koestler, in "The Logic of the Moist Eye," a brief chapter in his *The Act of Creation* (1964), lists five different occasions for tears in his explanation for "why we weep": rapture, mourning, relief, empathy, and self-pity. These tend to be the opposite of such self-assertive emotions as fear and rage, Koestler wrote, in that they do not tend toward action, toward the fight-or-flight option, but are instead associated with self-transcendence and quiescence. Self-transcending emotions "cannot be consummated by any specific voluntary action."

To be overwhelmed, enraptured, or entranced by love, beauty, or art—all of which can induce tears—is to eschew specific action in favor of luxuriating in the emotions themselves. This is clearest in the case of tears of rapture, relief, and self-pity, private emotions that demand no action beyond feeling them. But Koestler suggests that mourning is also a case in which there is nothing to be done, no action to be taken, just "passive surrender" to the grief. And empathy, he surmises, is similar. Empathy requires identification. To identify with another inhibits the self-asserting tendencies that lead us to action, and therefore empathy is a passive emotion that leads to no action.

Crying is for Koestler, too, therefore, a kind of escape from the world of action. He acknowledges that we all learn to use crying strategically in relationships, and that we learn this very early on, as infants. But the "true character" of weeping, he feels, is demonstrated by the person who weeps alone, "helpless in her surrender to an emotion which, by its nature, can find no other outlet, whether it is caused by the thunder of the church organ, or the fall of a sparrow."

But if we think of a teenage boy playing air guitar alone in his bedroom, wowing the stadium crowd, or a man alone in his house screaming at a phantasm of his boss about some indignity, we see that emotions experienced while we are alone often have an imagined audience. We can even think of the playing out of such scenarios as a close relative of empathy: the imaginative projection out of our current situation into another, complete with feelings of identification with the person we would like to be—the one playing the stadium, for instance, or the one that tells off the boss. In its combination of self-directedness and self-transcendence, in fact, crying while one is alone may be the paradigmatic example of the empathetic response.

Our empathetic tears, like our tears of contrition or our tears of love, are for ourselves and for others: they are both the stuff of self-absorption and a crying out, a call, an announcement. When we weep at a commercial about starving children on the television, we may do so in lieu of getting out the checkbook. I suspect that a study would show that when people jump up from the television or the newspaper and write their congressman, or make a donation to a charity, they are much more likely to do so when dry-eyed than when weeping, much more likely to be feeling anger, outrage, fear, or any number of emotions other than empathy.

And conversely, when we weep tears of empathy, the weeping itself becomes the action resulting from our feelings of that moment. It is not that our emotions, finding no outlet in action, are reduced to tears, but that certain emotions find their perfect outlet in tears. To the extent that we are feeling pushed beyond the boundaries of our selves by empathetic emotions, crying helps return us to our sense of self. Imagine, for instance, being brought to tears by two different visual stimuli: one a photograph of Bosnian prisoners, another a sublime work of art. And imagine the emotional arc of those two experiences. In both cases, we gradually come under the spell of very intense emotions. We experience a sense of being outside ourselves, outside our own experience. This feeling peaks, and then we well up or cry. That crying is inseparable from our sense of returning to ourselves, to our own bodies. We may cry during transcendent experiences, but what we transcend, when we cry, is rarely ourselves.

Adam Smith comes at the question of empathy from the other side. What is it, he wants to know, that we get from having others empathize with us?

> How are the unfortunate relieved when they have found out a person to whom they can communicate the cause of their sorrow? Upon his sympathy they seem to disburthen themselves of a part of

their distress: he is not improperly said to share it with them. . . . Yet by relating their misfortunes they in some measure renew their grief. They awaken in their memory the remembrance of those circumstances which occasion their affliction. Their tears accordingly flow faster than before, and they are apt to abandon themselves to all the weakness of sorrow. They take pleasure, however, in all this, and, it is evident, are sensibly relieved by it; because the sweetness of his sympathy more than compensates the bitterness of that sorrow, which, in order to excite this sympathy, they had thus enlivened and renewed.

Smith was an economist, among other things, and this kind of exchange, in which people actually transfer their grief into another's account and are "compensated" for it, serves him as an adequate explanation. But his language also suggests a sharing of pleasure in empathy, an abandoning of oneself to the sweetness of tears.

It would be nice, of course, if we could solve our problems of acting in the world simply by crying out our frustration with them. It would be nice if the world, like a good mother, answered our cries for sustenance and comfort. Miguel de Unamuno, Spain's most influential philosopher, has a passage in his *The Tragic Sense of Life* (1913) which most powerfully evokes this fantasy:

A pedant who beheld Solon weeping for the death of his son said to him, "Why do you weep thus, if weeping avails nothing?" And the sage answered him, "Precisely for that reason—because it does not avail." . . . And I am convinced that we should solve many things if we all went out into the streets and uncovered our griefs, and joined together in beweeping them and crying aloud to the heavens and calling upon God. And this, even though God should hear us not; but He would hear us. The chiefest sanctity of a temple is that it is a place to which men go to weep in common. A *misere* sung in common by a multitude tormented by destiny has as much value as a philosophy. It is not enough to cure the plague: we must learn to weep for it. Yes, we must learn to weep! Perhaps that is the supreme wisdom. Why? Ask Solon.

For Unamuno, recognizing the tragedy of life is the highest goal of philosophy. And so, "tormented by destiny," only a fool or a coward would refuse to weep.

Unamuno's vision of people coming together en masse to weep in the streets moves the theory of catharsis, obviously, from the personal to the social level, until it becomes a rite of mass empathy. More recently, the director James Cameron has written that "audiences around the world are celebrating their own essential humanity by going into a dark room and crying together" over his film *Titanic*. The suggestion, immodest though it may be, is that the world is finding peace in these scenes of communal weeping. For Unamuno and Cameron, we weep not just to make our selves better but to make a better world. Pragmatists might argue that this is delusional, that it substitutes symbolic action for real action. Unamuno argues that our emotional and nonemotional consciousness is already based on mass delusion—we place value on the wrong things, (such as blockbuster special-effects tearjerkers) and we mistake changes in the realm of material goods and technology for real progress Since our malaise is a crisis of belief—or ideology—it is precisely belief that can cure us.

The magical transformation of the world that some philosophers have identified as the weakness of emotional consciousness, in other words, is exactly what Unamuno feels is its strength. And perhaps it doesn't make sense to argue with a philosophical metaphor. We like to believe that to express our distress or dissatisfaction with the world is to annihilate that distress or dissatisfaction. We learned that this was possible as infants, whenever we cried out and were made to feel better with food, a change, or stroking. But our desire to continue to think in this way, despite what Unamuno or James Cameron has to say, is hard not to see as infantile.

7

Fictional Tears

I n the second act of *Hamlet*, a troupe of actors arrives at Elsinore and Hamlet asks one of them to give a speech. Give the one, Hamlet says, that describes the death of Priam, as watched by his wife Hecuba. The actor obliges Prince Hamlet and gives a powerful rendition. "Look whe'er he has not turn'd his color and has tears in 's eyes," says Polonious, moved to the point of discomfort. "Prithee no more." Hamlet himself is mesmerized by the actor's tears streaming from what he had earlier called the "the fruitful river in the eye." As the others leave the room, the prince ponders not only the nature of those tears but the basic mysteries of dramatic art and the riddle of human empathy as well, in one of the play's best-known soliloquies:

> O what a rogue and peasant slave am I!
> Is it not monstrous that this player here,
> But in a fiction, in a dream of passion,
> Could force his soul so to his own conceit
> That from her working all the visage wann'd,
> Tears in his eyes, distraction in his aspect,

A broken voice, an' his whole function suiting
With forms to his conceit? And all for nothing,
For Hecuba!
What's Hecuba to him, or he to Hecuba,
That he should weep for her?

Hamlet finds it "monstrous" that the actor can simulate the full bodily array of emotional expression while he himself remains incapable of carrying out the furious revenge he is sure he should wreak upon his uncle for killing his father. He regards the actor's performance as a judgment against him, as his grief at his father's death has still found no expression. "What would he do," he continues, "Had he the motive and the cue for passion/ That I have? He would drown the stage with tears."

The various motivations for tears—performative, expressive, and empathetic—are intertwined in this scene. We see an actor playing an actor reciting the words of a character from another story altogether, and we see him cry and we listen to Hamlet's soliloquy about his own inadequately expressed grief. We in the actual audience respond both to the first actor's tears and to the desire for tears that the actor playing Hamlet expresses. And in most productions we are more likely to cry in response to Hamlet's musing than we are to the actor playing the actor who cries on cue.

Most of us take for granted a certain amount of imitative behavior on our part as an audience. We are often moved to tears at the same time that actors on the stage or screen are, since they very often mark emotional climaxes in the drama. The Roman poet Horace assumed that this was not just a theatrical fact but a general one: "As man laughs with those who laugh,/ So he weeps with those that weep;/ If thou wish me to weep,/ Thou must first shed tears thyself;/ Then thy sorrows will touch me." We may just want to chalk this up to the fact that we are apes, that imitation is our natural mode of being and the basis not just of the way we learn but of our sociability.

But whatever the phylogenetic reason, Horace's scheme is a bit too simple. William Finn, the composer of *Falsettos* and other musicals, says that the actress Patti Lupone passed on to him the following primer on crying given to her by her acting teacher:

If you cry and the audience cries, that's fine.
If you don't cry and the audience does cry, that's very good
If you cry and the audience doesn't cry, that's very bad.

The basic principle by which this little mnemonic works is the same as Horace's: if an actor does a good job, the audience will laugh or weep along. The second line suggests that an actor can trigger an empathetic response stronger than the emotions he or she is portraying; often we cry because a character is strong enough not to cry—such as when Susan Sarandon finds out her son has a rare disease in *Lorenzo's Oil*, or when Cary Grant just barely tears up in *An Affair to Remember*. The last line is funny because it conjures up an image of an inept actor attempting to elicit tears through emotional blackmail and failing.

And, we might add, an actor playing Polonious may make the audience laugh when he weeps. When Polonius gets choked up at the actor's rendition, we do not imitate him. His pomposity has created an empathetic gulf between us. We can laugh at him as we have laughed at the tears of Stan Laurel or Lou Costello or other crying clowns—from Cochinella to Pierrot to Pee-wee Herman. Our response to these clowns may be partially empathetic, but it can also be cruel, akin to the perverse pleasures of watching people cry that authors like Dorothy Parker and Fyodor Dostoyevsky—to take just the two examples to be discussed here—relied on in their fiction.

In William Luce's play *Barrymore*, Christopher Plummer portrayed an aging John Barrymore, who was famous for his ability to cry on demand. An apocryphal story claims that he once asked a director what kind of crying was wanted in a particular scene and the director said, I don't care, just cry. Barrymore said, "Well, all right, I tell you what: I'll give you two big tears from the left eye, followed by three little ones from the right." Plummer plays Barrymore late in his career, rehearsing for his own Broadway comeback as Richard III. Being chronically drunk, Barrymore continually loses his place, goes off on tangents, and bursts into soliloquies from other Shakespeare plays, and does so with such brilliant pathos that much of the audience cries. The audience's tears at Plummer's performance are undoubtedly occasioned by many different things—Shakespeare's sublime verse, Plum-

mer's superb acting, an empathetic projection into Barrymore's experience, and, perhaps, some kind of perverse pleasure in watching a
man's downfall. Our response to fictional stories, some of which represent or use tears, some of which elicit them, can include a paradoxi-
cal combination of empathy and cruelty.

Empathy, cruelty, sublimity. If these are main springs of our tearful
response to stories and our pleasure at tearful scenes, they are far from
the only ones. Montaigne said that it was simply a desire for escape
that led people to the "laments of fiction, the tears of Dido and Adri-
ane." Our delight at the perfidious female tears in film noir or our
appreciation of modernist and postmodernist tears, such as the
patently inauthentic plastic tears in Man Ray's *Larmes*, are further
paradoxes and require further explanations. Some responses are time-
bound, of course—a play by Racine that had all of Paris in tears three
hundred years ago would not produce the same-sized puddles if it
were produced on Broadway today. And the crying heroes and heroines of the eighteenth and nineteenth centuries cannot move us in the
same way they did their original audiences because the very specific
social issues that produced those tears are no longer our issues. But
many works retain their power to move us deeply, and new ones are
constantly created with the intent of making us weep. What, finally, is
the relationship between the depths of despair and flights of aesthetic
transcendence, between tears written in ink and those dropped on the
page as we read, between those on the screen and those in the seats?

According to G. S. Brett, who wrote about the history of psychology
for the Wittenberg Symposium in 1927, "The subject of emotions was
saved from complete extinction" during the rise of scientific thinking
since Descartes by "the sudden emergence of the novel in the middle of
the eighteenth century." And imaginative literature, drama, and film
have been not only the most enduring record of our tears, but also perhaps the most important and certainly the most comprehensive of our
collective ruminations on the nature of emotion in social life. D. H.
Lawrence wrote that "the novel, properly handled, can reveal the most
secret places of life: for it is the *passional* secret places of life, above all,
that the tide of sensitive awareness needs to ebb and flow, cleansing

and refreshing." And indeed, unlike psychological or neurophysiological studies, literary examinations of emotion elicit emotion in response. We recognize, in the most famous cliché of critical prose, "I laughed, I cried," a comic reduction of the ideal aesthetic experience.

The pleasures afforded by stories—whether on film, on the stage, or in books—have been pondered by aestheticians and critics from the Greeks on. Most agree, despite reports of early film audiences ducking when actors shot guns toward the camera, that the fictionality of stories is central to our response. Hume summed this up in the eighteenth century and at the same time offered an explanation for our ability to take pleasure from others' pain:

> The heart likes naturally to be moved and affected. Melancholy objects suit it, and even disastrous and sorrowful, provided they are softened by some circumstance. . . . The theatre . . . has almost the effect of reality; yet it has not altogether that effect. However we may be hurried away by the spectacle; whatever dominion the senses and imagination may usurp over the reason, there still lurks at the bottom a certain idea of falsehood in the whole of what we see . . . [which] suffices to diminish the pain which we suffer . . . and to reduce that affliction to such a pitch as converts it into a pleasure. We weep for the misfortune of a hero, to whom we are attached. In the same instant we comfort ourselves, by reflecting, that it is nothing but a fiction: And it is precisely that mixture of sentiments, which composes an agreeable sorrow, and tears that delight us.

In other words, if we weep for Hecuba, we do so *because* Hecuba is nothing to us, finally. And we weep because of a "mixture of sentiments."

Socrates, in Plato's quasi-dialogue *Philebus*, had much earlier described the mixed nature of emotions. Socrates says that lamentation—along with anger, fear, longing and other emotions—are "pains of the soul itself" and yet "replete with immense pleasures." He quotes *The Iliad*, where Homer asserted that the "wrath that spurs the wisest mind to rage" is "sweeter by far than the stream of flowing honey." We do not just get pleasure by venting anger, Socrates says, we feel other "pleasures mixed up with the pains in lamentation and longing." Spectators at a tragedy, he says, "sometimes feel pleasure and weep at once," while at comedies, we take pleasure in the pains of others. Our own malice mixes pain into our pleasure, which accounts for why we can laugh and weep at the same time while watching comic drama. "In laments and tragedies and comedies—and not only in those of the stage but in the whole tragicomedy of life," he concludes, "pains are mixed with pleasures." Plato is certainly right—and well ahead of the legions who have since tried to isolate the nature of specific emotions—to suggest that all emotions are mixtures of varied and conflicting motives and feelings.

As Harriet Beecher Stowe wrote, "The bitterest tear shed over graves are for words left unsaid and deeds left undone," that is, not just for the loss itself but for a host of other regrets as well. Dylan Thomas's famous poem "Do Not Go Gently into That Dark Night" suggests a denser complexity:

> And you, my father, there on the sad height,
> Curse, bless, me now with your fierce tears, I pray.

The poem is full of oxymorons or near contradictions—praying to be cursed, fierce tears of blessing, sad heights, the desire for peace and the rejection of peace—and these are meant to relay the complex forces that determine the jumble of feelings we can have toward a parent and the idea of his or her mortality. Our emotions are "overdetermined," to employ the useful psychoanalytic coinage, in that they are multiply motivated, shaped by many different aspects of our relations, moods, understandings, habits, relationships, and emotional commitments. In Dostoyevsky's *The Brothers Karamazov* (1880), when Alyosha Karamazov's beloved mentor dies, he begins to cry, feeling the loss. He is bereft at his mentor's death and yet he realizes that he is free, now, to do whatever he wants. His crying gains momentum, he goes outside, falls down on the ground, and kisses the earth while weeping in "rapture." Both joyous and fearful at the prospect of leaving the monastery, he weeps just outside its gates in ecstasy while his dead mentor's wake is still under way inside.

Some psychologists have argued that this kind of explanation is much more complicated than is necessary, and that all such tears—those of Dylan Thomas's narrator, Dostoyevsky's character, or ours in response—are simple responses to loss. Psychoanalyst Sandor Feldman argued in 1956 that the very notion of tears of joy, for instance, is a mistake, that it is the result of a cultural misinterpretation. "There are no tears of joy," he wrote, "only tears of sorrow." Children do not cry at happy endings, he notes. Adults do so only because they are aware of death and the fleetingness of any happiness. As adults, he says, we cry at happy endings because we know they are false, illusory. It is our sorrow at the impossibility of happy endings in our real lives, and thus, finally, at our own loss of innocence, that leads us to weep at happy endings in fiction and film. Pleasure has nothing to do with it. From Feldman's perspective, Alyosha weeps in sorrow, pure and simple, at the loss of his mentor, at losing the security of the monastery, at the loss of his youth. He is kidding himself, or Dostoyevsky is, to think that he is experiencing rapture or ecstasy.

And some psychologists would suggest an even less complicated explanation. C. W. Valentine, a psychologist at the University of Birmingham in England who studied the development of fear in children, published a study in 1930 concluding that the fact that "children 'played at fear' even to the point of screams and tears suggests an innate craving for stimulation." Valentine was influenced both by Freud and by Cannon. Freud, in his *Three Essays on the Theory of Sexuality*, had written that for children, all excitation—even fear—has a sexual charge, and that similar forms of excitation explain the pleasurable effects of unpleasant emotions in later life as well. Valentine's argument suggests that in watching tragedies or melodramas, just as in the case of watching horror films, we feed our craving for stimulation, and thus associate crying with the pleasurable stimulations preceding and accompanying it. But the crying itself, he argues following Cannon, is simply a sign that the parasympathetic nervous system is doing its work of returning us to homeostasis after a run of pleasurable excitement. If we cry after reading Thomas's poem or a scene from a novel, it is simply because the poem or novel excited us, something we enjoy because of our innate desire for excitement.

This suggests that we respond to stories much as we respond to music, which, as one critic put it, "has its own unique entryway into people's emotional lives," and which can also induce tears. John Sloboda at the University of Keele had eighty-three people listen to musical passages and answer a battery of questions about their emotional responses. He found that shivers were most reliably provoked by relatively sudden changes in harmony. A racing heart was provoked by acceleration and syncopation. Tears were most reliably evoked by melodic appogiaturas, or grace notes, in which a note above or below the main tone precedes it, creating a certain amount of tension, which is then released when the main tone is sounded. (Tears were also caused, to a lesser extent, by sequences and harmonic movements that resolve tension by returning to the tonic, or the first note of the scale of the song's key.) Sloboda's conclusion, which others have also postulated, was that the emotional responses were caused by confirmations and violations of the listener's expectations—when we expect the melody to return to the tonic, both its delay and its arrival produce an emotional response. The tears we associate with the pleasure of a profound musical experience can be caused fairly mechanically, in other words, by stimulating our nervous system, and by arousing, frustrating, and satisfying our expectations.

But this is a most unsatisfying explanation for why we cry at complex fictions. If it were true, we would be equally likely to weep at the Marx Brothers' *A Night in Casablanca* as at *Casablanca* itself. Certainly the nature of what is represented is determining our response. When *First Blood*, the original Rambo movie, was released, many viewers found Sylvester Stallone's tears at the end to be quite moving. Rambo, after spending time in a brutal Viet Cong prison camp, has come home and gets arrested because he looks more like a hippie drifter than a war hero. He escapes from the local constabulary, which then chases him through the woods. After killing or maiming most of the posse, Rambo blows up most of the town before finally surrendering to his old Green Beret commander. As he gives in to his commander's pleas to stop the violence, he breaks down, slumps to the floor, and weeps. He does so as part of a change from a belief in his own right to vengeance to a belief in his responsibility to stop the killing. This belated spurt of "conscience" is accompanied by a radical change in his emotional state, along with all the physical signs of that change, from clenched jaw and fists to slumped posture, shaking, and sobbing. It is hard not to see this now without at least smirking, since the meanings of Vietnam, long hair, the military, "law and order," and any number of other issues of the day do not push the same buttons, do not make for the same profusion of conflicting emotions they did for audiences almost twenty years ago. The same tears appear on the screen (and the same amount of "excitement" in narrative and explosive terms), but they cannot produce the same quantity of tears in an audience. And since not everyone at a given historical moment weeps at the same fictional stimuli, clearly who we are and what we believe determines when we cry as well. These multiple factors are rarely studied, but one obvious place to look for clues is in the difference between men's and women's responses, and the different treatment of male and female tears in the weepier regions of Hollywood film.

The Roles of Drama, Melodrama, and Comedy

Popular films rely heavily on the depiction and eliciting of emotion. Many work simply by invoking and deploying our most commonly held assumptions about tears—the importance of having a good cry, for instance, or crying as a sign of sincerity. Robert Redford's *Ordinary People* (based on Judith Guest's novel), which won a raft of Academy Awards including Best Picture in 1980, is a case in point: cathartic tears are at the center of the film's examination of family dysfunction.

As the film opens, young Conrad Jarrett (Timothy Hutton) is suffering from a deep turmoil that neither a suicide attempt nor his stay at an institution has done much to alleviate. His father, Calvin (Donald Sutherland), despite a somewhat morbid or at least overbearing concern for his son's emotional state, remains incapable of reaching him, impeded largely by his denial that anything is wrong. Beth (Mary Tyler Moore), Conrad's distant mother, remains at all times cold and emotionally constipated. Conrad's problem, it turns out, is somehow related to the accidental death of his older brother, his mother's pet, and we begin to sense that Beth somehow blames Conrad for the accident. Beth responds to Conrad's meek attempts at closeness with an icy shudder of distaste, and Conrad responds to his father's guilty and overenthusiastic advances with surly or resigned withdrawl. There is little doubt about the lesson we are going to be taught: emotional repression is the very source of dysfunction.

When Conrad begins seeing a psychiatrist, Dr. Berger (Judd Hirsch), he gradually comes to understand his feelings of guilt and abandonment. The climactic scene is an emergency meeting with Berger in which Conrad breaks down, feels the pain he has been avoiding, and cries. His cathartic experience, made possible by Dr. Berger's reassurances—"I am your friend, you can count on it"—and his Socratic questions about Conrad's emotional life, is the result of a classic early Freudian therapeutic breakthrough. Conrad remembers the accidental drowning of his brother in a storm, at which he was present, and reexperiences it and all the anguish he felt at his own helplessness. He weeps and keens bitterly, talks, and weeps some more. And he is cured.

Pauline Kael wrote that *Ordinary People* is a romance about the ability of the Jewish doctor's emotional intelligence to combat the culturally acquired inability of WASPs to feel and express their emotions. After his own tearful meeting with Dr. Berger, even Calvin comes to recognize the emotional impoverishment of his married life. He sits, toward the end of the movie, in the family kitchen crying the night away. When his wife comes downstairs and asks him what could possibly be wrong, attempting to dismiss his worries, he slowly tells her how he, with help of Berger and his own tears, can now see her. We, the audience, have seen her this way all along. She hides behind proprieties, she doesn't really feel anything, she can't express love, she is avoiding the job of mourning. "I'm crying because I don't know who you are," he tells her, in obvious contradiction to the portrait he has just drawn, "or what it was that we've been playing at. So I was crying. I don't know if I love you anymore and I don't know what I'm going to do about that." She packs her bags and leaves. Father and son make an emotional connection in the backyard, in a mythically tinged winter scene, which now, watered by their tears, is preparing for another spring. They face their future with a new kind of stoicism, one but-

tressed by their own heroic catharses and their newfound ability to
feel, however little they seem to react, emotionally, to the departure of
the wife and mother. They are, at the end of the film, older, wiser,
freer, healthier. Conrad and Calvin are emotionally relieved, intellectually improved, and ennobled by the physically, sensually exhausting
and exhilarating catharses they have experienced.

Many, many movie characters have experienced similar cures. Gregory Peck's amnesia disappears after he remembers a very similar
childhood trauma and cries in Alfred Hitchcock's equally simplistic
therapy drama, *Spellbound* (1945). And Peck, this time playing the
doctor, cures Bobby Darin in *Captain Newman, M.D.* (1963). (Darin:
"Look at me, Doc, crying just like a little kid." Peck: "You're crying for
Big Jim and you ought to. You loved him and he's dead. Now you can
let yourself feel.") In *The Prince of Tides* (1991), Barbra Streisand, playing the therapist, finally convinces her patient (Nick Nolte) of the
theraputic necessity of crying. Nolte's character is apparently not a
film buff—the idea that tears can help comes as a big surprise to him.

There is an odd series of scenes about cathartic tears in James
Brooks's 1987 film *Broadcast News*. Early in the film, we see Jane
(Holly Hunter), a single, possibly repressed hot-shot producer of a TV
news show, take the phone off the hook, sit still for a minute, and
check her watch. She then starts to heave with sobs, tears washing
down her grimacing face. We are left in the dark, not knowing why she
is crying or what it means. Later in the film, Jane sits outside and again
checks her watch both before and after blubbering. We notice she has
brought Kleenex, and start to understand that this is a regularly sched-
uled activity. The third time, she cries in her office early in the morning, and as her coworkers in the newsroom arrive, they take no notice.
Clearly they have seen all this before and are unfazed. Is this an
uptight woman who times her crying jags as carefully as she times her
news segments, or a woman of such advanced emotional skills that she
can take care of herself through short sessions of self-administered
cathartic therapy?

The film pits Aaron (Albert Brooks), a shlumpy reporter with a
firm grasp of domestic and international politics, against Tom (William

Hurt), a telegenic, hunky numskull with no skill save an overweening desire to be an anchorman. In the battle between Aaron the true and Tom the false for an anchor spot and the heroine's love, the network's money is on Tom, who represents the triumph of Nielsen ratings over civilization and the intellect. When Tom does his first big story on date rape, he interviews a woman about her experience and she starts to sob, saying, "I promised myself I wasn't going to cry." In the edited interview that airs, the camera cuts to Tom, who, listening sympathetically, allows one large tear to roll down his cheek. The people in the newsroom watching this debut piece applaud. Even Jane, who has resisted Tom's charms so far, changes her mind. "It moved me," she tells him, although still a little skeptical of the self-congratulatory aspect of the interview. "It was unusual to cut to yourself when you teared up. But it was real. And it got me."

And it does. She falls in love with Tom and they begin the requisite torrid affair. Tom's tearful response to the rape victim proves to Jane that he is sincere and has depth. She then discovers (with Aaron's aid) that Tom's tearful sympathy was an act, filmed at the studio after the interview had taken place. She feels duped, and outraged at Tom's breach of journalistic ethics. He explains that it is easy for him to cry at will, having learned to do so in acting class, and he fails to see the ethical problem, explaining that he had in fact felt strong sympathy for the woman during the interview, that his staged cry was an accurate representation of his feelings. But his artificially induced tears condemn him irredeemably, and the romance is over. In a coda, they meet years later, he with his bimbo fiancée, she with her integrity.

The film seems to argue what we already know, that sincere tears are good and false tears are bad, and that people who display false emotions are not to be trusted emotionally. We are encouraged to see Jane as an eighties superwoman who can both love passionately and be devoted to her work, who can both express and control her emotions, and who can both sleep with and reject the leading man. She tears up when her coworkers get fired, when she sees goodness in a person, or when the news piece she is working on is tragic, and all these tears are viewed by those around her as tributes to her worthiness and their own, rather than as proof of her weakness.

The film was made at a time when women had recently entered many workplaces and professions previously closed to them, and when psychologists and sociologists were studying the impact of women's emotional styles on workplace politics and culture. These studies detailed the conflicts women experienced as they learned to balance the often incompatible demands of gender and professionalism, as well as the prejudice against both "feminine" and "masculine" women. Jane feels no such problems, and her crying creates none. She can cry easily, but she can control it easily as well. She is at the top of her profession because she is good at it, and her emotionality is never interpreted as the kind of feminine incapacity that all the real-world evidence suggests it would have been. Like a nineteenth-century heroine, she leads a charmed life. Although she can be seduced, her heart remains pure, and that purity is recognized by all around her. She struggles through her life with great emotional integrity. She maintains her dignity despite the temptations—like the dumb hunk—strewn in her path. She is sincere, and her tears prove it, even those she has on schedule.

Ordinary People and *Broadcast News* used tears as themes but were not classic tearjerkers. Of course, one man's tearjerker is another man's *Rocky*—while filmmakers have worked long and hard to produce films that jump-start tears, their "weepies" don't always work well, and sometimes don't work at all. Men and women tend to respond differently to melodramatic scenes, and Hollywood produced an enormous number of melodramas expressly for women in the 1930s and 1940s. These films quickly collected nicknames—weepie, weeper, tearjerker, sobstory, soaper, four-hankie job—and although they were indeed designed specifically to make women cry, they were marketed under the more sedate name of "women's films." In the late 1940s, people began making what were called "male weepies," featuring situations geared to elicit male tears. Both male and female weepies use tears as well as produce them, but we are not meant, as in *Broadcast News* and *Ordinary People*, to think about tears or other issues of emotional expression explicitly. The tears on the screen are instrumental in making us cry, but thematically they are incidental rather than significant.

Even in films not so clearly engineered to extract a gendered response, men and women will react differently. The climactic scene of Diane Keaton's *Unstrung Heroes* (1995), for instance, shows a father watching home movies of his dead wife with their young son. Father and son have been at odds with each other throughout the film, and only now, after the funeral, do they forget and forgive their grievances against each other. They reunite and hug, providing the emotional climax and resolution of the film. In this last scene, all three family members are shown fulfilling their familial roles in ways they had not managed to do before. The father hugs his son; the son is respectful and loving to his father for the first time. Even the mother, who had eariler appeared distracted and depressed by her illness, in the home movies is shown as a happy, young, nurturing mother. I watched this film with a group of friends, and I asked people why they had cried at the climactic scene. A married woman said she had cried because she imagined losing her husband. A younger woman said she imagined losing her mother. A middle-aged man said the catalyst was the relation between father and son. Each of them were more or less "easily moved to tears" based on the different ways that scene intersected with their own experience. The roles on the screen, in relation to the social roles of the individuals in the audience, combined to cue tears.

An actor friend told me that whenever he needed tears for a scene, he conjured up a daydream to elicit them and that he had used several over the course of his career, replacing them when they got stale. He had concocted his latest scenario after the birth of his son. He imagined that he was on the *Titanic* as it was sinking (this was before the James Cameron film), and that he was handing his wife and baby son into a lifeboat. This vision could make him break down into sobs almost immediately. When I asked why he thought this worked so well, he said that it was because the image produced the most intense feeling of loss he could imagine.

Although this makes perfect sense in a way, I suggested that it nevertheless struck me as a bit odd, since his wife and son were not dying in this fantasy. He was not losing them so much as they were losing him. As we talked more, he realized that the scene's effectiveness for him was based on the fact that others were watching and approving of what he was doing—the captain of the ship, the first mate, the other men taking charge of the situation. This daydream, this mini-melodrama, makes him weep because in it he consummately fulfills an iconographic social role.

My friend cries when imagining himself heroically fulfilling his duty—not only seeing to it that his family is taken care of but perfectly fulfilling other traditional male roles, such as calmly and valiantly administering in the face of disaster—and doing it all in the eyes of witnesses, including the local authorities and other heroic men who can fully appreciate his heroism. Since it was the *Titanic,* it also seemed as if the eyes of history itself were on his courageous self-sacrifice, his manly act. His way having been prepared by previous melodramas of male heroism, he can weep in a kind of role-fulfillment ecstasy.

Hollywood has long known that a hero or heroine's fulfillment of a specific social role is a surefire tear-starter, and film melodrama is the dramatic form that most stridently involves itself in both the performance of social roles and the production of audience tears. The films of Douglas Sirk and Vincente Minnelli are regularly used in college courses as paradigmatic classics of the genre, and their films always hinge on role fulfillment. Sirk's best-known film, *Imitation of Life* (1959), is the story of a daughter who has not been a very good daughter, but whose mother has persevered and always done her best despite the daughter's disrespect and delinquency. The climax of the film shows the wayward daughter weeping over her mother's coffin, finally realizing how perfectly her mother had always fulfilled her role. This act of piety, her grieving on her mother's bier, is her final submission to the role she has been avoiding, the role of the dutiful and grateful daughter. When she cries, we cry with her, and if the survey data for other melodramas holds up, women more than men. In King Vidor's *Stella Dallas* (1937), one of the classic women's films of the 1930s, the climactic moment comes when the poor character played by Barbara Stanwyck gives her beloved daughter up to her rich and powerful husband. She lets her maternal sense of responsibility— the child will have more opportunities and privileges with her father—take precedence over her own desire to be with her daughter. The desires are mutually exclusive, and as her dedication to her role triumphs, the audience weeps.

Minnelli's *Home from the Hill* (1959) is a male weepie that tells the story of a man with two sons, one legitimate and one illegitimate. The father (Robert Mitchum as a philandering, tyrannical patriarch) tries to make his somewhat effeminate legitimate son (George Hamilton) into a hunter and he-man like himself but fails. His illegitimate son (George Peppard) serves as his ranch foreman and is the one who carries him home when he gets drunk; in other words, the bastard son does all the work of being the good son and gets no parental respect or even recognition. The father dies, and in the final scene we see the father's headstone, which his wife has inscribed with the names of both sons. She thus recognizes the illegitimate son for the first time, and tells him that he has been a good son. Finally acknowledged by the family, he wells up, and so does the music, and again it is the recognition of role fulfillment that serves as the flashpoint for the audience's tears.

Virtually all classic weepies follow the same track. Sirk documented male role failure in several of his "impossible stories," as he called them, particularly in *Written on the Wind* (1956) and *Magnificent Obsession* (1954), both of which have millionaire bachelor protagonists who are wasting their lives in dissipation, avoiding the cultural imperatives to get married, have children, work, and take responsibility for their actions. In *Magnificent Obsession*, the rich wastrel has a conversion, quits drinking and carousing, and becomes a brilliant surgeon and settled family man. At first the other characters wonder if he can properly be forgiven and trusted. When the people around him accept his conversion, the woman he loves bursts into tears and we have reached our emotional peak.

The most successful melodramas, as one would suppose, appeal to both men and women. James L. Brooks's *Terms of Endearment* (1983), another Academy Award Best Picture, features a young mother dying of cancer. From her hospital bed she says good-bye to her two young sons, taking care of their emotions rather than her own. Her older son is morose and irritable. He sullenly resists her attempts to have a last talk with him and to make the connection she knows he needs. She tells him that years from now, when he remembers this day, he may regret his inability to express his love. And she says that when that day comes, he should remember that she understands, and that she forgives him. Not even death, she suggests, will keep her from fulfilling her maternal role. We all—mothers, people with mothers—weep.

Of course, in our everyday lives we constantly confront role failure, from the spectacular to the mundane, and rarely do we experience the kind of resolution these "impossible stories" offer. Melodrama's reputation as a low form comes from the improbability of its solutions. Critic Thomas Schatz calls such resolutions "narrative sleight-of-hand," and it is a form of chicanery, I suppose. But the melodramatic wish-fulfillment fantasies these films purvey do not even pretend to be real-world solutions to the problems of meeting our culture's demands with respect to role performance. No one could mistake them for advice manuals. Most of our role-performance failures never get resolved—when we or our parents or partners are not good enough parents or partners, we live with the consequences, which often means no forgiveness, no restitution, no recompense. Melodramas exploit our desire for perfect resolution, and the tears we cry at these stories are a sign that we know such resolutions to be impossible. Our tears are proof, in fact, that we know very well how false melodramatic conclusions are.

Comedies make laughs out of the same failures of role performance that animate melodramas. When Laurel cried ineffectual tears and Hardy got ineffectually angry, they were enacting comic exaggerations of normal male behavior. Neil Simon's Broadway comedy *The Odd Couple* (1966; film version, 1968), like the Laurel and Hardy routines (and again with a thread of homosexuality lurking in the jokes), presents two competing models for male emotional behavior, one angry, one weepy. Oscar, your basic, standard-issue slob both hygienically and ethically, finally lures the Pigeon sisters, Gwendolyn and Cecily, into the apartment he shares with Felix, the fussy, recently divorced prig. Oscar, in gleeful anticipation, goes off to mix cocktails, leaving Felix alone with the giggling women and his own nervous sweat. At a loss for chit-chat, Felix begins to tell them about his kids and his ex-wife—she's wonderful, a wonderful cook, wonderful with the kids, a wonderful decorator—showing them pictures and getting happily excited. His excitement and awkwardness eventually get the best of him and he begins to weep at his forced removal from his role as husband and father.

Gwendolyn and Cecily do their best to comfort him: "You mustn't be ashamed," Gwendolyn says. "I think it's a rare quality in a man to be able to cry. . . . I think it's sweet," she says with a little sniffle, "terribly, terribly sweet!" And by then she, too, is sobbing volubly, while Cecily, mourning her own divorce now, chimes in with tears as well. Cecily announces that this is the first time she's cried since she was fourteen. "Just let it pour out," advises Felix. "It'll make you feel much better. I always do." Oscar returns with a tray of drinks (asking "Is ev-rybuddy happy?!") to find this scene of mass weeping, and immediately yells at Felix, demanding to know what the hell is going on. The sisters plead with Oscar to quit scolding. "I think he's the dearest thing I've ever met," says Gwendolyn, dabbing at her eyes. "He's so sensitive," Cecily adds, "so fragile. I just want to bundle him up in my arms and take care of him."

Oscar is a dolt, unable at first to see that women respond better to an honest display of emotion than to leering bravado. But Felix is clearly not an acceptable model either, effeminate in his obsessive housecleaning, his pride in his cooking, and his wearing of aprons, and he, too, thinks his weeping unmans him. When the Pigeon sisters ask Felix and Oscar up to their apartment, Felix refuses to go: "Don't you understand?" he asks. "I cried, I cried in front of two women!" But by then Oscar has seen the light: "They loved it!" he answers. "I'm thinking of getting hysterical myself!" Oscar has relearned the lessons of the great eighteenth-century lovers and is ready to add crying to his meager seductive arsenal. Felix, though, refuses to think pragmatically, showing us (if not Oscar) that his sincerity is the key. "You're not going to make any effort to change?" Oscar asks in disbelief. "This is the person you're going to be until the day you die?" Felix responds, opting for authenticity over growth, "We are what we are." The movie sides with Felix; his sincerity redeems his unmanly tears.

The film follows the have-one's-cake-and-eat-it-too logic of popu-

lar entertainments, which tend to give their audiences both sides of
the cultural debates of their time without siding explicitly with either.
The Odd Couple encourages us both to ridicule Felix's femininity and
to understand the attraction his tears have for the Pigeon sisters. We
empathize with Oscar's frustration and see all the crassness of his masculine pose. We end up seeing that it is both noble and humiliating to
cry. In such comedies of role-based weeping, we are asked not to cry,
of course, but to laugh in response.

Stuart Smalley, the fragile self-help guru played by Al Franken on
"Saturday Night Live," parodies the excesses of the therapeutic culture's encouragement to feel and express emotion, as he, always on the
verge of tears, gives in to them and other emotional excesses on a regular basis. Franken's character is belittled for trying to construct an
entire person out of adherence to sincerity and self-expression, for
confusing self-approval with self-knowledge, and for comically confusing the effect of his tears when he sees them in the mirror with their
effect on his audience. He gives us a kind of antietiquette manual for
our emotional culture, a series of "how not to" exempla for a world
forever transformed by therapeutic ideas and ideals. When Stuart
whimpers his self-affirmations in the mirror, it is not self-affirmation
that is being flayed but its ersatz, formulaic invocation. He is pathetic
because he has the equipment—the sensitivity, the knowledge, the
concepts, the desire—to understand himself, but he opts over and over
for a willful misunderstanding. And he is comic in his tears because he
constantly fails to live up to his general social role as a "man," to his
other socially available option as a gay man (he remains closeted), or
to his chosen role as adviser and guru. It is this failure that, when he is
forced to recognize it, makes him weep. Like all crying clowns, he is
like us, except worse at it.

Cruel Tears

Crying for laughs is hardly new. Shakespeare asks, "How much better
is it to weep at joy than to joy at weeping?" but given the prevalence
of comic tears, the answer is far from clear. One can find comic tears
in Greek plays, in Chaucer, in Rabelais, and throughout the history of

the novel. Charlie Chaplin's Little Tramp often seems on the verge of tears, and lets a drop fall when the occasion merits it, much like the highly stylized crying clowns of the *commedia dell'arte*, all for our amusement, however sentimentally tinged. Lucille Ball's blubbering or Mary Tyler Moore breaking down into a tearful "Oh, Rob!" in "The Dick Van Dyke Show" has the same effect. As the tears start, so does our laughter.

And we take joy in watching tears in other ways as well. Some stories of weeping give us an intense, voyeuristic pleasure. In classic eighteenth-century novels like Samuel Richardson's *Pamela* (1741) or *Clarissa* (1748), when the heroine's chastity is threatened, she often breaks down in tears as she pleads with the bad men not to ruin her, and such scenes were the most widely enjoyed by their readers. Some of Richardson's more moralistic readers worried that such scenes of virtue besieged verged on the pornographic, and the Marquis de Sade, in his foray into the genre, *Justine* (1791), made clear why. When Justine asks her assailant, "Can you conceive of gleaning happiness in the depths of tears and disgust?" she quickly finds that the answer is yes, that her tears inflame her rapist's passion. In Sade's *Philosophy in the Bedroom* (1795) he argues that "one weeps not save when one is afraid, and that is why kings are tyrants," and according to his erotic theory, tyranny is one natural impulse of the sexually aroused person.

When Baculard d'Arnaud's character, in *Les Amans malheureux* (1746), says, "How ravishing and adorable are the eyes of a lover when they are filled with tears!" he might be suggesting just this, or that other people's tears give them a kind of aesthetic glow. D'Arnaud's contemporary Choderlos de Laclos, in his 1782 novel *Les Liaisons dangereuses*, more emphatically outlines the way cruelty can be found to be pleasurable. Set among the French aristocracy on the eve of the Revolution, the novel describes the underside of the culture of sensibility, in which lovers who shed naïve tears are used as pawns in the manipulative and masochistic games of the debauched, idle rich.

The film version, *Dangerous Liaisons* (1989), like the novel, focuses on the less pretty emotions—betrayal, revenge, humiliation—and the various deceptions that cause them. The film depicts the artifice at the center of eighteenth-century court culture, with its powdered wigs, its heavy makeup, its bustles and corsets, its very mannered manners. When we see a young innocent boy (Keanu Reeves) crying at the opera, enraptured by the love story onstage, saying earnestly, "It's sublime!" we are meant to find it amusing, as do the more sophisticated folk in the audience we see laughing at his naïveté. But we are also meant to see their cruelty. When the aristocrat Valmont (John Malkovich) gives a peasant money, he finds the man "gratifyingly tearful," and we are meant to see the lack of empathy, the cruelty in his appreciation of the other man's tears.

At the end of the film, when Valmont is dying from wounds sustained in a duel, we see a big tear gather in one eye and roll down his cheek as another tear forms in his other eye. Exquisitely timed, just like one of his character's barbed witticisms, the second tear rolls down the other cheek. But we are unsure what exactly to make of these tears. Are they a sign of self-pity? Regret? Self-regard? Guilt? Pain? Self-loathing? Petulance? None of the above? Just before he expires, he smiles; he finds the pleasure in pain to the end.

The last scene of the movie follows Glenn Close, who plays Valmont's sometime lover Madame Merteuil, as she realizes she has been fully ostracized from society. She goes into a screaming tantrum and then sits down to take off her makeup, wiping it from under her eyes as if wiping away tears. Then, staring in the mirror at her own face, its artificial charms wipped off with a handkerchief, she begins to silently weep. This scene is not in the novel, and represents an opposing view of the relation of tears to pleasure, one summed up by the Midwestern American proverb, "Tears are the natural penalties of pleasure." It is, in a sense, the final revenge against her: she is forced to feel an emotion that does not bring her pleasure. (In the novel, her "natural penalty" is a disfiguring venereal disease.) And the audience gets to enjoy her downfall in the same way she has enjoyed reducing the people around her to tears.

The mixture of sublime tears and bodily debility in the death scene may provide pleasure because of, as the French critic and novelist Georges Bataille put it, the voluptuousness of our own horror. Or it may be that we simply have a taste for the tragedies of others, that we take pleasure in other people's misfortune just as Valmont and

Madame Merteuil do, just as the weeping audience does when they go to see the *Titanic* sink down again and again.

Dorothy Parker, in her most famous story, "Big Blond," makes her heroine Hazel seem foolish, pathetic, and addicted to the pleasures of weeping. She thereby makes an interesting case for the perverse pleasure of crying and the voyeuristic pleasure that crying can afford. The narrator tells us that Hazel

> fell readily into the habit of tears during the first year of her marriage. Even in her good-sport days she had been known to weep lavishly and disinterestedly on occasion. Her behavior at the theater was a standing joke. She could weep at anything in a play—tiny garments, love both unrequited and mutual, seduction, purity, faithful servitors, wedlock, the triangle.
>
> "There goes Haze," her friends would say, watching her. "She's off again."
>
> Wedded and relaxed, she poured her tears freely. To her who had laughed so much crying was delicious. All sorrows became her sorrows; she was Tenderness. She would cry long and softly over newspaper accounts of kidnapped babies, deserted wives, unemployed men, strayed cats, heroic dogs.

What Parker's Hazel discovers is the private pleasure of tears. Her pleasure is due to the exalted place crying affords her ("she was Tenderness") and the comfort she finds in it, the escape from the tensions of her world. For us as readers, Hazel's tears are a sign of her undiscriminating taste in both theater and everyday life, and thus gives us a sense of our superiority, much as Valmont and Merteuil felt superior when they made their victims cry. Hazel's weepiness is a sign of what a pathetic, ineffective, hopeless person she is. The list of her empathetic identifications shows her to be overly sentimental, the opposite of the cosmopolitan, Algonquin wit who created her and the cosmopolitans we consider ourselves to be as we read.

"To her who had laughed so much crying was delicious," Parker writes, and our delight in Hazel's tearful humiliation can be delicious as well. Hazel's crying after she is married is a case of "letting herself

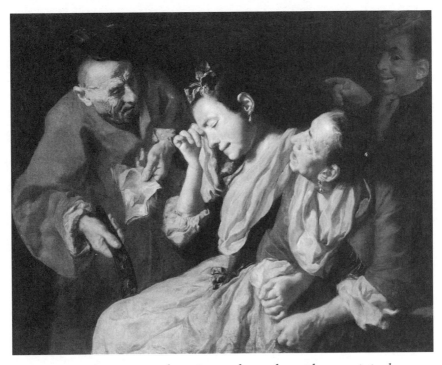

Tears can motivate some people to give comfort and provide voyeuristic pleasure to others. Gaspare Traversi, *The Detected Love Letter* (seventeenth century). Bequest of John Ringling, Collection of the John and Mable Ringling Museum of Art, the State Art Museum of Florida.

go," and the piece is a criticism of marriage more than it is a criticism of weeping. But the weeping is necessary to the pleasure we take in the story. Hazel's story is on one level tragic—a fun-loving, pretty, but not too bright young woman is reduced, in a few pages, from a popular model to an abused wife, and then to a desperate alcoholic with varicose veins and no companions except her maid. But Parker keeps us distanced from the human tragedy with cruel humor, using among other things these patronizing representations of Hazel's crying. In this Parker is relying on a stock and oft exploited response, part schadenfreude and part outrageousness, orchestrated by a narrator who makes the cruelty seem normal and deserved.

Fyodor Dostoyevsky makes Parker look like a piker when it comes to human cruelty and black humor. In *Notes from Underground* (1864), the narrator lets loose a tirade of accusations against and confessions to Liza, a prostitute he has been tormenting. As he rants at her, he explains why he made her cry on their first night together: "It was power, power that I needed then," he tells her in what is perhaps the most naked admission in literature of the relationship of power to tears. "I had to play with you, reduce you to tears, humble you, make you hysterical—that's what I needed!" The idiom is significant: to "reduce" people to tears is to diminish them, to deny their full being and shrink them into an image of their distress.

But the power of tears turns on him. After his diatribe, she runs to him sobbing, and throws her arms around his neck weeping. This then causes the underground man to "break down":

> I broke down too and sobbed as I had never sobbed before . . . and for a quarter of an hour sobbed in true hysterics. She clung to me, embraced me, and remained motionless in that embrace. Still, the trouble was that the fit of hysteria had to pass in the end. And then . . . lying prone on the sofa, pressing my face into the wretched leather cushion, I gradually, involuntarily, distantly at first, but irresistibly began to feel how embarrassing it would be for me now to raise my head and look straight into Liza's eyes.

Tears here do not, finally, do their work because the underground man refuses to allow the intimacy they imply. The dark comedy of his dilemma is that he cannot learn from these experiences and goes on abusing social interactions in an attempt to wield power, always falling victim to the power of the conventions he despises.

But Dostoyevsky shows that if oppression can cause tears, so can tears be oppressive. The underground man humiliates the prostitute until she cries, her tears humiliate him until he cries, and then his tears, when they inevitably stop, will humiliate him further. And yet the underground man's humiliation is a source of pleasure, however perverse. The service he is receiving from this prostitute is clearly a substitute satisfaction, and each instance of tears can be read as a kind of orgasm, followed by a characteristic *tristesse* and then renewed desire. We all grow up hearing of Georgie-Porgie, who kisses the girls and makes them cry, and most of us have some firsthand knowledge of the relationship between pleasure and cruelty, whether we explicitly acknowledge it or not, and whether we actively pursue it or bump into its more passive manifestations, such as the feeling of schadenfreude, a joke at the expense of a friend, the reading of a novelistic rendition of tears, or, like Hazel or the underground man, simply feeling sorry for our own plight in this cruel world.

And so while some readers may find the underground man's weepy pleasures sadomasochistic or pathetic, they are clearly pleasures nonetheless. Bataille, like Dostoyevsky, sees a connection between cruelty and pleasure. The mother in his novel *My Mother* (1966) says, in a phrase that regularly gets quoted, "Pleasure only starts once the worm has got into the fruit; to become delightful happiness must be tainted with poison." In Bataille's meditation on tears and love, *The Tears of Eros* (1961), he writes: "In the violence of the overcoming [of reason], in the disorder of my laughter and my sobbing, in the excess of raptures that shatter me, I seize on the similarity . . . between an ultimate pain and an ultimate joy." This, Bataille says, is what makes the great sadomasochists—Gilles de Rais, the Marquis de Sade, Chinese torturers—who they are.

There is a somewhat less sadistic spin we can put on this as well. John Irving's novel *The Cider House Rules* opens with a story of a baby in an orphanage named Homer. A late-middle-aged couple has come to adopt him. They have many children of their own at home, including, until recently, the eldest daughter and her baby. But she had packed the infant up and left because the rest of the family complained so much about the baby's crying. In Irving's fairy-tale-like universe, the family realizes that they miss the infant, and even more so they miss the infant's crying. Since the mother can't have any more children, they go to the orphanage and find and adopt Homer.

Unfortunately, Homer is a remarkably content baby, famous at the orphanage for never crying. When his adoptive family realizes this, they are disappointed, and they begin to do whatever they can to make him cry. They starve him, hurt him, startle him, frighten him, burn him, and beat him. Eventually, he cries so much he keeps the whole small town awake at nights, and news of his wailing reaches the nurses at the orphanage, who come to rescue him. The people in this family were not sadists, the narrator tells us, they just got a little carried away indulging a very normal human impulse. They wanted to feel needed, and they wanted to be called upon in a way that they felt confident they could answer. Hence they wanted, more than anything, to hear a baby's cry.

There is a basic human pleasure in fulfilling the desires of others, and tears are the lubricant for many of these interactions. The most obvious case, as Irving's fable suggests, is the crying of babies, in which unconsciousness and helplessness merge in a prototypically pure expression of need. As people get older, their demands on each other grow in complexity and dimension, and the likelihood of finding a fully satisfying response diminishes. Thus we become much more wary, as adults, of making demands through tears or offering to answer them. But infant's tears, when they are not uncannily inconsolable or uncannily absent, are never particularly difficult to satisfy. And fulfilling those needs is, as parents learn, where much of the joy of the relationship resides. We demand tears, Irving suggests, from our children, and often, we might add, from others as well, in order to enjoy the simple pleasure of comforting them.

Elizabeth Prentiss, who as a nineteenth-century preacher's wife claimed she had "the *right* to sympathize with those who mourn . . . to join them in their prayers and tears," wrote in her best-seller *Stepping Heavenward* (1869) that "it would be pleasant to spend one's whole time" thus employed. As the historian Ann Douglas has pointed out, the intimate pleasure of mourning was inextricably linked to the power it bestowed upon women and clergy, and what looked like (and in fact was) self-indulgence at the personal level was also the staking out of a certain kind of cultural authority. The weeping female figures that adorned family sepulchers in nineteenth-century graveyards convey not just the iconic power of weeping women but the fact that women controlled the mourning process. Prentiss's pleasure in attending the weeping of others was directly related, Douglas suggests, to her sense of her own power. The most disturbing corollary of this is the study which found that women who cried when they were being raped suffered more serious and more extensive injuries than women who did not, suggesting that whatever the combination of violence and pleasure that goes into rape, the impetus is heightened by the sight of the victim's tears. In a more mundane and obviously less violent way, we are perhaps responding to a similar principle when we thrill to the tears we see represented on the screen or on the page.

Modern Tears

The classic blues musician John Lee Hooker told an interviewer last year: "You can't get no deeper than me and my guitar. I open my mouth, and it's there. I get so deep the teardrops come to my eyes." The depths of Hooker's emotion and its expression are perfect mirrors of each other; the "deeper" you go, the more likely tears are to rise to the surface. "That's why I wear my dark glasses," Hooker adds, with the bluesman's dose of irony, "so you won't see the teardrops." John Waters's film *Cry-Baby* (1990), a faux rock musical, uses a similar combination of invocation and parody. *Cry-Baby* tells the story of a crying crooner, played by Johnny Depp, who, in every crucial scene, is seen with a single, pronounced tear rolling down his cheek. Called by people in the film "the Big Boo-Hoo," "the Terrible Teardrop," or "Cry-Baby," he is an apotheosis of the fifties teen idol. Like Waters's *Hairspray* (1988), the film is not just a parody of the pop stylings of the late 1950s and early 1960s, it is a loving re-creation of them. The Elvis effect is everywhere, from the hairdos to the jailhouse-rock number after Cry-Baby is arrested, in a fictional world only marginally more stylized than the one it mimics. The single tear that rolls down Cry-Baby's face again and again is not just mockery, it is also tinged with a certain reverence.

In the middle of the film, we cut back and forth between Cry-Baby's girlfriend Alison, collecting her tears in a mason jar in a parody of the ancient practice of collecting tears in a lacrimatory vial, and Cry-Baby, weeping as he strums a guitar made out of a tissue box and singing, in a style calmer than Johnnie Ray's but rawer than Elvis's:

Johnny Depp as the hero of John Waters's film Cry-Baby *(1990)*. © 1999 Universal City Studios, Inc. Courtesy of Universal Studios Publishing Rights. All Rights Reserved.

> *Teardrops are falling out of my eyes,*
> *Teardrops are falling, I wonder why,*
> *Teardrops are falling, for you make me cry.*

Waters shows us that this song, which seems to ignore not just all aesthetic rules of composition but the entire history of songwriting, nonetheless retains its power to affect.

As if she hears his song, Alison, home in her bedroom, drinks her jarful of collected tears, finishing it off as the song ends. Cry-Baby has a single tear tattooed on his cheek in jail so that his tear for Alison will last forever. Cry-Baby and Alison luxuriate in their pain and tears, and the Roman touch with the lacrimatories is supposed to add to the sense of decadent emotion. But Waters is also highly critical—through his depictions of the uptight society mothers and frat boys—of an emotional life that denies the reality of pain. Even more ridiculous than the weepy misfits, Waters suggests, are the codes of everyday modern life, especially in their 1950s suburban manifestations, that attempt to regulate and readjust all emotional perturbations. Waters shows crying to be the luxury of the disaffected, and indeed even suggests that crying is adequate recompense for falling through society's cracks. Better a weeping melancholic, in Waters's universe, than a sunny, well-adjusted citizen. The mixture of social criticism, the silly, the sentimental, the grotesque, and the reverential is one of Waters's trademarks, as is the way in which, at the end of the film, the parody spills into wanton excess, as we watch long, caressing shots of the ten main players, each of whom is shown weeping bizarrely profuse, abundant (and obviously glycerin) tears as the credits begin to roll. Although the film has celebrated tears, the exorbitant crying at the end manages to alienate us from the naturalness of tears themselves, just as Hooker's joke about the sunglasses gives the lie to his blues sentimentality, and just as the "natural" sign of sentiment on Cry-Baby's cheek has been replaced by a campy, tacky tattoo.

Modernist artists and writers questioned the naturalness of tears in their dramas of alienation. The French symbolist poet and grandfather of modernism, Charles Baudelaire, in his introduction to his masterpiece *Les Fleurs du mal*, mocks our belief that we can, in my own fairly literal translation, "wash away our blemishes with vile tears." In Robert Lowell's more poetic translation of the line, Baudelaire's distaste is rendered even stronger: "We pray for tears to wash our filthiness, / importantly pissing hogwash through our eyes." Many writers railed against conventionalized sentimentality in the late nineteenth century, one comic example being the end of *Huckleberry Finn*, in which Tom Sawyer makes Jim squeeze onions so that he can water the plant in his prison cell with tears: Sawyer says that in all of the books he's read, the prisoner waters a plant with his tears. The modernists not only criticized conventional understandings of emotion but also attempted to frustrate conventional emotional responses to their art, celebrating both emotional and aesthetic distance. Man Ray's photographs of fake tears, with their perfect, glistening, and yet plastic, inanimate effect, are perhaps the most obvious example. Man Ray is preceded by Alfred Jarry, who in his 1902 novel *The Supermale* has his protagonist, who is dying as the result of a scientific experiment, cry a single tear, which is zapped by electricity and turned into a jewel.

Modernism's emphasis on aesthetic control and distance was in direct opposition to romantic and sentimental modes, and part of the rise of a masculinist ethic: sentimentalism was derided as effeminate, romance dismissed as stuff for girls. All of this led T. S. Eliot, Ezra Pound, and other modernists to confine displays of emotion, as Maurizia Boscagli has argued, to the realm of mass culture and kitsch. Mass culture was at the same time saturating its audience's psyches with images of actors and actresses weeping, which, whatever general ideas about the value of tears it may reinforce, couldn't but suggest that crying was a form of play-acting.

The twenties also saw the rise of a masculinist style of writing, most famously that of Ernest Hemingway. Hemingway became famous as a big-game hunting, bullfight-loving, hard-drinking man's man, and a "tough guy" writer. His writing was celebrated for its terseness and economy, in which narrators speak in a kind of emotional monotone, eschewing emotional inflection. In the story "Indian Camp," part of Hemingway's first book, *In Our Time* (1925), a young boy is with his father, a doctor, as he performs an emergency cesarean on a poor Native American woman. "Oh, Daddy, can't you give her something to make her stop screaming?" the young boy asks. "No. I haven't any anæsthetic," his father answers. "But her screams are not important. I don't hear them because they are not important." They are important to the woman's husband, who commits suicide upon hearing his wife scream. The story ends with the young boy thinking to himself, in a line that has become famous, "He felt quite sure he would never die." The woman's husband died because he thought his wife's crying was important; the young boy is learning to feel his own power by not responding to the emotional appeals of others.

The other stories in the book, too, show the ways in which boys are trained to be stoics, and the ways that stoicism manifests itself in later life. Instead of crying at scenes of death and carnage during the war, men say things like "My word yes a most pleasant business." To their wives' appeals they say, "Oh shut up." Hemingway has often been naïvely considered a writer who celebrates such male continence or incompetence, but he was in fact, especially in his early work, a great chronicler and critic of what T. S. Eliot famously called the "dissociation of sensibility" at the heart of modern life and culture.

For Eliot, the divorce of rationality from emotion, of feeling from experience, and of bodies from minds, was the great curse of modernity. Before the modern era, feeling, thinking, perceiving, sensing, writing, reading—all were part of an organic whole, they had a "fidelity." But by his own time, Eliot thought, we were hopelessly divided. "In the seventeenth century," Eliot wrote, "a dissociation set in, from which we have never recovered." We are marooned, cut off, unable to think through even our own most trivial desires. "Do I dare?" the narrator of one of Eliot's best-known poems, J. Alfred Prufrock, asks. "Do I dare to eat a peach?" Prufrock and the other modern everymen of Eliot's poetry risk nothing, feel nothing strongly, and so live in a kind of emotional abeyance—they neither cry nor laugh, existing in a cloud of boredom that is itself a defense against feeling anything.

Of course, Parker shows that Hazel's false sentimentality is equally "dissociated." The novelist Nathanael West describes the crying of his antihero, Homer Simpson, in *The Day of the Locust* (1939) in ways reminiscent of Parker's Hazel. West describes the sound Homer makes crying in one scene as "like that of a dog lapping gruel" and in another

Lichtenstein's ironic take on being overwhelmed by tears. Roy Lichtenstein, *Drowning Girl* (1963). The Museum of Modern Art, New York. Philip Johnson Fund and gift of Mr. and Mrs. Bagley Wright.

as "like an ax chopping pine, a heavy, hollow, chunking noise. It was repeated rhythmically but without accent. There was no progress in it. Each chunk was exactly like the one that preceded. It would never reach a climax." And therefore it could never do him any good. Homer's crying, at once animalistic and mechanical, helps complete West's picture of a hopeless, primitive, degraded soul.

If Hemingway and Eliot show their time's antiemotionalism to be a form of cowardice, then Parker and West suggest that weeping is a form of bad taste and self-indulgence. D. H. Lawrence, too, attacked conventional emotional expression as moribund and in need of replacement. An emotion, for Lawrence, is a feeling that has been named, classified, and thereby falsified. But like Hemingway and Eliot, Lawrence also thought the problem was one of timidity as well as conventionality. The problem was not that men and women felt strong emotions, but that they were inadequately felt, and therefore inauthentic. We have barely begun "to educate ourselves in the feelings," Lawrence wrote, which we must do in order to counter our genteel civilization's diminution of emotion.

Lawrence assumed that male reticence was at best an only partially successful defense against pain, at worst an alienation from the self. In *Women in Love* (1920), when Birkin finds Gerald, whom he loved, dead, he at first talks himself out of feeling anything: "to rant, to rave, to be tragic, to make situations—it was all too late. Best be quiet and bear one's soul in patience and fullness." But moments later, he breaks down. "With a strange whimpering cry, the tears broke out. He sat down in a chair, shaken by a sudden access. Ursula, who had followed him, recoiled aghast from him as he sat with sunken head and body convulsively shaken, making a strange, horrible sound of tears." But whereas Homer Simpson's horrible sounds are animalistic and lack "progress," Birkin's are meaningful: in these tears he comes closest to overcoming his handicap, which Lawrence saw as a general affliction—his lack of female qualities. Sentimentality was the enemy for Lawrence, too, but passion was the corrective.

Gertrude Stein, another antisentimentalist, wrote with an affect so flat that she didn't need commas. Stein wrote, in one of her many enigmatic works, *The Geographical History of America; or, The Relation of Human Nature to the Human Mind* (1936), a running commentary on tears, interspersed almost as non sequiturs throughout the text: "It is exciting not to cry," we are told at one point, and later: "To cry does not make the human mind oh no to cry does not make the human mind it makes a piece of nature but it does not make the human mind." Many such sentences appear in this quasi-philosophical tone, along with some that are more narrative: "And so and so and there is no real use for tears. Only when her son has fallen off a cart and when the small bones of his ankle are broken in the midst of the harvest and he cannot work for two months. Then it is nervousness that makes water come to her eyes." These passages seem to stand alone in all their cryptic glory, but a pattern does finally emerge. Stein thinks that tearlessness is a twentieth-century phenomenon: "In the nineteenth century they did not surprise tears they dwelt with tears," she explains, but "gradually human nature has no tears." In the sentimental nineteenth century, people dwelt with tears as a regular part of their lives, but now we are at best momentarily surprised by them, or they are simply a form of nervousness. In the twentieth century, "Human nature has now no tears. . . . [T]here are no tears." The lack of emotion Stein describes is, in part, a fact of cultural history—even if only inasmuch as Eliot, Hemingway, Man Ray, and others invented it. But Stein does not confuse this with the idea that no one cries. "It is clearer than anyone that there are no tears," she writes. "Anyone" can cry, but there are no more tears of the sort that the nineteenth century cried.

Stein repeats this idea over and over again in the text—we used to have tears but now we do not—and she sounds almost nostalgic about it. The poet Laura Riding, like Stein, wrote about the diminishing number of occasions for tears, and she makes it clear that the change has something to do with communication. In "When Love Becomes Words," Riding wrote that we "extract the sincere drop of relief" from our disappointments that corresponds to the "tear in our thoughts / That we have no reason to shed." The tears are still in our thoughts, we just have no reason to shed them. We may feel like crying, but we have no one to cry to, not enough sense that our cries will be heard or answered, and therefore no reason to shed them.

The discussion of tearlessness by Stein, Eliot, and Hemingway and

One of Thomas Woodruff's series of crying clowns, in which real tears and modernist tears meld. Thomas Woodruff, *Chromatic Aberration, Crying Clown—Green* (1990). Courtesy the artist and P•P•O•W, New York.

the critique of tears by West and Parker signaled a new distrust of emotion among the literary elite. The kind of emotionalism represented by sentimental novelists like Dickens, Stowe, and Louisa May Alcott, the lachrymose poetry of the Victorian poets, and the weepy heroines and weepy audiences of stage melodrama had become irredeemably old-fashioned. The new masculinist ethos, the new feminism, along with developments in the social and natural sciences, especially the rise of behaviorism and the discovery of endocrinology, all helped usher in a brave new era of antiexpression in high culture. More recently, this can be seen in the series of paintings by Roy Lichtenstein, in the style of melodramatic cartoons, of women with puddles of tears falling from their eyes. Sentimentality is the stuff of bad culture, these paintings suggest, ironic distance the measure of art.

But there continued to be, in the twenties and thirties and beyond, many conventional novels and films that encouraged melodramatic or sentimental tears. Gene Stratton Porter, Harold Bell Wright, Kathleen Norris, and other best-selling authors wrote romance novels and historical novels that, like those of the previous century, were designed to elicit tears, and that featured tearful scenes meant to be taken in full seriousness. The rise of the weepie is proof enough that however seriously these critiques of emotional expression were, "anyone" could still cry.

Weepiness never disappears, it just gets reinvented. Laura Esquival's best-selling *Like Water for Chocolate* (1992) is a case in point. The protagonist, Tita, is a prodigious weeper, and this fact about her is as telling as the weepiness of any sentimental heroine in past centuries. But rather than being a physiomoral fact as it was for eighteenth-century novelists, or a quasi-religious fact as it was for nineteenth-century sentimentalists, for Esquival it is magically real.

> When she was still in my great-grandmother's belly her sobs were so loud that even Nacha, the cook, who was half-deaf, could hear them easily. Once her wailing got so violent that it brought on an early labor. And before my great-grandmother could let out a word or even a whimper, Tita made her entrance into this world, prematurely, right there on the kitchen table. . . . Tita had no need for the usual slap on the bottom, because she was already crying as she emerged; maybe that was because she knew then that it would be her lot in life to be denied marriage. The way Nacha told it, Tita was literally washed into this world on a great tide of tears that spilled over the edge of the table and flooded across the kitchen floor. That afternoon . . . Nacha swept up the residue the tears had left on the red stone floor. There was enough salt to fill a ten-pound sack—it was used for cooking and lasted a long time.

Unlike the preternatural tears at the end of *Cry-Baby*, these tears are not uncanny or bizarre, they are miraculous. And unlike Dickey Lee's 1950s hit "9,999,999 Tears," we are not supposed to immediately dismiss Tita's tears as exaggeration. Her feats of weeping are meant, as much as those of any sentimental heroine, to awe us with her emotional prowess. They are, of course, weirdly dissociated—Tita weeps just as prodigiously while chopping onions, and the sweeping up of the tears' residue is an oddly pragmatic response to them—but not because Tita is alienated from her own passions. Tita is just extraordinarily, abnormally endowed as an emotional being. She is born, and reborn, on a flood of her own tears. As Adrienne Rich wrote in her poem "Peddling Onions," as if in response: "Only to have a grief equal to all these tears!"

Conclusion

The End of Tears

Niobe, the queen of Thebes and granddaughter of Zeus, made a big mistake. She bragged about her fourteen children and let slip a snide remark about the goddess Leto's paltry total of two. Unfortunately, Leto's two children were the gods Artemis and Apollo, who avenged the insult to their mother by slaughtering all of Niobe's seven sons and seven daughters. Niobe's husband, seeing the carnage, killed himself. Weeping and wailing, Niobe pleaded with Zeus to put her out of her misery. As a gesture of mercy (although it seems a tardy gesture), he turned her into a stone, and this stone has been weeping ever since, or so the story goes.

The unending grief of the mother who has lost her children is a perennial image. Aurora, Roman goddess of the dawn, weeps every sunrise about the death of her son Memnon, which is how we get dewdrops on the morning ground. Hyria melted away in tears at the death of her son Cycnus, and in one version of the Greek myth her tears formed Lake Hyria, in which she then drowned herself; in another version she was turned by Zeus into the Cyncean Lake. The Pietà, the image of the mourning Mary holding the body of the crucified Christ, or the innumerable paintings of a weeping Mary at the foot of the cross, are Christian equivalents, as are the weeping statues of saints and visitations of the Virgin. Mexican children are told to watch out for "La Llorona," an eternally weeping ghost central to Mexican folklore who prowls the woods and other dark places.

These are prodigious tears. Even turning Niobe to stone—the emblematic emotionless material—cannot stop her weeping. The power of figures such as Niobe, the crying Madonna, or La Llorona resides not just in their obvious demand upon our sympathies, given their losses; they undoubtedly also represent our desire for eternal maternal devotion. But at the same time, nothing can bring back Niobe's or La Llorona's children—they cry forever precisely because their demands are unanswerable. If the tears of the eternally bereaved mother can make us feel the power of tears, they also mark the absolute limits of that power.

In nonmythological mourning, weeping does eventually cease, of course. Even in cases in which tears seem interminable—colic, for instance, or other forms of pathological crying—crying does come to an end. And so while Niobe never stops crying, we (and our mothers) do. As the German poet Heinrich Heine put it, "Whatever tears one may shed, one always blows one's nose." And while we know this, in the throes of extreme lamentation we forget. Whenever we begin to cry, the end of our own crying is unimaginable, and the myth's resonance comes from this—that when we are crying, it feels eternal. We can be taken out of time, plucked out of the narrative within which we had been seeing ourselves, as we ride crying's waves of sensation and absorption. The myth's most unreal aspect is also that which gets at the phenomenological truth of tears: until they end, they feel eternal.

How, then, do we stop crying?

In a story told in three of the Gospels of Mark, Luke, and John, Jesus is brought to the house of one of the rulers of a temple whose child has died. There is great weeping and wailing in the house, and Jesus says, "Do not weep; for she is not dead but sleeping." Jesus brings the child back to life and the weeping ceases.

Among the Tlingit of Alaska, it was the custom for a man, when his child died, to abstain from sex for several months while he worked and saved up what he needed to hold a feast in honor of the deceased. His wife, meanwhile, mourned and cried at night for the dead child. When the husband was ready, he said to his wife, "I wish to stop you from crying. So I will give a feast for your child."

At the final traditional ceremony of mourning among the Pawnee, the chief entered the lodge of the grieving family and told them that it was time to stop mourning. His assistant would bring a bowl of water that the chief then used to wash the faces of the family, washing away the last tears.

These stories suggest several of the ways—consolation, compensation, commandment, and coddling—in which people induce each other to stop crying. In the Gospel story, the man is offered a miracle and the reader is offered a spiritual satisfaction: the consolation that the soul lives even if the body "is sleeping." The Tlingit husband exchanges ritual for relief, and asks his wife to stop crying only when he is ready to exchange a feast for her tears. The Pawnee chief, like Jesus, commands that the weeping stop, and like the Tlingit husband he offers ritual compensation in the form of the symbolic washing away of the family's tears.

In *The Odyssey*, we are given an interesting parable of the end of crying. In book 4, Odysseus's son, Telemakhos, who is traveling in disguise, hears the story of his father's heroism and loss from Meneláos, the husband of Helen, and the whole company gets weepy as they remember the battles: "Thus did he speak, and his words set them all to weeping. Helen wept, Telemakhos wept, and so did Meneláos, nor could Nestor's son keep his eyes from filling, when he remembered his dear brother Antilochus whom the son of bright Dawn had killed." The remembrance of the dead, the retelling of the lost life, accompanied by testimonials and expressions of longing reignite the fires of mourning. Even Nestor's son, who first suggests that the company not just "weep away these hours," admits that mourning is right and proper. "What else can we bestow on the poor dead?" he asks, but a "lock of hair sheared, and a tear let fall."

Eventually, though, mourning must stop so that life may go on.

Helen arrives at a solution to the problem of eternal mourning and arranges the cessation of tears:

> Then Jove's daughter Helen . . . drugged the wine with an herb that banishes all care, sorrow, and ill humour. Whoever drinks wine thus drugged cannot shed a single tear all the rest of the day, not even though his father and mother both of them drop down dead, or he sees a brother or a son hewn in pieces before his very eyes.

Helen got the "mild magic" from the Egyptians, the acknowledged masters of medicine in Homer's time. After this magical therapy, storytelling can resume without mourning. This episode is an allegorical fable of the social functions of crying and not crying. The tears that are shed when the stories begin are signs of a deep social bond, arising not just out of Meneláos's debt to Ulysses for helping him win the war against the Trojans but also out of that debt's reversion to Telemakhos. The tears now shed are "bestowed" upon the dead as repayment of that debt, and at the same time they are shed in ways that acknowledge communal ideals even as they help define them. When we cry together, we agree—for that ephemeral time—on what is most important. When we cry together, we respond to each other's most profound desires.

But this moment of tearful communion must pass, for as Nestor's son points out, eventually they must sleep, and they must eat, and if they were to continue weeping forever, other opportunities would pass. These opportunities—for more storytelling, for games, for camaraderie, for ritual—are all, too, the sign and making of communal bonds. To cry together is to create community, to recognize each other, and to then stop crying is to forge ahead with that community. Something always acts as Helen's potion, as the mild magic of forgetfulness.

Parents learn as they go along that one emotion can replace another. They tickle their babies to pull them out of crankiness, or make them feel safe and loved so as to allay their fears, or shame them in order to stop their tirades or demands. Learning not to cry, then, is often a matter of learning how to feel something else. These substitutions are the stuff of our daily emotional lives, and if they can be thought of at one level as a form of repression, they are also essential to what we call conscience, socialization, and maturation. Sometimes crying is a reasonable request for solace, redress, attention, apology, comfort, peace, or help, and if such appeals are answered, people stop crying. But weeping often constitutes an unreasonable demand, or even an impossible demand, directed against the fates, as in the case of inconsolable mourning. In such cases, we need, eventually, to stop of our own volition. And whenever we know that weeping will fall on deaf ears, or cause us to be ridiculed, we try to stop tears before they start. It is one of the jobs of a parent to teach, and one of the jobs of a child to learn, these skills.

Emily Brontë wrote a poem in the 1830s that suggests what it is we commonly do when we don't cry—we perform an act of concealment:

> *She dried her tears and they did smile*
> *To see her cheeks' returning glow;*
> *Nor did discern how all the while*
> *That full heart throbbed to overflow.*
> *With that sweet look and lively tone,*
> *And bright eye shining all the day,*
> *They could not guess, at midnight lone,*
> *How she would weep the time away.*

This trope is achingly familiar from its television and cinematic uses, as when people blink back their tears in displays of strength and fortitude. What is essential in such scenes, as in Brontë's poem, is that the tears are not entirely hidden, that they are both hidden and revealed. The "bright eye shining all the day" reveals the hidden tears; those who can't see this lack discernment.

A scene from *The Odyssey* centers on manly concealment. Odysseus is at a feast at the palace of Alkínoös, where no one knows his true identity. The minstrel begins to sing of the great fight between Odysseus and Achilles, already a legend since Odysseus has been working his way home for ten years and is presumed dead. When he hears the song, Odysseus cries, and we are told in some detail about the concealing of his tears.

Ulysses drew his purple mantle over his head and covered his face, for he was ashamed to let the Phaeacians see that he was weeping. When the bard left off singing he wiped the tears from his eyes, uncovered his face, and, taking his cup, made a drink-offering to the gods; but when the Phaeacians pressed Demodocus to sing further, for they delighted in his lays, then Ulysses again drew his mantle over his head and wept bitterly. No one noticed his distress except Alkínoös, who was sitting near him, and heard the heavy sighs that he was heaving.

At this point Alkínoös calls a halt to the singing and declares that they should have a track meet instead. After the track meet, once again the minstrel begins singing of the battle for Troy. Upon hearing it, Odysseus

> was overcome, and his cheeks were wet with tears. He wept as a woman weeps when she throws herself on the body of her husband who has fallen before his own city and people, fighting bravely in defense of his home and children. She screams aloud and flings her arms about him as he lies gasping for breath and dying, but her enemies beat her from behind about the back and shoulders, and carry her off into slavery, to a life of labor and sorrow, and the beauty fades from her cheeks—even so piteously did Ulysses weep, but none of those present perceived his tears except Alkínoös, who was sitting near him, and could hear the sobs and sighs that he was heaving. The king, therefore, at once rose and said, "From the moment that we had done supper and Demodocus began to sing, our guest has been all the time groaning and lamenting. He is evidently in great trouble, so let the bard leave off."

We are never explicitly told why Odysseus is crying here, but we assume that the cause lies in his remembrance of tragedy and his longing for home. But more important than the cause is the effect. Odysseus is hiding his tears—because they are unmanly? because he doesn't want to be found out? And yet he is not hiding them very well, since his host knows both times, and both times the revealing of tears causes things to change. To try to hide one's tears is as effective, as a means of communication, as letting them flow freely. The two forms of crying—open and concealed—work the same magic, they just demand slightly different responses. And that difference, in testimony as widely separated as Brontë's and Homer's, is that concealed tears demand more respect. Open crying can be childish, or tragic, or peevish, or hysterical, but hidden tears are heroic.

Darwin noted that when we repress an emotion, only those muscles that are under voluntary control are affected, and Freud was convinced that "no mortal can keep a secret. If his lips are silent, he chatters with his finger-tips; betrayal oozes out of him at every pore." More recently, Ekman and Freisen have written about what is called "nonverbal leakage," the way suppressed emotions are revealed in gestures and other bodily cues. But Odysseus's tears suggest something else, since he is not really suppressing his tears at all.

This scene has also been discussed by the German philosopher Martin Heidegger, who examined Odysseus's concealment in an essay he wrote on Heraclitus, an early Greek philosopher known as "Heraclitus the Obscure" and, because of his pessimism, "the weeping philosopher." Heidegger claims that in the original Greek, Odysseus is not concealing his tears but rather concealing himself; the Greek reads, "He remained concealed." Heidegger's philosophical notions are themselves famously difficult, and it probably will not help many of my readers when I quote Heidegger's conclusion to this essay:

> The invisible shining of the lighting streams from wholesome self-keeping in the self-restraining preservation of destiny. Therefore the shining of the lighting is in itself at the same time a self-veiling—and is in that sense what is most obscure.

Indeed. Heidegger makes the point that self-revealing and self-concealing are necessarily intertwined, that one cannot occur without the other, that they can be said, in fact, to be the same. From this perspective, Odysseus is unveiling himself as he cries at the very same time that he remains concealed. No one's being can remain completely concealed, and being can never be completely revealed.

And although Heidegger doesn't remark on this aspect of the text,

Heraclitus (c. 540–475 B.C.) was known as the weeping philosopher because of his dark view of human nature. This painting has been variously identified as "The Weeping Heraclitus" and "St. Jerome." Jerome (c. 347–420) translated the Bible from Hebrew into Latin. Hendrick ter Brugghen, Dutch, 1588–1629. *St. Jerome,* 1621. Oil on canvas, 145 x 120 cm. © The Cleveland Museum of Art, 1999, Mr. and Mrs. William H. Marlett Fund, 1977.2.

the self-revealing that Odysseus does here has to do with memory, with hearing tales of his own past. Odysseus cries in part because he feels revealed, he feels a kind of public recognition in hearing the bard's song. He cries because he hears his presence, which he is hiding, made public. Learning not to cry is one way in which we attempt to control the amount we reveal to others, not only of what we feel but, thereby, of who we feel we are. Crying is itself always a mask, and conceals as it reveals; surreptitious crying does the same, differently. And Odysseus's semiconcealed tears do in fact reveal something about him. As Alkínoös observes his partially concealed tears, he responds to them: the harper is told to stop and new activities are instituted. As a guest in Mycenaean culture, Odysseus was entitled to the utmost consideration; if he cried, everyone needed to adjust accordingly. The assumption is that since only some dire emotional distress allows one to make the demands on the attention and sympathy of the group that crying entails, the crying person must feel that he or she has a right to our sympathies. We may decide that he or she is wrong, but our first reaction will necessarily be to respond.

Adam Smith, the economic and moral philosopher, wrote that partially concealed tears compel us to respond more respectfully than we otherwise might. "We are disgusted with that clamorous grief which, without any delicacy, calls upon our compassion with sighs and tears and importunate lamentations. But we reverence that reserved, that silent and majestic sorrow, which discovers itself only in the swelling of the eyes, in the quivering of the lips and cheeks, and in the distant, but affecting coldness of the whole behaviour." Our respect for this particular form of crying leads us to "regard it with respectful attention," and to do whatever we can to help the crier maintain his or her composure, "lest by any impropriety we should disturb that concerted tranquillity, which it requires so great an effort to support." And so Alkínoös breaks off the song.

In this way, the rules of crying are maintained as they are broken. We can cry in public as long as we look like we are trying not to: we are less likely to get in trouble for breaking the rules if we pretend that we are not breaking them. Thus we can continue to issue those tearful demands we supposedly stopped making at the age of five or eight by employing conventional gestures that both disguise and display our weeping. Please respond to my tears, the quickly wiped eye insinuates, but pretend along with me that I'm not really crying. Like Odysseus's hood, our performances with Kleenex, handkerchiefs, and averted looks allow us to announce our private desires on the public stage, and to make known those desires in ways that don't incur the social costs associated with open tears.

A world without tears has at various times devoutly been wished. Revelation 7:17–21 promises a paradise without tears: "For the Lamb who is in the midst of the throne will shepherd them and lead them to living fountains of waters. And God will wipe away every tear from their eyes. And death shall be no more; neither shall there be mourning, nor crying, nor pain any more, for the former things have passed away." For the Hebrew desert dwellers two millennia ago, the idea of constant, "living" fountains of water and the idea that tears might be wiped away forever together contributed to the idea of heaven.

And again, philosophers from the Stoics and Plato on have argued for a tearless world. The pride in not crying, the arrogance of emotional stoicism, perhaps finds its most eloquent defense in William Wordsworth's "Ode: Intimations of Immortality from Recollections of Early Childhood," an examination of youth, loss, and nostalgia completed in 1804, six years after his *Lyrical Ballads* announced the arrival of the Romantic sensibility:

> *Though nothing can bring back the hour*
> *Of splendour in the grass, of glory in the flower;*
> *We will grieve not, rather find*
> *Strength in what remains behind;*
> *In the primal sympathy*
> *Which having been must ever be;*
> *In the soothing thoughts that spring*
> *Out of human suffering;*
> *In the faith that looks through death,*
> *In years that bring the philosophic mind.*

The "years that bring the philosophic mind" are then echoed in the last verse of the poem, when Wordsworth declares that "the meanest flower" can evoke "thoughts that do often lie too deep for tears." Philosophy here is the consoler, and the majestic cadence of these verses and their joyous sonority replace mourning with victory, tears with elation. This is a romance of transformed loss, a fantasy of emotional satisfaction unseating the deepest despair, and it is described in terms that deny the conflict between rationality and emotion. The ode says that the strength we find is a kind of philosophy, a philosophy that brings us not out of the depths but into a deeper place. Authenticity of feeling is not denied here but arrogated to the mind. Tears may go very deep, but philosophical thought lies deeper.

In this world, however, tears will always be with us. If learning to stop crying is necessary to maturation, to stop altogether is to be less than human. In the classic cult film *Invasion of the Body Snatchers* (1956), it is possible to recognize a child whose body has been snatched because it doesn't cry. But this world is not likely to run out of tears. Like the Tin Man in *The Wizard of Oz*, who is constantly in danger of rusting himself from crying—we might worry that we don't have enough heart, but we needn't worry that the world will run out of tears.

In *Waiting for Godot*, Pozzo muses that "the tears of the world," in fact, "are a constant quality. For each one who begins to weep, somewhere else another stops." Beckett suggests the inevitability and the essential meaningless of tears—they start, they stop, they are a constant, like the rotation of the earth, and therefore have no meaning other than that which we give them in our promiscuous desire to make meaning. But Beckett did not always believe this. Elsewhere he wrote: "My words are my tears," suggesting the opposite of Pozzo's contention, that tears and meaning-making are twinned, intertwined acts.

Such analogies, rather than offering explanations of the mystery of tears, simply refer to that mystery. Are tears words? Well, no. There has been a long tradition of letting these two fundamental forms of expression stand in for each other, as when Ovid says that "tears are sometimes as weighty as words," or Voltaire says that "tears are the silent language of grief," or Heinrich Heine writes, "What poetry there is in human tears!" Psychotherapist Jeffrey A. Kottler titled his recent book *The Language of Tears*, and in it he discusses the "language system" of tears, which he claims to have learned to decode. He suggests that the best way to learn the language is to "look inward," "be reflective," and "experiment with letting yourself go." Kottler intends to be inspirational, and promises in his introduction that *"this book will move you emotionally. . . . This book will change your life."* And like many popular psychologists, he does so by invoking the most positive connotations and possibilities of our emotional lives.

But if tears are a language, they are simply a gestural one, and like other gestural languages, they are culture-specific rather than universal, and in many cases much more open to interpretation than verbal language. When we see someone crying and feel that we understand—say, in the famous photograph of a young girl crying as she wanders out of her napalmed village in Vietnam—it doesn't matter how removed we are from her culture, her place, her time. We feel that some tears express themselves with perfect universality, with an authenticity too obvious and powerful to question. But we are also familiar with the more problematic type of tears, in which abandon and willfulness, hope and despair, self-affirmation and self-abnegation, sincerity and deception, surrender and manipulation, authenticity and disguise can all be mixed up. Alfred Lord Tennyson, in one of the most famous poems of the Victorian era, "Tears, Idle Tears," suggests that tears are always explainable, and at the same time always ineffable: "Tears, idle tears, I know not what they mean, / Tears from the depth of some divine despair / Rise in the heart, and gather to the eyes, / In looking on the happy autumn-fields, / And thinking of the days that are no more." He can list their causes—divine despair, nostalgic loss—but still know "not what they mean." As a communication medium, tears are like very early radio: they grab everyone's attention and sometimes the signals can be picked up quite clearly, but they are at best diffuse in their broadcast and spotty in reception. And like any language, they can be used to persuade or evade, to clarify or obscure, to reveal or disguise the self and its motives. They can be used, like any language, in the full gamut of human projects, from the sublime to the ridiculous.

Our own language about tears continues to evolve. Daniel Goleman's book *Emotional Intelligence: Why It Can Matter More than IQ* (1995), for instance, has added its title to our lexicon. At first glance, *Emotional Intelligence* and its subtitle announce the priority of emotion over rationality and might seem to be a clear inheritor of the emotivist paradigms of the 1970s. But the title is a marketing ploy, and Goleman in fact makes the opposite argument. Every day in the news, he writes, we hear about someone else—boy, girl, man, woman—losing control of his or her emotions and running amok. Given this seemingly increasing tendency to "go postal," Goleman claims that what we need is self-restraint. Yes, emotions are important and repression is bad. But however important it is for us to be "in touch" with our emotions, Goleman argues, it is more important still to control them:

> Our passions, when well exercised, have wisdom; they guide our thinking, our values, our survival. But they can easily go awry, and do so all too often. As Aristotle saw, the problem is not with emotionality, but with the *appropriateness* of emotion and its expression. The question is, how can we bring intelligence to our emotions—and civility to our streets and caring to our communal life.

If the 1970s and its emphasis on expression was made possible by economic prosperity, Goleman's book is much more tied to a 1990s sense of increasing limitations. It retains the 1970s belief in the power of emotion to transform the world, but is less optimistic about what changes will be wrought. It is a book, finally, about emotional downsizing.

Steven Pinker, the MIT neuroscientist, takes a similar approach in his best-selling *How the Mind Works* (1997). He begins his chapter on the emotions with a discussion of the massacre of twenty-eight schoolchildren in Dunblane, Scotland. Pinker's conclusion is that emotions are part of our basic adaptive machinery, that they are all "engineered" (in the metaphor he prefers) to help us adapt to life's demands. For Pinker, emotions "have a cold logic of their own," since even people who run amok do so in the service of some idea—that they have been wronged by a society, that they are not being recognized, that they deserve the revenge they are wreaking. For Pinker and Goleman, emotions all tend to adaptive behavior, but for both emotional flooding is a perversion of the normal functioning of the emotions, and the body holds no truth. To *feel* something may be necessary for us to act rationally, as Damasio suggests, but for all three of these writers, acting rationally, not feeling intensely, is the goal.

What is important about the cathartic viewing of films or reading of novels, according to Pinker, is that films and novels help us to cogni-

tively assess our world. Pinker's argument here is a very old one. In his
commentaries on Aristotle's *Poetics* in 1570, the Italian Renaissance
aesthetician Lodovico Castelvetro argued that tragic catharsis "expels
terror and pity from the hearts of men" and that we feel a resulting
"health of mind gotten through bitter medicine." But we find real
pleasure in tragedy because we glean moral lessons from it for which
we can then congratulate ourselves. We weep in proud appreciation of
our own rational abilities. In a similar vein, the German philosopher
Ernst Cassirer argued that our emotional life "changes its form"
through catharsis and that our emotions are "relieved of their material
burden" through art and become objects of pure contemplation. John
Crowe Ransom argued in the 1950s that catharsis is at best a necessary evil akin to "the point of view of a modern military authority
legalizing prostitution in the neighborhood of the camp," and claims
that its object is to "intensify the aesthetic moment in order to mini-
mize and localize it, and clear the way for the scientific moment."
Lionel Trilling in the 1960s located the pleasure of the tragic catharsis
in the knowledge, which we gain through watching the great tragedies,
of the complexity of life. In each case, we are pleased not by our emotional transformation but by our "health of mind," by our progress as
thinkers. "A tear," as the philosopher Jerome Neu put this position in
the 1980s, "is an intellectual thing."

It may be, then, given the renewed popularity of such ideas—*Emotional Intelligence* spent forty-nine weeks on the *Publishers Weekly* best-
seller list—that we are in the midst of a transition away from the
cathartic beliefs of the 1970s. The teenagers who are crying at *Titanic*
do not say, after all, like the baby-boomer director of the film, that
they are saving the world, or that they are "celebrating their own
essential humanity." And they don't claim to be resolving any buried
issues. They weep, they say, because it makes the movie more enjoyable, and they weep more each time they see it. They do not say that
they are experiencing catharsis. They are not cathecting, not adapting,
not releasing, not improving, not expressing. They are simply enjoying
the warm bath of their own sensations. The turn-of-the-century Harvard philosopher George Santayana, in one of his many pithy remarks,
wrote: "The young man who has not wept is a savage; the old man

who will not laugh is a fool." But of course "savages" and "fools" are very much like the rest of us, who weep and laugh our whole lives long if we are lucky, even if these basic human responses can do nothing to restrain our tendency to be either savage or foolish. This may be less pithy and quotable, but it is more accurate.

Nor is it true, as the British Romantic poet Thomas Moore wrote, that "it is only to the happy that tears are a luxury." Tears are a luxurious respite, even for many who suffer. Mark C. Taylor, a deconstructionist literary critic, has played on the etymological relationship between emotional tears and tears as rips, or ruptures, or rending, and tears are always experienced as a radical change from whatever state preceded them, whether we take that to be the Sartrean idea of tears as an escape, the physiological understanding of tears as a return to homeostasis, or our everyday understanding of tears as a breakdown, a collapse from a state of holding things together to one of letting them go. Taylor also plays on the relation between secretions and secrets, writing that both come from the same root, meaning "to separate": "A secret is an outside that is inside," he writes, "a secretion is an inside that is outside." It is this uncanny categorical mixing, Taylor suggests, that give tears their cultural power.

Here Taylor is borrowing from the anthropologist Mary Douglas, who has argued that bodily secretions—urine, sweat, semen, bile, mucous, pus—tend to be considered dangerous in cultures around the world. The secretions of the body are impure, dirty, threatening. While tears have remarkably found their way out of the general ban against excretions in most cultures, even so, as we have seen, they are fraught with danger because they can incite people to revenge, or cause social embarrassment, harassment, miscommunication, and disappointment. That we cry so often in seclusion is one sign that no matter how much poetic talk we hear of tears as pearls and jewels and tributes, these secretions, too, require a level of secrecy. And like secrets, they are best shared with one or a few people. When secrets leave the arena of intimacy, they stop being secrets.

And Douglas also argues (along with other anthropologists and some theologians) that there is a link between that which a culture considers dangerous and that which they consider sacred. The "holy tears" of the medieval saints may seem like relics of a bygone era to some of us, and Madonna's use of a crying statue of a saint in her video "Like a Prayer" may seem like a purely degraded version of the religious meaning of tears. But there is still a great deal of talk about sacral tears. One, for instance, comes from the Meher Baba homepage on the Internet, which quotes New Age guru Baba: "The spiritual path is closely connected with feelings; that's true. However, this does not mean that inner passion should be exposed through an outer display, such as the shedding of tears." Sacred tears are sullied by their profane appearance, just as they were for St. Augustine sixteen hundred years earlier. Nonetheless, someone with "a pure and sensitive heart" should weep spiritual tears, they should "weep within continuously." Baba's advice to never cry and to weep internally is another summing up of our age's double vision.

So is the latest entry in the quack-cure sweepstakes, Peter Van Oosterum's *Tears: A Key to the Remedy* (1998), in which homeopath Van

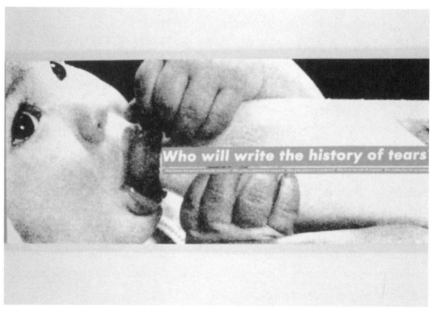

Barbara Kruger, *Untitled (Who will write the history of tears?)* (1991). Courtesy Mary Boone Gallery, New York.

Oosterum suggests drinking a solution containing one's own tears to cure whatever it is that is making one cry. Straight tears would be too powerful, Van Oosterum suggests, and so he recommends about one two-hundreths of a single tear, shaken in a solution two hundred times. Never mind that whenever we cry, the majority of our tears drain through our nasolacrimal ducts, and from there into the stomach, at a rate thousands of times the dose this cure suggests. This arbitrary, faux-magic formula suggests that tears are the problem, and still tears are somehow the solution.

And so it goes. Van Oosterum hit upon his idea for homeopathic tears when he heard that the ancient Greeks, Romans, and Hebrews, as part of their funeral rites, would cry into lacrimatories. These small vials, full of tears, were often sealed up and buried with the dead, which on the one hand was a way of burying one's feelings, but which on the other hand was a way of offering a tribute to the dead, giving of one's own tears as if they were flowers or gifts. When Psalm 56 says, "Put Thou my tears in Thy bottle," we assume that the psalmist is asking God to accept the tribute of tears. John Waters imagines the romantic ad absurdum by having his characters in Cry-Baby drink whole mason jars full of tears. Profound or grotesque? It is hard to say, since tears are in the eye of the beholder, as it were. The desire they express can always be as easily ridiculed as revered.

And they continue to change their spots as well. The historical change for men over this last century is fairly obvious, one that makes crying, however infrequent, the rule rather than the exception. And this is undoubtedly a good thing. To deny tears is to deny a fundamental pleasure as well as a fundamental capability—the human ability to magically transform the world into one of our own making, even if only temporarily. And for women, the change is also obvious. Crying is no longer women's prerogative, with all that entails. And of course for both men and women, tears are sure to start in this life, and just as sure to end. And it is not only the changing culture that alters the meanings of such things as imbibing our own tears. Our emotional life changes as we age, and changes in relation to what we feel we need from others in the way of emotional expression and what kinds of emotional demands we feel we have the right to make. Such changes are most obvious in the movement from infancy to childhood to adolescence to adulthood. But even though there is no research on this topic, it is safe to say that every serious life change results in a reevaluation of one's emotional options. "Who will write the history of tears?" Roland Barthes asked. We all will.

References

[A.B.]. "Moral Weeping" (1755). In Brady, Cope, Millner, Mitric, Puckett, and Seigel, *A Dictionary of Sensibility.*
http://www.engl.virginia.edu/~enec981/dictionary/19anonV1.html.

Acebo, Christine, and Evelyn B. Thoman. "Role of Infant Crying in the Early Mother-Infant Dialogue." *Physiology and Behavior* 57:3 (Mar. 1995): 541–47.

Acquarone, Stella. "What Shall I Do to Stop Him Crying? Psychoanalytic Thinking About the Treatment of Excessively Crying Infants and Their Mothers/Parents." *Journal of Child Psychotherapy* 18 (1992): 33–56.

Addison, Joseph. *Essays of Joseph Addison.* Edited by John Richard Green. New York: St. Martin's, 1960.

Adler, Alfred, et al. *Feelings and Emotions: The Wittenberg Symposium.* Edited by Martin L. Reymert. Worcester, Mass: Clark University Press, 1928.

Adriani, N., and Albert C. Kruyt. *De bare'e sprekende Toradjas van Midden-Celebes (de Oost Toradjas)* (The bare-speaking Toradja of central Celebes [the East Toradja]). Vol. 2. Amsterdam: N.V. Noord-Hollandsche Uitgevers Maatschappij. Translated for the HRAF by Jenni Kerding Moulton, 1951.

Aeschylus. *The Complete Plays of Aeschylus.* Translated by Gilbert Murray. London: Allen & Unwin, 1952.

Aggleton, John P., ed. *The Amygdala: Neurobiological Aspects of Emotion, Memory, and Mental Dysfunction.* New York: Wiley-Liss, 1992.

Ahern, Emily Martin. *The Cult of the Dead in a Chinese Village.* Stanford, Calif: Stanford University Press, 1973.

Ainsworth, Mary D. Salter, Silvia M. Bell, and Donelda J. Stayton. "Individual Differences in the Development of Some Attachment Behaviors." *Merrill Palmer Quarterly* 18 (1972): 123–43.

————. "Infant-Mother Attachment and Social Development: 'Socialisation' as a Product of Reciprocal Responsiveness to Signals" (1974). In *Becoming a Person: Child Development in Social Context*, vol. 1, edited by Martin Woodhead, Ronnie Carr, and Paul Light. London: Routledge, 1991.

Albee, Edward. *Three Tall Women.* New York: NAL, Dutton, 1994.

Alexiou, Margaret. *The Ritual Lament in the Greek Tradition.* New York: Cambridge University Press, 1974.

Alvarez, M., and Ian St. James-Roberts. "Infant Fussing and Crying Patterns in the First Year in an Urban Community in Denmark." *Acta Paediatrica* 85:4 (1996): 463–66.

Anand, K. J. S., and P. R. Hickey. "Pain and Its Effects in the Human Neonate and Fetus." *New England Journal of Medicine* 317 (1987): 1321–29.

Anderson, E. N. *Ecologies of the Heart: Emotion, Belief, and the Environment.* New York: Oxford University Press, 1996.

"Annals of Blubbering." *Time,* 17 Oct. 1994, 18.

Aquinas, St. Thomas. *Summa Theologica.* Translated by the Fathers of the English Dominican Province. Westminster, Md.: Christian Classics, 1981.

Ariès, Philippe. *The Hour of Our Death* (1977). Translated by Helen Weaver. New York: Vintage, 1982.

Aristotle. *Poetics* and *History of Animals.* In *The Works of Aristotle,* translated by W. D. Ross (1908). New York: Oxford University Press, 1952.

————. *Poetics.* Translated by S. H. Butcher (1895). In *Criticism: The Major Texts,* edited by Walter Jackson Bate. New York: Harcourt Brace Jovanovich, 1970.

Arnold, Magda. *Emotion and Personality.* New York: Columbia University Press, 1960.

Auchincloss, Kenneth. "The Year of the Tear." *Newsweek,* 29 Dec. 1997, 40–42.

Augustine (St. Augustine, Bishop of Hippo). *Confessions.* Translated by Henry Chadwick. New York: Oxford University Press, 1991.

Austin, Alfred. *Lyrical Poems.* New York: Macmillan, 1891.

Averill, James R. "The Acquisition of Emotions During Adulthood." In *The Social Construction of Emotions. See* Harré, 1986.

————. *Anger and Aggression: An Essay on Emotion.* New York: Springer, 1982.

————. "A Constructivist View of Emotion." In *Emotion: Theory, Research, and Experience,* vol. 1: *Theories of Emotion,* edited by R. Plutchik and H. Kellerman. New York: Academic Press, 1980.

Azzarolo, A. M., A. K. Mircheff, R. L. Kaswan, F. Z. Stanczyk, E. Gentschein, L. Becker, B. Nassir, and D. W. Warren. "Androgen Support of Lacrimal Gland Function." *Endocrine* 6:1 (1997): 39–45.

Badinter, Elisabeth. *XY: On Masculine Identity.* New York: Columbia University Press, 1995.

Bakker, Tammy Faye. *I Gotta Be Me* and *Run to the Roar.* In *What Counts: The Complete Harper's Index,* edited by Charis Conn and Ilena Silverman. New York: Henry Holt, 1991.

Banker, James A. "Mourning a Son: Childhood and Paternal Love in the Consolateria of Giannozzo Manetti." *History of Childhood Quarterly* 3 (1976): 351–62.

Barr, Ronald G. "The Crying Game." *Natural History* 106:9 (1997): 47.

————. "Normality: A Clinically Useless Concept: The Case of Infant Crying and Colic." *Journal of Developmental and Behavioral Pediatrics* 14:4 (1993): 264–70.

————. "The Normal Crying Curve: What Do We Really Know?" *Developmental Medicine and Child Neurology* 32:4 (1990): 356–62.

————. "Recasting a Clinical Enigma: The Case of Infant Crying." In *Challenges to Developmental Paradigms: Implications for Theory, Assessment and Treatment,* edited by Philip R. Zelazo and Ronald G. Barr. Hillsdale, N.J.: Lawrence Erlbaum, 1989.

Barthes, Roland. *On Racine.* Translated by Richard Miller. New York: Hill & Wang, 1964.

————. *The Pleasure of the Text.* Translated by Richard Miller. New York: Hill & Wang, 1975.

Basedow, Herbert. *The Australian Aboriginal.* Adelaide, Australia: F. W. Preece & Sons, 1929.

Bataille, Georges. *My Mother, Madame Edwarda, The Dead Man* (1966). Translated by Austryn Wainhouse. New York: Marion Boyars, 1989.

————. *The Tears of Eros* (1961). Translated by Peter Connor. San Francisco: City Lights, 1989.

Baudelaire, Charles. *Les Fleurs du mal.* Paris: Labiche, c. 1949.

Bayne, Sheila Page. *Tears and Weeping: An Aspect of Emotional Climate Reflected in Seventeenth-Century French Literature.* Tübingen, Germany:

Gunter Narr Verlag, 1981.

Beauvoir, Simone de. *Memoirs of a Dutiful Daughter*. Translated by James Kirkup. Cleveland, Ohio: World Publishing, 1959.

Becher, Hans. *Die Surara und Pakidai, zwei Yanonami-Stamme in Nordwest-brasilien* (The Surara and Pakidai, two Yanoama tribes in northwest Brazil). Museum für Volkerkunde (Hamburg), Mitteilungen, no. 26. Hamburg, Germany: Kommissionsverlag Cram, De Gruyter & Co., 1960. Translated for the HRAF by Frieda Schutze.

Beckett, Samuel. *Waiting for Godot*. New York: Grove, 1956.

Beebe, Susan A., Rosemary Casey, and Jennifer Pinto-Martin. "Association of Reported Infant Crying and Maternal Parenting Stress." *Clinical Pediatrics* 32:1 (1993): 15–19.

Benedict, Ruth. *Patterns of Culture*. New York: Houghton Mifflin, 1934.

Benedict, St. *The Rule of St. Benedict*. Translated by Anthony C. Meisel and M. L. del Mastro. Garden City, N.Y.: Image Books, 1975.

Bennett, Wendell C., and Robert M. Zingg. *The Tarahumara: An Indian Tribe of Northern Mexico*. Chicago: University of Chicago Press, 1935.

Bentham, Jeremy. *Defence of Usury: Shewing the Impolicy of the Present Legal Restraints on the Terms of Pecuniary Bargains*. Dublin: D. Williams, 1788.

Bentley, Margaret E., Laura E. Caulfield, and Malathi Ram. "Zinc Supplementation Affects the Activity Patterns of Rural Guatemalan Infants." *Journal of Nutrition* 127 (1997): 1333–38.

Beowulf. Translated by David Wright. New York: Penguin, 1957.

Berenger-Feraud, L. J. B. "Les Ouolofs." In *Les Peuplades de la Sénégambie*, edited by Ernest Leroux. Paris: Librairie de la Société Asiatique de l'Ecole des Langues Orientales Vivantes, 1879.

Beyer, H. Otley, and Roy Franklin Barton. "An Ifugao Burial Ceremony." *Philippine Journal of Science* 6 (1911): 227–52.

Birbaumer, Neils, and Arne Öhman, eds. *The Structure of Emotion*. Seattle: Hogrefe & Huber, 1993.

Blackwood, Beatrice. *Both Sides of Buka Passage: An Ethnographic Study of Social, Sexual and Economic Questions in the North-Western Solomon Islands*. Oxford: Clarendon Press, 1935.

Blankenship, Vicki Ann. "A Comparative Study of Student Nurses, Nursing Faculty, and Staff Nurses in their Perceptions of Weeping, Their Weeping Behaviors, and Their Interaction with the Weeping Patient." Ph.D. dissertation, University of Texas at Austin, 1984.

Blatz, W. E, and D. Millichamp. "The Development of Emotion in the Infant."

University of Toronto Studies, Child Development Series, no. 4 (1935): 44.

Blatz, W. E., D. Millichamp, and M. Fletcher. *Nursery Education.* New York: Morrow, 1935.

Blesius, R. "The Concept of Empathy." *Psychology* 26:4 (1989): 10–15.

Bloom, Floyd E. *Brain, Mind, and Behavior.* 2nd ed. New York: Freeman, 1988.

Bly, Robert. *Iron John: A Book About Men.* Reading, Mass.: Addison-Wesley, 1990.

Boettner, Loraine. *Roman Catholicism.* Philadelphia: Presbyterian and Reformed Publishing, 1962.

Bohannan, Paul, and Laura Bohannan. "Three Source Notebooks in Tiv Ethnography." Unpublished manuscript. New Haven, Conn.: HRAF, 1958.

Bollig, Laurentius. *Die Bewohner de Truk-Inseln: Religion, Leben und kurze Grammatik eines Mikronesiervolkes* (The inhabitants of the Truk Islands: Religion, life and a short grammar of a Micronesian people). Münster, Germany: Aschendorffsche Verlags-buchhandlung, 1927. Translated for the Yale Cross-Cultural Survey, 1942.

Borquist, A. "Crying." *American Journal of Psychology* 17 (1906): 149–205.

Boscagli, Maurizia. "A Moving Story: Masculine Tears and the Humanity of Televised Emotions." *Discourse* 15.2 (Winter 1992–93): 64–79.

Bowlby, John. *Attachment and Loss.* New York: Basic Books, 1969.

Boyle, Robert. *Medicinal Experiments; or, A Collection of Choice and Safe Remedies, for the Most Part Simple, and Easily Prepared: Useful in Families, and Very Serviceable to Country People.* 2nd ed. London: Sam. Smith, 1694.

Bradburn, Beth. "The Apprenticeship of Tears." Unpublished manuscript. 1998.

Braza, Kathleen. "Families and the Grief Process." ARCH fact sheet no. 21, Mar. 1993. http//www.counselingforloss.com/elle/artilce16.htm.

Brett, G. S. "Historical Development of the Theory of the Emotions." In *Feelings and Emotions: The Wittenberg Symposium. See* Adler, et al., 1928.

Bright, Timothie. *A Treatise of Melancholie* (1586). New York: Columbia University Press, 1940.

Bronstein, Phyllis, Maria Briones, Teri Brooks, and Brookes Cowan. "Gender and Family Factors as Predictors of Late Adolescent Emotional Expressiveness and Adjustment: A Longitudinal Study." *Sex Roles* 34 (1996): 739–65.

Brontë, Emily. *The Poems of Emily Brontë.* Edited by Derek Roper. New York: Oxford University Press, 1995.

Brooks, Peter. *The Melodramatic Imagination: Balzac, Henry James, Melodrama, and the Mode of Excess*. New Haven, Conn.: Yale University Press, 1976.

Bryan, Yvonne E., and John D. Newman. "Influence of Infant Cry Structure on Heart Rate of the Listener." In *The Physiological Control of Mammalian Vocalization*, edited by John D. Newman. New York: Plenum Press, 1988.

Buck, Peter. *The Coming of the Maori*. Wellington, New Zealand: Maori Purposes Fund Board, 1950.

Buck, Ross. *The Communication of Emotion*. New York: Guilford, 1984.

Budd, Malcolm. *Music and the Emotions: The Philosophical Theories*. New York: Routledge, 1992.

Byars, Jack. *All That Hollywood Allows: Rereading Gender in 1950s Melodrama*. Chapel Hill: University of North Carolina Press, 1991.

Byrne, Mike. "The Crying Game: Doheny Researchers Follow the Hormonal Tracks of Our Tears." USC News Service. http://cwis.usc.edu/dept/News_Service/chronicle_html/1995.02.20./crying.html.

Camus, Albert. *The Stranger*. Translated by Stuart Gilbert. New York: Vintage, 1954.

Cannon, Walter B. *Bodily Changes in Pain, Hunger, Fear, and Rage*. New York: D. Appleton, 1929.

———."The James-Lange Theory of Emotions: A Critical Examination and an Alternative Theory." *American Journal of Psychology* 40 (1927).

Carmichael, Kay. *Ceremony of Innocence: Tears, Power and Protest*. St. Martin's, 1991.

Carr, Harvey A. *Psychology: A Study of Mental Activity*. London: Longmans, Green, 1925.

Carroll, Lewis. *Alice's Adventures in Wonderland; and, Through the Looking-Glass* (1865, 1872). New York: Three Sirens, 1930.

Carroll, Michael P. "The Virgin Mary at LaSalette and Lourdes: Whom Did the Children See?" *Journal for the Scientific Study of Religion* 24 (1985): 56–74.

Castelvetro, Lodovico. *Castelvetro on the Art of Poetry*. Edited and translated by Andrew Bongiorno. Binghamton, N.Y.: Medieval and Renaissance Texts and Studies, 1984.

Chanticleer [pseudo]. "Decay of Weeping." *Independent*, 19 Sept. 1925, 329.

Chapman, George. *The Widow's Tears* (1612). London: Methuen, 1975.

Chen, Shing-jen. "The Development of Spontaneous Crying of an Infant: The

First Three Months." *Research and Clinical Center for Child Development* 12 (1990):" 49–57.

Chewings, Charles. *Back in the Stone Age: The Natives of Central Australia.* Sydney: Angus & Robertson, 1936.

Choti, S. E., A. R. Marston, S. G. Holston, and J. T. Hart. "Gender and Personality in Film-induced Sadness and Crying." *Journal of Social and Clinical Psychology* 5 (1987): 535–44.

Chupak, Cindy. "Can You Stand to See a Grown Man Cry?" *Glamour,* June 1994, 128.

Church, Lousia "No Time for Tears." *American Home,* June 1945, 16–19.

Cioran, E. M. *Tears and Saints* (1937). Translated by Ilinca Zarifopol-Johnston. Chicago: Chicago University Press, 1995.

Cixous, Hélène. *The Hélène Cixous Reader.* Edited by Susan Sellers. New York: Routledge, 1994.

Clément, Catherine. *Syncope: The Philosophy of Rapture* (1990). Translated by Sally O'Driscoll and Deirdre M. Mahoney. Minneapolis: University of Minnesota Press, 1994.

Condry, John, and Sandra Condry. "Sex Differences: A Study of the Eye of the Beholder." *Child Development* 47 (1976): 812–19.

Cook, William Azel. *Through the Wilderness of Brazil by Horse, Canoe and Float.* New York: American Tract Society, 1909.

Cooley, D.G. "Your Emotions Can Make You Sick." *Better Homes and Gardens,* June 1945, 8.

Cooper, Jame Fenimore. *The Spy: A Tale of Neutral Ground* (1821). New York: Penguin, 1997.

Copway, George. Quoted in M. Inez Hilger, *A Social Study of One Hundred Fifty Chippewa Indian Families of the White Earth Reservation of Minnesota.* Washington: Catholic University of America Press, 1939.

Cornelius, Randolph R. *The Science of Emotion: Research and Tradition in the Psychology of the Emotions.* Upper Saddle River, N.J.: Prentice Hall, 1996.

Corwin, M. J., B. M. Lester, and H. L. Golub. "The Infant Cry: What Can It Tell Us?" *Current Problems in Pediatrics* 26 (1996): 325–34.

Cretser, Gary A., William K. Lombardo, Barbara Lombardo, and Sharon Mathis. "Reactions to Men and Women Who Cry: A Study of Sex Differences in Perceived Societal Attitudes Versus Personal Attitudes." *Perceptual and Motor Skills* 55 (1982): 479–86.

Crile, George W. *The Origin and Nature of the Emotions.* Philadelphia: W. B.

Saunders, 1915.

Crits-Christoph, Paul, Lester Luborsky, Ellen Gay, Thomas Todd, Jacques P. Barber, and Ellen Luborsky. "What Makes Susie Cry? A Symptom-Context Study of Family Therapy." *Family Process* 30 (1991): 337–45.

Cudworth, Ralph. *A Treatise Concerning Eternal and Immutable Morality* (1678). New York: Garland, 1976.

Cunha, Euclides da. *Rebellion in the Backlands* (1902). Translated by Samuel Putnam. Chicago: University of Chicago Press, 1944.

Cuthbertson-Johnson, Beverly, David D. Franks, and Michael Dornan. *The Sociology of Emotions: An Annotated Bibliography*. New York: Garland, 1994.

Damasio, Antonio. *Descartes' Error: Emotion, Reason, and the Human Brain*. New York: Grosset, Putnam, 1996.

D'Arnaud, Baculard. *Les Amans malheureux; ou, Le Comte de Comminges* (1746). La Haye, France: Gosse & Pinet, 1776.

Darwin, Charles. *The Expression of Emotions in Man and Animals* (1872). Chicago: University of Chicago Press, 1965.

Davidson, Richard J., and Nathan Fox. "Frontal Brain Asymmetry Predicts Infants' Response to Maternal Separation." *Journal of Abnormal Psychology* 98 (1989): 127–31.

Davis, Wendy Ellen. "Crying It Out: The Role of Tears in Stress and Coping of College Students." Ph.d. dissertation, University of Colorado at Boulder, 1990.

Demos, Virginia. "Crying in Early Infancy: An Illustration of the Motivational Function of Affect." In *Affective Development in Infancy*, edited by T. Berry Brazelton and Michael W. Yogman. Norwood, N.J.: Ablex Publishing Corp., 1986.

Descartes, René. *The Passions of the Soul* (1649). Translated by Stephen Voss. Indianapolis, Ind.: Hackett, 1989.

Detterman, Douglas K., and Lee Salk. "The Effect of Heartbeat Sound on Neonatal Crying." *Infant Behavior and Development* 1 (1978): 49–50.

Dewey, John. "The Theory of Emotion" (1894). In *The Early Works, 1882–1898*, edited by Fredson Bowers and Jo Ann Boydston. Carbondale, Il.: Southern Illinois University Press, 1967–72.

Diamond, Norma Joyce. *K'un Shen: A Taiwan Village*. New York: Holt, Rinehart & Winston, 1969.

Dickens, Charles. *Oliver Twist* (1838) and *The Old Curiosity Shop* (1841). In *The Works of Charles Dickens*. New York: Bigelow, 1924.

Diderot, Denis. *Oeuvres complètes*. Paris: Hermann, 1975.

Dinnage, Rosemary. "Delightful Tears." *New York Review of Books*, 19 Feb. 1998, 32–34.

Dobb, J., and M. Small. "Crying Together, Laughing Together." *Nursing Times* 93:31 (1997): 36–37.

Dolan, Deirdre. "New York's Streetwise Adolescents Drowning in Their *Titanic* Tears." *New York Observer*, 23 Feb. 1998, 1, 12.

Dorsey, George A., and James R. Murie. "Notes on Skidi Pawnee Society." *Field Museum of Natural History, Anthropological Series* 27:2 (1940): 65–119.

Dorsey, John M. *Psychology of Emotion: Self-discipline by Conscious Emotional Continence.* Detroit, Mich.: Center for Health Education, 1971.

Dostoyevsky, Fyodor. *The Brothers Karamazov* (1880). Translated by David Magarshack. New York: Penguin, 1982.

———. *Notes from Underground* (1864). Translated by Mirra Ginsburg. New York: Bantam, 1974.

Douglas, Ann. "Heaven Our Home: Consolation Literature in the Northern United States, 1830–1880." In *Death in America. See* Stannard, 1975.

Douglas, Mary. *Purity and Danger: An Analysis of Concepts of Pollution and Taboo.* London: Routledge & Kegan Paul, 1966.

Downey, J., and R. T. Bidder. "Perinatal Information on Infant Crying." *Child Care, Health and Development* 16 (1990): 113–21.

Drummond, Jane E., C. Faye Wiebe, and Ruth M. Elliott. "Maternal Understanding of Infant Crying: What Does a Negative Case Tell Us?" *Qualitative Health Research* 4:2 (May 1994): 208–23.

Dry, E. A. "The Social Development of the Hausa Child." *Proceedings of the III International West African Conference Held at Ibadan, Nigeria.* Lagos: Nigerian Museum, 1949.

Durham, Mary Edith. *Some Tribal Origins, Laws, and Customs of the Balkans* (1928). New York: AMS Press, 1979.

Durkheim, Emile. *The Rules of Sociological Method and Selected Texts on Sociology and Its Method* (1895). Translated by W. D. Halls and edited by Steven Lukes. London: Macmillan, 1982.

Egerton, Muriel. "Passionate Women and Passionate Men: Sex Differences in Accounting for Angry and Weeping Episodes." *British Journal of Social Psychology* 27 (1988): 51–66.

Eggan, Fred. *Social Organization of the Western Pueblos.* Chicago: University of Chicago Press, 1950.

Eisenberg, Nancy, ed. *Empathy and Related Emotional Responses.* San Francisco: Jossey-Bass, 1989.

Eisenberg, Nancy, and Janet Strayer, eds. *Empathy and Its Development*. Cambridge: Cambridge University Press, 1987.

Eisenberg-Berg, Nancy, and P. Mussen. "Empathy and Moral Development in Adolescence." *Developmental Psychology* 14:2 (1978): 185–86.

Ekman, Paul J. "Facial Expression and Emotion." *American Psychologist* 48 (1993): 384–92.

———. "Biological and Cultural Contributions to Body and Facial Movement in the Expression of Emotion." In *Explaining Emotions*, edited by Amelie O. Rorty. Berkeley: University of California Press, 1980.

———, ed. *Darwin and Facial Expression: A Century of Research in Review*. New York: Academic Press, 1973.

Ekman, Paul, and Richard J. Davidson. *The Nature of Emotion: Fundamental Questions*. New York: Oxford University Press, 1994.

Ekman, Paul J., and W. V. Friesen. "Nonverbal Leakage and Clues to Deception." *Psychiatry* 32 (1969): 88–105.

Elias, Norbert. *The Civilizing Process: The Development of Manners* (1939). New York: Urizen, 1978.

Elliott, M. R., J. Drummond, and K. E. Barnard. "Subjective Appraisal of Infant Crying." *Clinical Nursing Research* 5:2 (1996): 237–50.

Elliott, M. R., E. L. Pedersen, and J. Mogan. "Early Infant Crying: Child and Family Follow-up at Three Years." *Canadian Journal of Nursing Research* 29:2 (1997): 47–67.

"Emotional Male." *Newsweek*, 8 Nov. 1948, 44.

Ephron, Nora. *Heartburn*. New York: Knopf, 1983.

Erlich, Vera St. *Family in Transition: A Study of Three Hundred Yugoslav Villages*. Princeton, N.J.: Princeton University Press, 1966.

Esquival, Laura. *Like Water for Chocolate*. Translated by Carol and Thomas Christensen. New York: Doubleday, 1992.

Euripides. *Medea and Other Plays*. Translated by Philip Vellacott. Baltimore: Penguin, 1963.

Evitt, Marie Faust. "Crying Games: How to Help Your Child Avoid Breaking Down into Tears." *Parenting*, Jan. 1995, 130.

Ewers, John Canfield. *The Blackfeet: Raiders of the Northwestern Plains*. Civilization of the American Indian Series, no. 49. Norman, Okla.: University of Oklahoma Press, 1971.

Fagan, J., and I. L. Shepherd, eds. *Gestalt Therapy Now*. Palo Alto, Calif.: Science and Behavior Books, 1970.

"Fashions in Emotion." *Living Age*, 15 July 1911, 185–87.

Feet, P. O., K. G. Götestam, and N. Norman. "Gender Differences in Pro-lactin and Aldosterone in Primary Non-agitated Depressed Patients and Normal Controls." *European Journal of Psychiatry* 7 (1993): 133–45.

Feld, Steven. *Sound and Sentiment: Birds, Weeping, Poetics, and Song in Kaluli Expression.* Philadelphia: University of Pennsylvania Press, 1982.

Feldenkrais, Moshé. *The Body and Mature Behavior.* London: Routledge & Kegan Paul, 1949.

Feldman, Sandor S. "Crying at the Happy Ending." *Journal of the American Psychoanalytic Association* 4 (1956): 477–85.

Fell, Joseph P., III. *Emotion in the Thought of Sartre.* New York: Columbia University Press, 1965.

Ffoulkes, Arthur. "Funeral Customs of the Gold Coast Colony." *Journal of the African Society* 8 (1909): 154–64.

"Finally, It's OK to Cry." *Your Health,* 8 Oct. 1991, 22–23.

Fisher, Philip. *Hard Facts: Setting and Form in the American Novel.* New York: Oxford University Press, 1985.

Folk Tales from China. 1st series. Translated by Chou Chia-tsan. Peking: Foreign Languages Press, 1957.

"49er Loville Cries Tears of Strength." *San Francisco Examiner,* 19 Dec. 1995.

Fourier, Charles. *The Passions of the Human Soul and Their Influence on Society and Civilization* (1851). New York: Kelley, 1968.

Franks, David D., and E. Doyle McCarthy, eds. *The Sociology of Emotion: Original Essays and Research Papers.* Greenwich, Conn.: JAI Press, 1989.

French, Thomas M. "Psychogenic Factors in Asthma." *American Journal of Psychiatry* 96 (1939).

Freud, Sigmund. *Three Essays on Sexuality* (1905) and "Mourning and Melancholia" (1917). In *The Standard Edition of the Complete Psychological Works of Sigmund Freud,* edited by James Strachey et al. London: Hogarth, 1953–74.

———, and Josef Breuer. *Studies in Hysteria* (1895). Translated by A. A. Brill. New York: Nervous and Mental Disease Publishing Co., 1936.

Frey, William H., II, and Muriel Langseth. *Crying: The Mystery of Tears.* New York: Harper & Row, 1985.

Freyre, Gilberto. *The Masters and the Slaves: A Study of the Development of Barzilian Civilization* (1943). New York: Knopf, 1956.

Frodi, Ann M., Michael E. Lamb, Lewis A. Leavitt, and Wilberta L. Donovan. "Fathers' and Mothers' Responses to Infant Smiles and Cries." *Infant Behavior and Development* 1 (1978): 187–98.

Fuller, Barbara F., Maureen R. Keefe, and Mary Curtin. "Acoustic Analysis of Cries from 'Normal' and 'Irritable' Infants." *Western Journal of Nursing Research* 16:3 (1994): 243–53.

Fulton, Robert. "The Sacred and the Secular: Attitudes of the American Public Toward Death, Funerals, and Funeral Directors." In *Death and Identity*, edited by Robert Fulton and Robert Bendiksen. Bowie, Md.: Charles Press Publishers, 1976.

Furedy, John J., Alison S. Fleming, Diane N. Ruble, Hal Scher, et al. "Sex-Differences in Small-Magnitude Heart-Rate Responses to Sexual and Infant-Related Stimuli: A Psychophysiological Approach." *Physiology and Behavior* 46:5 (1989): 903–05.

Gallin, Bernard. *Hsin Hsing, Taiwan: A Chinese Village in Change*. Berkeley: Univesity of California Press, 1966.

Gallo, D. "Educating for Empathy, Reason and Imagination." *Journal of Creative Behavior* 23:2 (1989): 98–115.

Gennep, Arnold van. *The Rites of Passage* (1909). Translated by Monika B. Vizedom and Gabrielle L. Caffe. Chicago: University of Chicago Press, 1960.

Gilkey, J. L. "How to Gain Emotional Poise." *Reader's Digest*, October 1945, 39–40.

Gladwin, Thomas, and Seymour B. Sarason. *Truk: Man in Paradise*. Viking Fund Publications in Anthropology, no. 20. New York: Wenner-Gren Foundation for Anthropological Research, 1954.

Glass, David C., ed. *Neurophysiology and Emotion*. New York: Rockefeller University Press and Russell Sage Foundation, 1967.

Goethe. *The Sorrows of Young Werther* (1774). Translated by Elizabeth Mayer and Louise Bogan. New York: Modern Library, 1984.

Golden, Tom. *Swallowed by a Snake: The Gift of the Masculine Side of Healing*. http:/www2.dgsys.com/~tgolden/3tribal.html.

Goldman, Irving. *The Cubeo: Indians of the Northwest Amazon*. Illinois Studies in Anthropology, no. 2. Urbana, Ill.: University of Illinois Press, 1963.

Goldstein, A. P., and G. Y. Michaels. *Empathy: Development, Training, and Consequences*. Hillsdale, N.J.: Lawrence Erlbaum, 1985.

Goleman, Daniel. *Emotional Intelligence: Why It Can Say More Than IQ*. New York: Bantam, 1995.

Gomes, Edwin H. *Seventeen Years Among the Sea Dyaks of Borneo: A Record of Intimate Association with the Natives of the Bornean Jungles*. London: Seeley & Co., 1911.

Gorer, Geoffrey. *Death, Grief and Mourning.* Garden City, N.Y.: Doubleday, 1965.

Grant, Peter. "The Saulteaux [Ojibwa] Indians About 1804. In *Les Bourgeois de la Compagnie du Nord-Ouest*, edited by L. F. R. Masson, vol. 2. Quebec: De L'Imprimerie Générale A. Cote et Cie., 1890.

Gregory of Narek. *Book of Lamentation.* In *Lamentations of Narek: Mystic Soliloquies with God*, translated by Mischa Kudian. London: Mashtots, 1977.

Griffis, William Elliot. *Corea: The Hermit Nation.* New York: Scribner's, 1882.

Grinker, R. R. *Psychosomatic Research.* New York: Norton, 1953.

Grinnell, George Bird. *Blackfoot Lodge Tales: The Story of a Prairie People* (1888). Lincoln, Nebr.: University of Nebraska Press, 1962.

Gross, James J., Barbara L. Fredrickson, and Robert W. Levenson. "The Psychophysiology of Crying." *Psychophysiology* 31:5 (1994): 460–68.

Guinagh, Barry. *Catharsis and Cognition in Psychotherapy.* New York: Springer, 1987.

Gusinde, Martin. *Die Feuerland Indianer, Band 1, Die Selk'nam; vom Leben und Denken eines Jägervolkes auf der grossen Feuerlandinse* (The Fireland Indians, vol. 1, The Selk'nam; on the life and thought of a hunting people of the Great Island of Tierra del Fuego). Mödling bei Wien: Verlag der Internationalen Zeitschrift "Anthropos," 1931. Translated for the HRAF by Frieda Schutze.

Gustafson, Gwen E., and Karen L. Harris. "Women's Responses to Young Infants' Cries." *Developmental Psychology* 26:1 (1990): 144–52.

Hallock, K. "Don't Be Afraid to Cry." *American Journal of Nursing* 95:4 (1995): 80.

Hammond, Ruth Anne. "RIE Tears." *Educaring: Resources for Infant Educators* 16:3 (1995): 3.

Hardy, Barbara. *Forms of Feeling in Victorian Fiction.* Athens, Ohio: Ohio University Press, 1985.

Harper, Sue, and Vincent Porter. "Moved to Tears: Weeping in the Cinema in Postwar Britain." *Screen* 37:2 (1996): 152–73.

Harré, Rom, ed. *The Social Construction of Emotions.* New York: Basil Blackwell, 1986.

Harrell, Clyde Stevan. *Belief and Unbelief in a Taiwan Village.* Dissertation (anthropology), Stanford University, Stanford, Calif., 1975. University Microfilms, Publication, 75-6860. Ann Arbor, Mich.: University Microfilms, 1975.

Harrison, Aaron. "Crying Is Music." *Hygeia* 19 (Apr. 1941): 338–40.

Hastrup, Janice L., John G. Baker, Deborah L. Kraemer, and Robert F. Bornstein. "Crying and Depression Among Older Adults." *Gerontologist* 26:1 (1986): 91–96.

Heidegger, Martin. *Early Greek Thinking: The Dawn of Western Philosophy.* Translated by David Farrell Krell and Frank A. Capuzzi. New York: Harper & Row, 1984.

Hemingway, Ernest. *In Our Time* (1925). New York: Scribner's, 1970.

Heritage, Timothy. "'Weeping Bolshevik' Gets Tough Before Russian Poll." Reuters News Service, 13 Nov. 1995.

Hiaasen, Carl. *Lucky You.* New York: Knopf, 1997

Hilger, M. Inez. "Chippewa Child Life and Its Cultural Background." *Bureau of American Ethnology Bulletin* 146. Washington, D.C.: Smithsonian Institution, 1951.

Hillman, James. *Emotion: A Comprehensive Phenomenology of Theories and Their Meanings for Therapy.* London: Routledge & Paul, 1960.

Hilton, Stanley G. *Senator for Sale: An Unauthorized Biography of Senator Bob Dole.* New York: St. Martin's, 1995.

Hippocrates. *Hippocratic Writings.* Edited by G. E. R. Lloyd and translated by J. Chadwick and W. N. Mann. New York: Penguin, 1978.

Hobbes, Thomas. *The Leviathan* (1651), *De Corpore* (1650), and *De Homine* (1658). In *The English Works of Thomas Hobbes of Malmesbury,* edited by William Molesworth (1839–45). Aalen, Germany: Scientia, 1966.

Hochschild, Arlie Russell. "Emotion Work, Feeling Rules, and Social Structure." *American Journal of Sociology* 85 (1979): 551–75.

———. *The Managed Heart: The Commercialization of Human Feeling.* Berkeley: University of California Press, 1983.

Holst-Warhaft, Gail. *Dangerous Voices: Women's Laments and Greek Literature.* London and New York: Routledge, 1992.

Homan, William E., M.D. *Child Sense: A Pediatrician's Guide for Today's Families.* New York: Basic Books, 1969.

Homer. *The Odyssey.* Translated by Robert Fitzgerald. Garden City, N.Y.: Anchor, Doubleday, 1961.

———. *The Iliad.* Translated by Robert Fitzgerald. Garden City, N.Y.: Anchor, Doubleday, 1974.

———. *The Odyssey.* Translated by Samuel Butler. London: J. Cape, 1922.

Hooke, S. H. *Middle Eastern Mythology: From the Assyrians to the Hebrews* (1963). New York: Penguin, 1991.

Hooker, John Lee. Quoted in Ted Drozdowski, "Blue Blood." *Los Angeles Mag-*

azine, Mar. 1995, 63–67.

Hoover-Dempsey, Kathleen V., Jeanne M. Plas, and Barbara Strudler Wallston. "Tears and Weeping Among Professional Women: In Search of New Understanding." *Psychology of Women Quarterly*, 10 (1986): 19–34

Howell, William. "The Sea Dyak." *Sarawak Gazette* 38–40 (1908–10).

Huffman, Lynne C., Yvonne E. Bryan, Frank A. Pedersen, Barry M. Lester, et al. "Infant Cry Acoustics and Maternal Ratings of Temperament." *Infant Behavior and Development* 17:1 (1994): 45–53.

Huizinga, Johann. *The Waning of the Middle Ages: A Study of the Forms of Life, Thought, and Art in France and the Netherlands in the XIVth and XVth Centuries*. London: E. Arnold, 1924.

Hume, David. *Essays Moral, Political, and Literary* (1741). Edited by Eugene F. Miller. Indianapolis, Ind.: Liberty Classics, 1985.

Humphries, S. C. *The Family, Women and Death: Comparative Studies*. London: Routledge, 1983.

Hunziker, U. A., and R. G. Barr. "Increased Carrying Reduces Infant Crying: A Randomized Control Trial." *Pediatrics* 77 (1986): 641–48.

Hurst, Fannie. *Imitation of Life*. New York: Perennial Library, 1990.

Hutcheson, Francis. *An Essay on the Nature and Conduct of the Passions and Affections with Illustrations on the Moral Sense* (3rd ed., 1742). Gainesville, Fla.: Scholars' Facsimiles and Reprints, 1969.

Huxley, Aldous. *Vulgarity in Literature: Digressions from a Theme*. London: Chatto & Windus, 1930.

Hvidberg, Flemming Friis. *Weeping and Laughter in the Old Testament*. Leiden, Holland: E. J. Brill, 1962.

Ignatius of Loyola, St. *Inigo: Original Testament. The Autobiography of Ignatius Loyola*. Translated by William Yeomans. London: Inigo International Centre, 1985.

Irigaray, Luce. "When Our Lips Speak Together." Translated by Carolyn Burke. *Signs: Journal of Women and Culture in Society* 6 (1980): 69–79.

Irving, John. *The Cider House Rules* (1985). New York: Ballantine, 1993.

Izard, Carroll, ed., *Emotion, Personality and Psychopathology*. New York: Plenum Press, 1979.

James, Henry. *The Aspern Papers* (1888). In *The Novels and Tales of Henry James*. New York: Scribner's, 1907–17.

James, William. *Principles of Psychology*. 2 vols. New York: Henry Holt, 1890.

———. *Varieties of Religious Experience* (1902). New York: Penguin, 1982.

——— "What is an Emotion." *Mind* 9 (1884): 188–205.

Janet, Pierre. *The Mental State of Hystericals: A Study of Mental Stigmata and Mental Accidents.* Translated by Caroline Rollin Corson. New York: Putnam, 1901.

Janov, Arthur. *The Primal Scream: Primal Therapy, the Cure for Neurosis.* New York: Putnam, 1970.

Jarry, Alfred. *The Supermale* (1902). Translated by Ralph Gladstone and Barbara Wright. New York: New Directions, 1977.

Jefferson, Thomas. *Papers.* Vol. 10. Edited by Julian P. Boyd et al. Princeton, N.J.: Princeton University Press, 1950.

Jenkins, Nicholas. "Veil of Tears: The Candidates Are Having a Bawl." *New Yorker,* 22 Apr. 1996.

Jenness, Diamond. *The Life of Copper Eskimos: Report of the Canadian Arctic Expedition, 1913–1918.* Ottawa: F. A. Acland, 1922.

Johansson, E. E., K. Hamberg, G. Lindgren, and G. Westman. " 'I've Been Crying My Way': Qualitative Analysis of a Group of Female Patients' Consultation Experiences." *Family Practice* 13:6 (1996): 498–503.

Johnson, B. "Educating the Emotions." *North American Review* 247:2 (1939): 355–64.

Jones, Livingston F. *A Study of the Thlingets of Alaska.* New York: Fleming H. Revell, 1914.

Jones, Maxine B., Mary K. Peacock, and Jan Christopher. "Self-reported Anger in Black High School Adolescents." *Journal of Adolescent Health* 13:6 (1992): 461–65.

Joubert, Laurent. *Treatise on Laughter* (1579). Translated by David de Rocher. University, Ala.: University of Alabama Press, 1980.

Kang, Younghill. *The Grass Roof.* New York: Scribner's, 1931.

Kaplan, Fred. *Sacred Tears: Sentimentality in Victorian Literature.* Princeton, N.J.: Princeton University Press, 1987.

Karsten, Rafael. "Indian Tribes of the Argentine and Bolivian Chaco: Ethnological Studies." In *Societas Scientiarum Fennica, Commentationes Humanarum Litterarum,* vol. 4. Helsingfors, Finland: Akademische Buchhandlung, 1932.

Kaufman, Howard Keva. *Bangkhuad: A Community Study in Thailand.* Association for Asian Studies, Monographs, no. 10. Locust Valley, N.Y.: J. J. Augustin, 1960.

Kay, Dennis. *Melodious Tears: The English Funeral Elegy from Spenser to Milton.* New York: Oxford University Press, 1990.

Kemper, Theodore D. "Sociological Models in the Explanation of Emotions."

In *Handbook of Emotions*. *See* Lewis and Haviland, 1993.

Kepecs, J. G., et al. "Relationship Between Certain Emotional States and Exudation into the Skin." *Psychosomatic Medicine* 13 (1951): 1–10.

Ketterman, Grace. *Mothering: The Complete Guide for Mothers of All Ages.* Boston: Beacon Hill, 1998.

Kimball, A. M. "Big Babies Are Bad Citizens." *Independent Woman* 20 (Nov. 1941): 326–27.

Kimmel, Michael. *Manhood in America: A Cultural History*. New York: Free Press, 1996.

Klass, Dennis, et al., eds. *Continuing Bonds: New Understandings of Grief.* Bristol, Pa.: Taylor & Francis, 1996.

Klineberg, Otto. "Expressing Emotions the World Over." *Science Digest* 8 (1940): 56–62.

———. *Social Psychology*. New York: Henry Holt, 1940.

Knez, Eugene Irving. *Sam Jong Dong: A South Korean Village*. Dissertation, Syracuse University, Syracuse, N.Y., 1959. University Microfilms, Publication 59-6308. Ann Arbor, Mich.: University Microfilms, 1960.

Koestler, Arthur. *The Act of Creation* (1964). New York: Penguin Arkana, 1989.

Kohl, J. G. *Kitchi-Gami*. London: Chapman & Hall, 1860.

Kottler, Jeffrey A. *The Language of Tears*. San Francisco: Jossey-Bass, 1996.

Kraemer, Deborah L., and Janice L. Hastrup. "Crying in Adults: Self-control and Autonomic Correlates." *Journal of Social and Clinical Psychology* 6:1 (1988): 53–68.

———. "Crying in Natural Settings: Global Estimates, Self-monitored Frequencies, Depression and Sex Differences in an Undergraduate Population." *Behaviour Research & Therapy* 24: 3 (1986): 371–73.

Kramer, Richard Ben. *Bob Dole*. New York: Vintage, 1996.

Kristeva, Julia. *Black Sun: Depression and Melancholia*. Translated by Leon S. Roudiez. New York: Columbia University Press, 1989.

Kübler-Ross, Elizabeth. *On Death and Dying*. New York: Collier, 1969.

Labarre, Weston. "The Cultural Basis of Emotions and Gestures." *Journal of Personality* 16 (1947): 49–68

Labott, Susan M., Randall B. Martin, Patricia S. Eason, and Elayne Y. Berkey. "Social Reactions to the Expression of Emotion." *Cognition and Emotion* (special issue, Emotion in Social Life) 5:5–6 (Sept–Nov. 1991): 397–417.

Laclos, Choderlos de. *Les Liaisons dangereuses* (1782). Paris: Imprimerie

Nationale, 1981.

The Ladies' Indispensable Companion and Housekeepers Guide, Embracing Rules of Etiquette; Rules for the Formation of Good Habits; and a Great Variety of Medical Recipes to which is Added one of the Best Systems of Cookery Ever Published. New York: H. Dayton, 1860.

Laird, D. A., and T. McClumpha. "Sex Differences in Emotional Outlets." *Science*, n.s., 62 (25 Sept. 1925): 292.

Lambert, Gavin. *On Cuckor.* New York: Putnam, 1972.

Lambrecht, Francis. "The Mayawyaw Ritual." *Catholic Anthropological Conference, Publications* (Washington, D.C.) 4:1–5 (1932–41).

Landis, E. B. "Mourning and Burial Rites in Korea." *Journal of the Anthropological Institute of Great Britain and Ireland* 25 (1896): 340–61.

Landow, George P. *The Victorian Web.* http://www.stg.brown.edu/projects/hypertext/landow/victorian/victov.html

Lang, Peter J. "The Three-System Approach to Emotion." In Neils Birbaumer and Arne Öhman, eds., *The Structure of Emotion.* Seattle: Hogrefe & Huber, 1993.

Lang, Robert. *American Film Melodrama: Griffith, Vidor, Minnelli.* Princeton, N.J.: Princeton University Press, 1989.

Lange, Marjory E. *Telling Tears in the English Renaissance.* Studies in the History of Christian Thought, no. 70. New York: E. J. Brill, 1996.

Lawrence, D. H. "The Novel and the Feelings." In *Phoenix: The Posthumous Papers of D. H. Lawrence* (1936). New York: Viking, 1968.

———. *Women in Love* (1920). New York: Cambridge University Press, 1987.

Leach, Penelope. *Babyhood: Infant Development from Birth to Two Years.* New York: Penguin, 1974.

———. *Your Baby and Child from Birth to Age Five.* New York: Knopf, 1986.

LeDoux, Joseph. *The Emotional Brain: The Mysterious Underpinnings of Emotional Life.* New York: Simon & Schuster, 1996.

Lee, Keun. "The Crying Pattern of Korean Infants and Related Factors." *Developmental Medicine and Child Neurology* 36:7 (1994): 601–07.

Leger, D. W., R. A. Thompson, J. A. Merritt, and J. J. Benz. "Adult Perception of Emotion Intensity in Human Infant Cries: Effects of Infant Age and Cry Acoustics." *Child Development* 67:6 (1996): 3238–49.

Lendrum, Susan, and Gabrielle Syme. *Gift of Tears: A Practical Approach to Loss and Bereavement Counseling.* New York: Routledge, 1992.

Lerner, Laurence. *Angels and Absences: Child Deaths in the Nineteenth Cen-*

tury. Nashville, Tenn.: Vanderbilt University Press, 1998.

Lester, Barry M., and C. F. Zachariah Boukydis. "No Language but a Cry: Nonverbal Vocal Communication: Comparative and Developmental Approaches." In *Studies in Emotion and Social Interaction*, edited by Hanus Papousek, Uwe Jurgens, and Mechthild Papousek. New York: Cambridge University Press, 1992.

Lester, Barry M., Michael Corwin, and Howard Golub. "Early Detection of the Infant at Risk through Cry Analysis." In *The Physiological Control of Mammalian Vocalization*, edited by John D. Newman. New York: Plenum Press, 1988.

Lester, Barry M., Cynthia T. Garcia-Coll, and Marta Valcarcel. "Perception of Infant Cries in Adolescent and Adult Mothers." *Journal of Youth and Adolescence* 18:3 (June 1989): 231–43.

Levine, Jennifer, and Debra Noell. "Embracing Fears and Sharing Tears: Working with Grieving Children." In *Interventions with Bereaved Children*, edited by Susan C. Smith and Margaret Pennells. London: Jessica Kingsley, 1995.

Levine, Murray, Jennifer Freeman, and Cheryl Compaan. "Maltreatment-related Fatalities: Issues of Policy and Prevention." *Law and Policy* 16 (1994): 449–71.

Lewis, Michael, and Jeanette M. Haviland, eds. *Handbook of Emotions*. New York: Guilford Press, 1993.

Lipps, Theodore. *Psycholoical Studies* (1913). Translated by Herbert C. Sanborn. Baltimore: Williams & Wilkins, 1926.

Lohaus, Arnold, Heidi Keller, Suzanne Volken, Martina Cappenberg, and Athanasios Chasiotis. "Intuitive Parenting and Infant Behavior: Concepts, Implications and Empirical Validation." *Journal of Genetic Psychology* 158:3 (1997): 276–86

Lombardo, William K., Gary A. Cretser, Barbara Lombardo, and Sharon L. Mathis. "For Cryin' Out Loud—There Is a Sex Difference." *Sex Roles* 9 (1983): 987–95.

Lovell, Deborah M., Graham Hemmings, and Andrew B. Hill. "Bereavement Reactions of Female Scots and Swazis: A Preliminary Comparison." *British Journal of Medical Psychology* 66:3 (1993): 259–74.

Lowell, Robert. *The Voyage and Other Versions of Poems by Baudelaire*. New York: Farrar, Straus & Giroux, 1961.

Lowen, Alexander. *The Betrayal of the Body*. New York: Macmillan, 1967.

———. *Bioenergetics*. New York: Coward, McCann & Geoghagen, 1975.

———. *The Language of the Body*. New York: Collier, 1958.

————. *Narcissism: Denial of the True Self.* New York: Macmillan, 1983.

Lumholtz, Carl. *Unknown Mexico: A Record of Five Years' Exploration of the Western Sierra Madre; in the Tierra Caliente of Tepic and Jalisco; and Among the Tarascos of Michoacán.* Vol. 1. New York: Scribner's, 1902.

Lutz, Catherine A., and Lila Abu-Lughod, eds. *Language and the Politics of Emotion.* New York: Cambridge University Press, 1990.

Mackenzie, Henry. *The Man of Feeling* (1771). New York: Norton, 1958.

MacLean, Paul D. "Cerebral Evolution of Emotion." In *Handbook of Emotions. See* Lewis and Haviland, 1993.

————. "Psychosomatic Disease and the 'Visceral Brain': Recent Developments Bearing on the Papez Theory of Emotions." *Psychosomatic Medicine* 11 (1949): 338–53.

Maddox, Richard. *El Castillo: The Politics of Tradition in an Andalusian Town.* Urbana, Ill.: University of Illinois Press, 1993.

Mailer, Norman. *The Gospel According to the Son.* New York: Random House, 1997.

Mair, Lucy P. *An African People in the Twentieth Century.* London: George Routledge & Sons, 1934.

Maldonado-Duran, Martin, and Juan-Manuel Sauceda-García. "Excessive Crying in Infants with Regulatory Disorders." *Bulletin of the Menninger Clinic* 60:1 (1996): 62–78

"Male Declared More Emotional Than Female." *Science News-Letter,* 13 Nov. 1948, 312.

Malinowski, Bronislaw. *Crime and Custom in Savage Society.* London: Kegan Paul, Trench, Trubner, 1926.

————. *The Sexual Life of Savages in North-western Melanesia.* New York: Halcyon House, 1929.

Man, Edward Horace. *On the Aboriginal Inhabitants of the Andaman Islands.* London: Royal Anthropological Institute of Great Britain and Ireland, 1932.

Manstead, Anthony S. R., ed. *Emotion in Social Life.* Hillsdale, N.J.: Lawrence Erlbaum, 1991.

Marañon, Gregorio. "Contribution à l'étude de l'action émotive d'adrénaline. *Revue Française d'Endocrinologie* 2 (1924): 301–25.

Margolin, Leslie. "Child Abuse by Baby-sitters: An Ecological-Interactional Interpretation." *Journal of Family Violence* 5 (1990) 95–105.

Maslach, Christina. "Negative Emotional Biasing of Unexplained Arousal." In *Emotion, Personality and Psychopathology. See* Izard, 1979.

Masters, William M. "Rowanduz: A Kurdish Administrative and Mercantile

Center." Dissertation submitted in partial fulfillment of the requirements for the degree of Doctor of Philosophy at the University of
Michigan, Ann Arbor, 1953.

Mather, Cotton. *The Angel of Bethesda* (1724). Edited by Gordon W. Jones.
Barre, Mass.: American Antiquarian Society and Barre, 1972.

May, Herbert G. and Bruce M. Metzger, eds. *The Oxford Annotated Bible.* New
York: Oxford University Press, 1977.

McCarthy, Susan, and Jeffrey Moussaieff Masson. *When Elephants Weep: The
Emotional Lives of Animals.* New York: Doubleday, 1995.

McDevitt, T. M., R. Lennon, and R. J. Kopriva. "Adolescents' Perceptions of
Mothers' and Fathers' Prosocial Actions and Empathic Responses."
Youth and Society 22:3 (1991): 387–409.

McEntire, Sandra J. *The Doctrine of Compunction in Medieval England: Holy
Tears.* Lewiston, N.Y.: Edwin Mellen, 1990.

———, ed. *Margery Kempe: A Book of Essays.* New York: Garland, 1992.

McKinley, James C., Jr. "Anguish of Rwanda Echoed in a Baby's Cry." *New
York Times,* 21 Feb. 1996, A1, A4.

McNaughton, Neil. *Biology and Emotion.* New York: Cambridge University
Press, 1989.

Mead, Margaret. *Coming of Age in Samoa: A Psychological Study of Primitive
Youth for Western Civilization.* New York: Morrow, 1928.

Meinwald, Dan. "Memento Mori: Death and Photography in Nineteenth-
Century America." *CMP Bulletin* 9:4 (1990): 1–33.

Melville, Herman. *Redburn; White-Jacket; Moby-Dick.* New York: Literary
Classics of the United States, 1983.

Messing, Simon David. "The Highland-Plateau Amhara of Ethiopia." Dissertation in anthropology presented to the faculty of the Graduate School of
the University of Pennsylvania in partial fulfillment of the requirements
for the degree of Doctor of Philosophy, Philadelphia, 1957.

Messner, Michael A. "'Changing Men' and Feminist Politics in the United
States." *Theory and Society* 22 (1993): 723–27.

Milder, Benjamin, and Bernardo A. Weil, eds. *The Lacrimal System.* Norwalk,
Conn.: Appleton Century Crofts, 1983.

Mills, R. S., and J. E. Grusec. "Cognitive, Affective, and Behavioral Consequences
of Praising Altruism." *Merrill-Palmer Quarterly* 35:3 (1989): 299–326.

Milner, Joel S., Lea B. Halsey, and Jim Fultz. "Empathic Responsiveness and
Affective Reactivity to Infant Stimuli in High- and Low-Risk for Physical Child Abuse Mothers." *Child Abuse and Neglect* 19:6 (1995):

767–80.

Molière. *The Misanthrope* (1666). Translated by John Wood. New York: Penguin, 1987.

Montagu, Ashley. "Natural Selection and the Evolution of Weeping in Man." *Journal of the American Medical Association* 174:4 (1961).

Montague, J. F. "Emotion Can Ruin Your Health." *Science Digest* 13 (Apr. 1943): 7–10.

Montaigne, Michel de. *The Complete Essays*. Translated and edited by M. A. Screech. New York: Penguin, 1991.

Moore, Thomas. *Lalla Rookh* (1817). London: Longman's, 1849.

Moose, J. Robert. *Village Life in Korea*. Nashville, Tenn.: M. E. Church, 1911.

Moreno, Kasia. "Some Weep, Some Don't." *Forbes*, 15 Dec. 1997, 12.

Morley, J. K. *Some Things I Believe*. London: Macmillan, 1937.

Mrs. Hale's New Book of Cookery and Complete Housekeeper. New York: H. Long & Brother, 1852.

Munroe, Ruth H., and Robert L. Munroe. "Infant Experience and Childhood Cognition: A Longitudinal Study Among the Logoli of Kenya." *Ethos* 12 (1984): 291–306.

Myers, Garry Cleveland, M.D. *The Modern Family*. New York: Greenberg, 1934.

Nash, June. *In the Eyes of the Ancestors: Belief and Behavior in a Maya Community*. New Haven, Conn.: Yale University Press, 1970.

Natu, Bal. *Glimpses of the God-Man*. 1982. http://www.sunyerie. edu/mb/erics/tearsjoy.html.

Nelson, J. Daniel. "Dry Eye in Sjögren's Syndrome." National Sjögren's Syndrome Association. http://www.sjogrens.org/eye.htm.

Nelson, Judith Kay. "The Meaning of Crying Based on Attachment Theory." *Clinical Social Work Journal* 26 (1998): 9–22.

Nichols, Michael P., and Melvin Zax. *Catharsis in Psychotherapy*. New York: Gardner, 1977.

Niemeier, Susanne, and René Dirven, eds. *The Language of Emotions: Conceptualization, Expression, and Theoretical Foundation*. Philadelphia: John Benjamins, 1997.

Okada, Fumihiko. "Weeping and Depression: Neural Mechanism." *Neuropsychiatry, Neuropsychology, and Behavioral Neurology* 8:4 (1995): 293–96.

Olsen, Paul, ed. *Emotional Flooding*. New York: Human Sciences Press, 1976.

Olson, Ronald L. *Social Structure and Social Life of the Tlingit in Alaska*. Berkeley: University of California Press, 1967.

O'Moore, A M., R. R. O'Moore, R. F. Harrison, G. Murphy, and M. E. Carruthers. "Psychosomatic Aspects in Idiopathic Infertility: Effects of Treatment with Autogenic Training." *Journal of Psychosomatic Research* 27:2 (1983): 145–51.

Orans, Martin. *The Santal: A Tribe in Search of a Great Tradition.* Detroit, Mich.: Wayne State University Press, 1965.

Ortony, Andrew, Gerald L. Clore, and Allan Collins. *The Cognitive Structure of Emotions.* New York: Cambridge University Press, 1988.

Ovid. *Heroides and Amores.* Translated by Grant Showerman. Cambridge, Mass.: Harvard University Press, 1977.

———. *Tristia.* Translated by L. R. Lind. Athens, Ga.: University of Georgia Press, 1975.

Palmer, Gretta. "Why Do Women Cry?" *Ladies' Home Journal,* Oct. 1948, 259–65.

Papanicolaou, A. C. *Emotion: A Reconsideration of the Somatic Theory.* New York: Gordon & Breach, 1989.

Papez, James W. "A Proposed Mechanism of Emotion." *Archives of Neurology and Psychiatry* 38 (1937): 725–43.

Parker, Dorothy. *Here Lies: The Collected Stories of Dorothy Parker.* New York: Viking, 1939.

Parry, Richard. *Basic Psychotherapy.* New York: Churchill Livingstone, 1983.

Paulme, Denise. *Organisation sociale des Dogon (Soudan français)* Paris: Domat-Montchrestien, 1940.

Peacham, Henry. *Minerva Britanna* (1612). Leeds, England: Scolar Press, 1966.

Pearsall, Marion. "Klamath Childhood and Education." *Anthropological Records* 9 (1950): 339–51.

Perls, Frederick S. [Fritz]. *Ego, Hunger, and Aggression: The Beginning of Gestalt Therapy.* New York: Random House, 1969.

———. *Gestalt Therapy Verbatim.* New York: Bantam, 1969.

Perry, Bruce D. "Death, Grief and Mourning: The Koreshian Children." http://www.bcm.tmc.edu/civitas/.

Phelps, Elizabeth Stuart. *The Gates Ajar* (1869). Edited by Helen Sootin Smith. Cambridge, Mass.: Harvard University Press, 1964.

Pinker, Steven. *How the Mind Works.* New York: Norton, 1997.

Pinyerd, Belinda J. "Infant Colic and Maternal Mental Health: Nursing Research and Practice Concerns." *Issues in Comprehensive Pediatric Nursing* 15:3 (1992): 155–67.

Plato. *Phaedrus* and *Philebus*, translated by R. Hackforth; *The Republic*, translated by Paul Shorey. In *The Collected Dialogues of Plato*, edited by Edith Hamilton and Huntington Cairns. Princeton, N.J.: Princeton University Press, 1961.

Plessner, Hellmuth. *Laughing and Crying: A Study of the Limits of Human Behavior*. Translated by James Spencer Churchill and Marjorie Grene. Evanston, Ill.: Northwestern University Press, 1970.

Plutchik, Robert. *Emotion: A Psychoevolutionary Synthesis*. New York: Harper & Row, 1980.

Poem of the Cid. Translated by Paul Blackburn. New York: American RMD, 1966.

Powers, Thomas. "The Last Hurrah." *New York Review of Books*, 15 Feb. 1996.

Prentiss, E. [Elizabeth]. *Stepping Heavenward* (1869). New York: A. D. F. Randolph, 1897.

Prévost, Abbé. *Mémoires et aventures d'un homme de qualité qui s'est retiré du monde* (1728–32). Paris: Librairie Ancienne Honoré Champion, 1934.

Propertius, Sextus. *Elegies*. Translated by G. P. Goold. Cambridge, Mass.: Harvard University Press, 1990.

Pruneau de Pommegorge, Antoine Edmé. *Description de la Nigritie*. Amsterdam: no publisher, 1789. Translated for the HRAF by Frieda Schutze.

Rabinowitz, Peter J. "'With Our Own Dominant Passions': Gottschalk, Gender, and the Power of Listening." *Nineteenth Century Music* 16:3 (Spring 1993): 242–52.

Radcliffe-Brown, A.R. *The Andaman Islanders: A Study in Social Anthropology*. Cambridge, England: The University Press, 1922.

Rafiqul-Haqq, M., and P. Newton. "The Place of Women in Pure Islam." http//debate.domini.org/newton/womeng.htm/.

Ransom, John Crowe. *The World's Body*. Scribner's, 1938.

Rattray, R. S. *Hausa Folk-lore, Customs, Proverbs, etc., Collected and Transliterated with English Translation and Notes* (1913). Oxford: Clarendon Press, 1969.

Reich, Wilhelm. *Character-Analysis*. Translated by Theodore P. Wolfe. New York: Farrar, Straus & Giroux, 1949.

———. *The Sexual Revolution: Toward a Self-governing Character Structure*. Translated by Theodore P. Wolfe. New York: Orgone Institute Press, 1945.

Reichel-Dolmatoff, Gerardo. *Los Kogi: Una tribu de la Sierra Nevada de Santa Marta, Colombia*. Bogotá: Editorial Iqueima, 1951. Translated for the HRAF by Sydney Muirden.

Reid, Guynel Marie. "Maternal Sex Stereotyping of Newborns." *Psychological Reports* 73:3 (Dec. 1994): 1443–50.

Reifler, D. M. "Early Descriptions of Horner's Muscle and the Lacrimal Pump." *Survey of Ophthalmology* 41:2 (1996): 127–34.

Restif de Bretonne, Edmé. *La Vie de mon Père* (1779). Ottawa: Cercle du Livre de France, 1949.

Reynolds, Cecil E. "Why Do We Weep?" *Literary Digest* 93 (30 Apr. 1927): 20.

Reynolds, Edward. *A Treatise of the Passions and Faculties of the Soul of Man* (1640). Gainesville, Fla.: Scholar's Facsimiles and Reprints, 1971.

Ribot, Th. [Théodule]. *La Psychologie des sentiments* (1889). Paris: Alcan, 1939.

Rich, Adrienne. *Snapshots of a Daughter-in-Law: Poems, 1954–1962*. New York: Norton, 1967.

Riding, Laura. *A Selection of the Poems of Laura Riding*. New York: Persea, 1996.

Riessman, Catherine Kohler. "Gender and the Social Construction of Emotions: The Feminization of Psychological Distress." Paper given to the American Sociological Association, 1989.

Riessman, Catherine Kohler, and Naomi Gerstel. "Gender Differences in Idioms of Distress after Divorce." Paper given to the American Sociological Association, 1989.

Rivers, W. H. R. *The History of Melanesian Society*. Cambridge: Cambridge University Press, 1914.

Robinson, Robert G., et al. "Pathological Laughing and Crying Following Stroke: Validation of a Measurement Scale and a Double-Blind Treatment Study." *American Journal of Psychiatry* 150:2 (1993): 286–93.

Rogers, Carl R. *Person to Person: The Problem of Being Human; a New Trend in Psychology*. Walnut Creek, Calif.: Real People Press, 1967.

Rorty, Amélie Oksenberg, ed. *Explaining Emotions*. Berkeley: University of California Press, 1980.

Rosaldo, Michelle Zimbalist. *Knowledge and Passion: Ilongot Notions of Self and Social Life*. New York: Cambridge Unversity Press, 1980.

Rosaldo, Renato. *Culture and Truth: The Remaking of Social Analysis*. Boston: Beacon Press, 1989.

Rosenblatt, Paul C. *Bitter, Bitter Tears: Nineteenth-Century Diarists and Twentieth-Century Grief Theories*. Minneapolis, Minn.: University of Minneapolis Press, 1983.

Ross, Catherine E., and John Mirowsky. "Men Who Cry." *Social Psychology Quarterly* 47 (1984): 138–46.

Rotundo, Anthony. *American Manhood: Transformations in Masculinity from the Revolution to the Modern Era*. New York: Basic Books, 1993.

Rousseau, Jean-Jacques. "A Discourse on the Origin of Inequality." In *The Social Contract and the Discourses*. Translated by G. D. H. Cole. New York: Knopf, 1993.

———. *Julie; or The New Heloïse* (1761). Translated by Philip Stewart and Jean Vache. Hanover, N.H.: Dartmouth College and University Press of New England, 1997.

Sade, Marquis de. *The Complete Justine, Philosophy in the Bedroom, and Other Writings*. Translated by Richard Seaver and Austryn Wainhouse. New York: Grove, 1966.

Sadoff, Robert L. "On the Nature of Crying and Weeping." *Psychiatric Quarterly* 40 (1996): 490–503.

St. James-Roberts, Ian, J. Bowyer, S. Varghese, and J. Sawdon. "Infant Crying Patterns in Manali and London." *Child Care, Health and Development* 20:5 (1994): 323–37.

St. James-Roberts, Ian, S. Conroy, and K. Wilsher. "Bases for Maternal Perceptions of Infant Crying and Colic Behaviour." *Archives of Disease in Childhood* 75:5 (1996): 375–84.

St. James-Roberts, Ian, Gillian Harris, and David Messer, eds. *Infant Crying, Feeding and Sleeping: Development, Problems and Treatments*. London: Harvester Wheatsheaf, 1993.

Sanders, Barry. *Sudden Glory: Laughter as Subversive History*. Boston: Beacon Press, 1995.

Santayana, George. *Dialogues in Limbo*. New York: Scribner's, 1925.

Sarbin, T.R. "Emotions as Narrative Emplotments." In *Entering the Circle: Hermeneutic Investigation in Psychology*, edited by M. J. Packer and R. B. Addison. Albany, N.Y.: State University of New York Press, 1989.

Sartre, Jean Paul. *The Emotions: Outline of a Theory*. Translated by Bernard Frechtman. New York: Philosophical Library, 1948.

Schachter, Stanley, and Jerome E. Singer. "Cognitive, Social, and Physiological Determinants of Emotional State." *Psychological Review* 69 (1962): 379–99.

Schaden, Egon. *Aspectos fundamentais da cultura Guarani* (Fundamental aspects of Guarani Culture). São Paulo: Difusão Europeia do Livro, 1962. Translated for the HRAF by Lars-Peter Lewinsohn.

Schaffer, H. Rudolph. "The Development of Interpersonal Behaviour." In *Introducing Social Psychology: An Analysis of Individual Reaction and Response*, edited by Henri Tajfel and Colin Fraser. New York: Penguin, 1978.

Schatz, Thomas. *Hollywood Genres: Formulas, Flimmaking and the Studio System*. Philadelphia: Temple University Press, 1981.

Scheff, Thomas J. *Catharsis in Healing, Ritual, and Drama*. Berkeley: University of California Press, 1979.

———. *Emotions, the Social Bond, and Human Reality: Part/Whole Analysis*. New York: Cambridge Univesity Press, 1997.

———. *Microsociology: Discourse, Emotion, and Social Structure*. Chicago: University of Chicago Press, 1990.

Scheper-Hughes, Nancy. *Death Without Weeping: The Violence of Everyday Life in Brazil*. Berkeley: University of California Press, 1992.

Schleidt, Margret. "An Ethological Perspective on Infant Development." In *Infant Development: Perspectives from German-speaking Countries*, edited by Michael E. Lamb and Heidi Keller. Hillsdale, N.J.: Lawrence Erlbaum, 1991.

Schreder, Mary Anne. "Special Needs of Bereaved Children: Effective Tools for Helping." In *Bereaved Children and Teens: A Support Guide for Parents and Professionals*, edited by Earl A. Grollman. Boston: Beacon Press, 1995.

Schwarzkopf, Norman. Interview with Barbara Walters. "20/20," shows 1111 and 1112. ABC News, New York, 15 and 22 Mar. 1991.

Sears, William. *Nighttime Parenting: How to Get Your Baby and Child to Sleep*. Franklin Park, Ill.: La Leche League, n.d.

Sedgwick, Eve Kososfky. *Epistemology of the Closet*. Berkeley: University of California Press, 1990.

Shaibani, Aziz Taher, Marwan N. Sabbagh, and Rachelle Doody. "Laughter and Crying in Neurological Disorders." *Neuropsychiatry, Neuropsychology, and Behavioral Neurology* 7:4 (1994): 243–50.

Shakespeare, William. *The Riverside Shakespeare*. Edited by G. Blakemore Evans. Boston: Houghton Mifflin, 1997.

Sherif, C. W. "Needed Concepts in the Study of Gender Identity." *Psychology of Women Quarterly* 6 (1982): 375–98

Shorvon, H. J., and W. B. Sargent. "Excitatory Abreaction: with Special Reference to Its Mechanism and the Use of Ether." *Journal of Mental Science* 93 (1947): 709–32.

Shott, S. "Emotion and Social Life: A Symbolic Interactionist Analysis." *American Journal of Sociology* 84 (1979): 1317–34.

Silva, Alcionilio Bruzzi Alves da. *A civilização indígena do Uaupes* (The indigenous civilization of the Uaupes). São Paulo: Centro de Pesquisas de Iauarete, 1962.

Simonov, P. V. *The Emotional Brain: Physiology, Neuroanatomy, Psychology, and Emotion.* Translated by Marie J. Hall. New York: Plenum Press, 1986.

Skinner, B. F. *The Behavior of Organisms: An Experimental Analysis.* New York: D. Appleton-Century, 1938.

Skrefsrud, Lars Olsen. *Traditions and Institutions of the Santals.* Translated by P. O. Bodding. Oslo, Norway: Oslo Etnografiske Museum, 1942.

Sloboda, John A. "Music Structure and Emotional Response: Some Empirical Findings." *Psychology of Music* 19:2 (1991) 110–20.

Smith, Adam. *The Theory of Moral Sentiments* (1759). In *Adam Smith's Moral and Political Philosophy,* edited by. Herbert W. Schneider. New York: Hafner, 1948.

Smith, E. H. "Your Emotions Will Get You If You Don't Watch Out!" *American Magazine,* Aug. 1925, 32–33.

Smith, Mary F. *Baba of Karo: A Woman of the Muslim Hausa.* London: Faber & Faber, 1954.

Solomon, Robert C. *The Passions.* Garden City, N.Y.: Anchor, Doubleday, 1976.

Solter, Aletha. "Why Do Babies Cry?" *Pre- and Peri-Natal Psychology Journal* 10:1 (1995): 21–43.

Song of Roland. Translated by Patricia Terry. Indianapolis, Ind.: Bobbs-Merrill, 1965.

Sophocles. *Ajax.* Translated by W. B. Stanford. New York: St. Martin's, 1963.
———. *The Theban Plays.* Translated by E. F. Watling. Baltimore, Md.: Penguin, 1947.

Southwell, Robert. *The Complete Poems of Robert Southwell.* Edited by Alexander B. Grosart. Westport, Conn.: Greenwood Press, 1970.

Spencer, Herbert. *Principles of Psychology* (1855). New York: D. Appleton, 1897.

Spencer, Walter Baldwin, and Francis James Gillen. *The Arunta: A Study of a Stone Age People.* London: Macmillan, 1927.

Spinoza, Baruch. *The Collected Works of Spinoza.* Edited and translated by Edwin Curley. Princeton, N.J.: Princeton University Press, 1985.

Spock, Benjamin. *The Common Sense Book of Baby and Child Care.* New York: Duell, Sloan & Pearce, 1946. Rev. ed. New York: Dutton, 1985.

Spock, Benjamin, and Anna David. "For Crying Out Loud." *Parenting,* Nov. 1994, 76–80.

Stanford, William Bedell. *Greek Tragedy and the Emotions: An Introductory Study.* Boston: Routledge & Kegan Paul, 1983.

Stannard, David E. "Where All Our Steps Are Tending: Death in the American Context." In *A Time to Mourn: Expressions of Grief in Nineteenth Century America,* edited by Martha V. Pike and Janice Gray Armstrong. Stony Brook, N.Y.: Museums at Stony Brook, 1980.

————, ed. *Death in America.* Philadelphia: University Pennsylvania Press, 1975.

Stasiewicz, Paul R., and Stephen A. Lisman. "Effects of Infant Cries on Alcohol Consumption on College Males at Risk for Child Abuse." *Child Abuse and Neglect* 13:4 (1989): 463–70.

Stearns, Peter. *Be a Man!: Males in Modern Society.* 2nd ed. New York: Holmes & Meier, 1990.

————. "History of Emotions: The Issue of Change." In *Handbook of Emotions. See* Lewis and Haviland, 1993.

Stearns, Peter, and Carol Z. Stearns. "Emotionology: Clarifying the History of Emotions and Emotional Standards." *American Historical Review* 90:4 (1985): 813–36.

————, eds. *Emotion and Social Change: Toward a New Psychohistory.* New York: Holmes and Meier, 1988.

Stein, Gertrude. *The Geographical History of America; or, The Relation of Human Nature to the Human Mind.* New York: Random House, 1936.

Stein, Lawrence B., and Stanley L. Brodsky. "When Infants Wail: Frustration and Gender as Variables in Distress Disclosure." *Journal of General Psychology* 122:1 (1995): 19–27.

Steinen, Karl von den. *Von den Steinen's Marquesan Myths.* Translated by Marta Langridge. Canberra, Australia: Target Oceania, Journal of Pacific History, 1988.

Stern, Daniel N. *The Interpersonal World of the Infant.* New York: Basic Books, 1985.

Stern, William. *Psychology of Early Childhood.* Translated by Anna Barwell. New York: Henry Holt, 1924.

Stifter, Cynthia A., and Julia Braungart. "Infant Colic: A Transient Condition with No Apparent Effects." *Journal of Applied Developmental Psychology* 13:4 (1992): 447–62.

Stowe, Harriet Beecher. *Uncle Tom's Cabin* (1850). New York: Modern Library, 1996.

The Successful Housekeeper; A Manual of Universal Application, Especially Adapted to the Every Day Wants of American Housewives. Detroit, Mich.:

M. W. Ellsworth & Co., 1888.

Symonds, Percival M. "A Comprehensive Theory of Psychotherapy." *American Journal of Orthopsychiatry* 24 (1954): 697–714.

Taylor, Mark C. *Tears*. Albany, N.Y.: State University of New York Press, 1990.

Ten Foot Square Hut and The Tales of the Heike. Translated by A. L. Sadler. Rutland, Vt.: Charles E. Tuttle, 1972.

Tennyson, Alfred. *In Memoriam* (1850) and "Tears, Idle Tears" (1847). In *The Poems of Tennyson*, edited by Christopher Ricks. Harlow: Longman's, 1969.

Terweil, Barend Jan. *Monks and Magic; An Analysis of Religious Ceremonies in Central Thailand*. Scandinavian Institute of Asian Studies, Monograph Series, no. 24. London: Curzon Press, 1975.

Thomas, Dylan. *Collected Poems*. New York: New Directions, 1957.

Thomas, Jo. "Lawyers Seek to Disqualify U.S. Attorney in Bomb Trial." *New York Times*, 14 Aug. 1997, A8.

Thompson, Jack George. *The Psychobiology of the Emotions*. New York: Plenum Press, 1988.

Thompson, Nicholas S., Carolyn Olson, and Brian Dessureau. "Babies' Cries: Who's Listening? Who's Being Fooled?" *Social Research* 63 (1996): 763–84.

Thurman, Wallace. *The Blacker the Berry . . . : A Novel of Negro Life* (1929). New York: Macmillan, 1970.

Tims, Hilton. *Emotion Pictures: The 'Women's Picture,' 1930–55*. London: Columbus Books, 1987.

Tomkins, Silvan. *Affect, Imagery, Consciousness*. 4 vols. New York: Springer, 1962–92.

———. *Shame and Its Sisters: A Silvan Tomkins Reader*. Edited by Eve Kososfky Sedgwick and Adam Frank. Durham, N.C: Duke University Press, 1995.

Tomkins, Silvan, and Carroll E. Izard, eds. *Affect, Cognition, and Personality: Empirical Studies*. New York: Springer, 1965.

Trilling, Lionel. *Sincerity and Authenticity*. Cambridge, Mass.: Harvard University Press, 1972.

Tschopik, Harry, Jr. "The Aymara." *Bureau of American Ethnology Bulletin* 143:2 (1946): 501–73.

———. "The Aymara of Chucuito, Peru: 1. Magic." *Anthropological Papers of the American Museum of Natural History* 44 (1951): 133–308.

Turnbull, Colin M. *The Forest People*. New York: Simon & Schuster, 1961.

———. *Wayward Servants: The Two Worlds of the African Pygmies*. Garden

City, N.Y.: Natural History Press, 1965.

Turner, Thomas Reed. *Beware the People Weeping: Public Opinion and the Assassination of Abraham Lincoln*. Baton Rouge, La: Louisiana State University Press, 1982.

Twain, Mark. *Mississippi Writings*. New York: Literary Classics of the United States, 1982.

Ullman, Sarah E., and Raymond A. Knight. "The Efficacy of Women's Resistance Strategies in Rape Situations." *Psychology of Women Quarterly* 17 (1993): 23–38.

Unamuno, Miguel de. *The Tragic Sense of Life* (1913). Translated by J. E. Crawford Flitch. New York: Dover, 1954.

Valentine, C. W. "The Innate Bases of Fear" (1930). *Journal of Genetic Psychology* 152:4 (1991): 501–27.

Van Haeringen, N. J. "Clinical Biochemistry of Tears." *Survey of Ophthalmology* 26 (1981): 84–96.

Van Oosterum, Peter. *Tears: A Key to a Remedy* (1995). Bath, England: Ashgrove, 1998.

Villa-Rojas, Alfonso. "The Tzeltal." In *Handbook of Middle American Indians*, vol. 7, edited by Robert Wauchope. Austin, Tex.: University of Texas Press, 1969.

Vincent-Buffault, Anne. *The History of Tears: Sensibility and Sentimentality in France*. Translated by Teresa Bridgeman. New York: St. Martin's, 1991.

Vingerhoets, Ad J., J. Assies, and K. Poppelaars. "Prolactin and Weeping." *International Journal of Psychosomatics* 39 (1992): 81–82.

Vingerhoets, Ad J., Marielle P. Van den Berg, Robert T. Kortekaas, Guus L. Van Heck, et al. "Weeping: Associations with Personality, Coping, and Subjective Health Status." *Personality and Individual Differences* 14:1 (1993): 185–90.

Virgil. *The Aeneid*. Translated by Edward McCrorie. Ann Arbor, Mich.: University of Michigan Press, 1995.

Voltaire. *Alzire* (1736). In *The Complete Works of Voltaire*, edited by Theodore Besterman. Toronto: University of Toronto Press, 1968.

von Staden, Heinrich. "Introduction: Alexandrian and Egyptian Medicine." In *Herophilus: The Art of Medicine in Early Alexandria*. New York: Cambridge University Press, 1989.

Wagner, R. E., M. Hexel, W. W. Bauer, and U. Kropiunigg. "Crying in Hospitals: A Survey of Doctors', Nurses' and Medical Students' Experience and Attitudes." *Medical Journal of Australia* 166:1 (1997): 13–6.

Waldman, Jane Lori. *Breakthrough or Breakdown: When the Psychotherapist*

Cries During the Therapy Session. Psy.D. dissertation, Massachusetts
    School of Professional Psychology, Boston, Mass.,1995.

Walker, Amanda M., and Samuel Menahem. "Intervention of Supplementary
    Carrying on Normal Baby Crying Patterns: A Randomized Study." *Jour-
    nal of Developmental and Behavioral Pediatrics* 15:3 (1994): 174–78.

Warhol, Robyn. "As You Stand, So You Feel and Are: The Crying Body and the
    Nineteenth Century Text." In *Tattoo, Torture, Mutilation, and Adornment:
    The Denaturalization of the Body in Culture and Text,* edited by Francis
    E. Mascia-Lees and Patricia Sharpe. Albany, N.Y.: State University of
    New York Press, 1992.

Warren, D. W., A. M. Azzarolo, Z. M. Huang, B. W. Platler, R. L. Kaswan, E.
    Gentschein, F. L. Stanczyk, L. Becker, and A. K. Mircheff. "Androgen
    Support of Lacrimal Gland Function in the Female Rabbit." *Advances in
    Experimental Medicine & Biology* 438 (1998): 89–93.

Watson, John B. *Behaviorism.* New York: Norton, 1925.

———. *Psychology from the Standpoint of a Behaviorist.* Philadelphia: Lippin-
    cott, 1924.

———. *The Psychological Care of Infant and Child.* New York: Norton, 1928.

Waugh, Evelyn. *The Loved One: An Anglo-American Tragedy.* Boston: Little,
    Brown, 1948.

Wegman, Cornelius. *Psychoanalysis and Cognitive Psychology.* New York: Aca-
    demic Press, 1985.

Weiss, Albert P. "Feeling and Emotion as Forms of Behavior." In *Feelings and
    Emotions. See* Adler et al., 1928.

Wells, R., J. McCann, J. Adams, J. Voris, and B. Dahl. "A Validational Study of
    the Structured Interview of Symptoms Associated with Sexual Abuse
    (SASA) Using Three Samples of Sexually Abused, Allegedly Abused,
    and Nonabused Boys." *Child Abuse and Neglect* 21:12 (1997): 1159–67.

Werb, Abraham. "The Anatomy of the Lacrimal System." In *The Lacrimal Sys-
    tem. See* Milder and Weil, 1983.

West, Nathanael. *The Day of the Locust* (1939). New York: New Directions,
    1962.

Whipple, Leon. "What is Your EQ?" *Survey Graphic* 30 (Nov. 1941): 640–41.

Whiteside, Jonny. *Cry: The Johnnie Ray Story.* New York: Barricade Books, 1994.

Whitman, Walt. "A Song of Joys." In *Complete Poetry and Collected Prose.* New
    York: Literary Classics of the United States, 1982.

Wied, Maximilian, Prinz von. *People of the First Man: Life Among the Plains
    Indians in Their Final Days of Glory. The Firsthand Account of Prince*

Maximilian's Expedition Up the Missouri River, 1833–1834. New York: Dutton, 1976.

Wikander, B., and T. Theorell. "Father's Experience of Childbirth and Its Relation to Crying in His Infant." *Scandinavian Journal of Caring Sciences* 11:3 (1997): 151–58.

Wilce, J. M., Jr. "The Pragmatics of 'Madness': Performance Analysis of a Bangladeshi Woman's 'Aberrant' Lament." *Culture, Medicine & Psychiatry* 22:1 (1988): 1–54.

Wilcox, Ella Wheeler. *Poems of Pleasure.* Chicago: Morril, Higgins & Co., 1892.

Wilkie, Colleen F., and Elinor W. Ames. "The Relationship of Infant Crying to Parental Stress in the Transition to Parenthood." *Journal of Marriage and the Family* 48 (1986): 545–50.

Williams, D. G., and G. H. Morris. "Crying, Weeping or Tearfulness in British and Israeli Adults." *British Journal of Psychology* 87:3 (1996): 479–505.

Wolf, Margery. *Women and the Family in Rural Taiwan.* Stanford, Calif.: Stanford University Press, 1972.

Wolke, Dieter. "The Treatment of Problem Crying Behaviour." In *Infant Crying, Feeding and Sleeping: Development, Problems and Treatments*, edited by Gillian Harris, Ian St. James-Roberts, and David Messer. London: Harvester, Wheatsheaf, 1993.

Wood, Edwin C., and Constance D. Wood. "Tearfulness: A Psychoanalytic Interpretation." *Journal of the American Psychoanalytic Association* 32 (1984): 117–36.

Young, P. T. "Studies in Affective Psychology." *American Journal of Psychology* 38 (1927): 157–93.

Zajonc, Robert B. "Emotional Expression and Temperature Modulation." In *Emotions: Essays of Emotion Theory*, edited by Stephanie H. M. Van Goozen, Nanne E. Van de Poll, and Joseph A. Sargent. Hillsdale, N.J.: Lawrence Erlbaum, 1994.

Zilboorg, Gregory. *History of Medical Psychology.* New York: Norton, 1941.

Index

Note: Page numbers in *italics* refer to illustrations.